# A DICTIONARY
## OF COLORFUL FRENCH SLANGUAGE
### AND COLLOQUIALISMS

# A DICTIONARY OF
# COLORFUL FRENCH SLANGUAGE
# AND COLLOQUIALISMS

*By*

## ETIENNE AND SIMONE DEAK

*A Dutton*  *Paperback*

NEW YORK
E. P. DUTTON & CO., INC.

*This paperback edition of*
"A DICTIONARY
OF COLORFUL FRENCH SLANGUAGE
AND COLLOQUIALISMS"
*First published 1961 by E. P. Dutton & Co., Inc.*
*All rights reserved. Printed in the U.S.A.*
*Copyright, ©, 1959, by Robert Laffont*

SBN 0-525-47087-5

*This short dictionary is dedicated from A to Z to our American friends whose never-lagging interest in the French slanguage has been an inspiration and a valuable incentive to us.*

E. and S. Deak.

A DICTIONARY
OF COLORFUL FRENCH SLANGUAGE
AND COLLOQUIALISMS

# FOREWORD

*Dear American Friend,*

*Our* Dictionary of Colorful French Slanguage and Colloquialisms *is not an ordinary dictionary. This is a special selection of French slang and colloquial terms with their equivalent in plain American language or <u>slanguage</u>, or both. This concise little book has been compiled for the benefit of all Americans who, having gone through standard classes of the French language and wishing a wider acquaintance with popular speech, want to go a step further in the field of that exciting and fascinating lingo popularly known as the <u>French argot</u>.*

*Yes, dear American Friend, this book, so full of practical and funny stuff, has been written especially for you. We know you are an ardent Francophile, we know you have many reasons to love France and the French language. We know you have studied French in your school days and we also know you have long since felt the necessity of possessing a handy bilingual dictionary that should be able to teach you the meaning of pictur-*

esque French slang words you so often hear from Frenchmen but whose meaning may not be quite clear to you.

Now this book is here. The dictionary that follows, containing words and phrases like you never learned in school, will teach you thousands of the most vivid, most colorful terms from French argot and popular speech. These expressive, sparkling words and spicy phrases have one thing in common : from whatever angle you look at them, they are 100 % French.

An exhaustive list of terms could not, of course, be included in such a limited number of pages, but the authors of this special dictionary have selected for you from A to Z the very cream of the lingo, that is to say 5000-odd slang words and colloquialisms you hear most often in France. One category of terms, however, may need a « danger signal » : we refer to those words and phrases that are of a rather coarse or vulgar type. Such terms are indicated in this dictionary with an *, signifying that, though currently used by certain enthusiasts, they are to be carefully avoided in conversation by all foreigners.

For those who think that pictures are funnier than words, this dictionary will have rewarding dividends : Jean Dugué, a Parisian artist who sees people and things as they really are, boldly illustrates with his pen more than a hundred different slang and popular terms. These humorous and witty drawings will make the use of the dictionary more entertaining to Americans.

This book is yours, dear American Friend. Read it, use it and learn from it. While we cannot, of course, guarantee that the first perusal will turn you into an expert on French argot, we can, however, assure you of one thing : you will have a fine time and you will enjoy a good laugh every time you glance through the pages of this fun-packed dictionary.

Paris, January 1959.

E. and S. DEAK.

# AVANT-PROPOS

*Le* Dictionary of Colorful French Slanguage and Colloquialisms, *que nous avons le plaisir de présenter à nos amis américains, n'est pas un dictionnaire ordinaire, mais un ouvrage spécial contenant des milliers de termes et de vocables familiers, populaires et argotiques de la langue française, avec leur équivalent en américain. Il s'adresse à cette catégorie d'Américains qui, après avoir étudié le français classique aux Etats-Unis et non contents de savoir la langue des lettrés, veulent connaître en plus le langage du peuple avec ses expressions familières et ses termes d'argot.*

*Mais oui, chers amis américains, c'est à vous que notre dictionnaire est destiné, car vous, qui êtes d'ardents francophiles, qui avez des raisons historiques et sentimentales d'aimer la France, vous, qui avez « potassé » la langue de Molière dans vos* high schools *ou l'avez étudiée à fond dans vos Universités, qui venez nombreux chaque année visiter notre pays, vous êtes certainement de ceux qui souhaitent, depuis longtemps, posséder un petit « bouquin » de ce genre : un dictionnaire qui ne soit pas comme les autres et qui puisse, dans votre langue élastique et pétrissable, vous faire comprendre ce que les Français veulent* dire par leurs innombrables termes imagés, que vous trouvez en France sur toutes les lèvres, mais dont la vraie signification vous échappe neuf fois sur dix. Qui ne vous le pardonnerait pas du reste, puisque peu de dictionnaires français-anglais vous enseignent l'usage de ces vocables populaires et qu'aucun ne vous explique le vrai sens des mots d'argot avec leur équivalent en slang *américain*.

*Le* Dictionary of Colorful French Slanguage and Colloquialisms *vous apprendra donc à connaître plus de 5.000 expressions populaires et argotiques, toutes pleines de verve, de pittoresque, de saveur et de couleur locale, parce que, nées sur le sol français, toutes « disent bien ce qu'elles veulent dire ». Elles sont les caractéristiques d'un peuple qui aime le parler imagé et dont l'argot, pour être moins riche que le* slang *américain, n'en est pas moins expressif.*

*Une liste complète ne pouvant être reproduite dans un manuel aussi restreint, les auteurs de cet ouvrage ont limité leur choix aux expressions que vous êtes susceptibles d'entendre le plus fréquemment en France. Nous signalons cependant aux lecteurs qui auront l'occasion de se servir de ce dictionnaire que certains des vocables qui y figurent présentent un caractère de vulgarité plus ou moins prononcée ; aussi avons-nous tenu à les faire précéder d'un astérisque \*, précisant par là que, bien que très connus et employés par le peuple, ils doivent être soigneusement évités par les étrangers.*

*Les petits dessins qui illustrent notre livre — et qui sont dus à l'habile plume du dessinateur parisien Jean Dugué — tendent à égayer cette étude et à rendre le sens de l'argot français plus accessible à ceux qui utilisent notre manuel.*

*Qu'il nous soit permis, pour terminer, de formuler le souhait que le* Dictionary of Colorful French Slanguage and Colloquialisms *devienne un instrument de travail utile entre les mains de nos amis d'Outre-Atlantique.*

Paris, Janvier 1959.

E. et S. DEAK.

# ABBREVIATIONS USED IN THIS DICTIONARY

| | | | |
|---|---|---|---|
| *abbr.* | abbreviated, abbreviation. | *pej.* | pejorative. |
| *adj.* | adjective. | *pl.* | *pluriel* (plural). |
| *adv.* | adverb. | *pop.* | popular(ly). |
| *coll.* | colloquial, colloquialism. | *q.* | *quelqu'un* (someone). |
| *dimin.* | diminutive, pet name. | *q. ch.* | *quelque chose* (something). |
| *Ex.* | example. | *sf.* | *substantif féminin* (feminine noun). |
| *excl.* | exclamation. | | |
| *(F)* | familiar (term or expression). | *(Sl)* | slang. |
| *f. i.* | for instance. | *sm.* | *substantif masculin* (masculine noun). |
| *fig.* | figurative sense, figurative(ly). | | |
| *interj.* | interjection. | *s.o.* | someone. |
| *joc.* | jocular(ly). | *s.th.* | something. |
| *(P)* | popular language. | *syn.* | synonym. |
| | | *v.* | verb. |

# A

**abatis** *sm. pl. (Sl)*. Arms and feet, "fins and kickers".

**abat(t)age** *sm. (P)*. Scolding, reprimand, bawling-out. Carelessly or hurriedly produced literary or artistic piece of work, "quickie", "potboiler".

**à bouche que veux-tu** *(F)*. Good and plenty, galore, enough and to spare.

**abouler** *v. (Sl)*. To pay, to cough up, to bring along, to hand over (the dough). *Aboule ton fric!* Come around with the dough !

**aboyeur** *sm. (P)*. One who solicits patronage for a cheap side-show, side-show barker, ballyhoo man, spieler.

**abracadabrant** *adj. (F)*. Extraordinary, fantastic, astonishing, stunning, "fantabulous".

**à brûle-pourpoint** *(F)*. Point-blank, bluntly.

**abruti** *sm. (P)*. Stupid guy, dope, chump, dumbbell. *Espèce d'abruti!* You, big mutt ! You, big fathead !

**acabit** *sm. (P)*. Type, nature. Ex. : *Deux coquins de même acabit,* two rascals of the same stripe.

**accommodé aux petits oignons** *(Sl)*. First class, tip-top, dandy, hotsytotsy.

**accommoder q. au beurre noir** *(Sl)*. To beat up, to bruise one badly, to give one a " shiner ".

**accommoder (assaisonner) q. aux petits oignons** *(Sl)*. To treat one roughly, to manhandle. Also sarcastically : to do up brown.

**accoucher** *v. (P)*. To confess, to " sing ". *Accouche ! Accouchez !* Speak up ! Shoot ! Fire away !

**accoutrer (s')** *v. (F)*. To attire oneself in.

**accroc** *(F)*. Hitch, snag, " bug ".

**accroche-cœur** *sm. (F)*. " Heart-breaker ", " kiss-curl ", a curl over the ear or on the forehead.

**accroche-pipe** *sm. (Sl)*. Mouth, " spitter ".

**accrocher (se l')** *v. (P)*. To tighten one's belt, to whistle for. Ex. : *Tu peux te l'accrocher,* you can whistle for it !

**acheter q.** *v. (P)*. To poke fun at s.o., to rib, to needle, to " guy " one.

**acheter à la foire d'empoigne** *(P)*. To steal, to " grab ".

**acheter une conduite** *(F)*. To turn over a new leaf.

**à court d'argent** *(F)*. To be short of money, to be hard up.

**à court de q. ch. (être)** *(F)*. To be short of s. th.

ADJUPÈTE.

**à cran (être)** *(P)*. To be very angry, to be mad, exasperated.

**acrobate** *sm. (Sl)*. Peculiar person, eccentric guy, odd stick, queer fish.

**activer** *v. (P)*. *Active(z) !* Hurry up ! Make it snappy ! Step lively !

**à d'autres !** *(F)* Excl. conveying disbelief : My eye ! You can't fool me ! I don't believe a word of what you say !

**adjupète** *sm. (Sl)*. Humorous military slang name for the traditionally strict *adjudant* ("top kick", "topper"), the highest ranking non-commissioned officer.

**afanaf** *adv. (Sl)*. Frenchified slang for : half-and-half.

**affaire (une)** *sf. (F)*. A bargain. *C'est une affaire,* that's a real bargain.

**affaires sont les affaires (les)** *(F)*. Business is business.

**affaler (s')** *v. (Sl)*. To confess, to " sing " (under the " third degree " or after a severe examination).

**afficher (s')** *v. (P)*. To show off, to spread oneself.

**affranchi(e)** *sm. sf.* Man (or woman) of no scruples and living on the fringe of society, man (or woman) belonging to the so-called " *milieu* ". (See this word).
*adj.* Smarted-up, hepped up.

**affubler (s')** *v. (F)*. To rig oneself out, to attire oneself in.

**à flot (être)** *(F)*. To be flush of money, to be well-heeled.

**à gogo** *adv. (F)*. Superabundant, more than plenty, in great quantity, enough and to spare, galore.

**agonir q. de sottises** *(P)*. To shower one with abuses, insults. To chew a person's ears off.

**agrafer** *v. (P)*. To catch, to get hold of one, to buttonhole one.

*(Sl)*. To arrest, to "nab", to capture, to "collar". *Se faire agrafer*, to get "nabbed".

AGRAFÉ PAR LE FLIC.

**Agro** *(F)*. Abbr. *Institut Agronomique* or student at *I.A.*

**aigrefin** *sm. (F)*. Crook, phoney.

**aile** *sf. (Sl)*. Arm, "fin".

**aileron** *sm. (Sl)*. Arm, "fin".

**aimable comme une porte de prison (être)** *(P)*. Gruff as a bear.

**air et la chanson (l')** *(F)*. Semblance and truth.

**à la bonne franquette** *(F)*. Quite simply, without any ceremony, "freewheeling". *Homme à la bonne franquette*, a freewheeler.

**à la bonne heure !** *(F)*. Excl. of pleasure or approval : That's the goods ! That's the ticket !

**à la côte (être)** *(Sl)*. To be on the bum, on the beach, on the rocks, broke, penniless.

**à la coule** *(Sl)*. Hep on (hep to). Said of a person who "knows the ropes", who is "in", smart guy, brighty, nobody's fool.

**à la diable** *(P)*. Reckless(ly).

**à la gare !** *(Sl)*. Rude term for : Go about your business ! Scram out of here ! The heck with you !

**à la godille** *(P)*. No-account, worthless, lousy, phoney, bogus, wash-out, cut-rate, "tinhorn".

**à la gomme** *(Sl)*. A variant of *à la godille*.

**à la hauteur** *(F)*. Capable, able, hep to, "in", one who "knows".

**à la manque** *(P)*. Another variant of *à la godille*.

**à l'anglaise (filer)** *(F)*. To take French leave.

**à la noix** *(P)*. Another pop. variant of *à la godille*.

**à la noix de coco (faire q. ch.** *(Sl)*. To bungle (up).

**à la page (être)** *(F)*. To be well acquainted with, to be hep to, to be hip, to be "in", to be in the know.

**à la papa** *(P)*. In a quiet, leisurely way, comfortably.

**à la queue leu leu** *(F)*. In Indian file.

A LA QUEUE LEU LEU.

**à la revoyure !** *(Sl)*. Good-by ! I'll be seeing you ! See you later, alligator ! See you in church !

**à l'article de la mort (être)**
*(F)*. To be at death's door.

**à l'eau de rose** *(P)*. Fig. sense :
Without pep, inoffensive, inefficient,
weak, watery.

**à l'estomac** *(P)*. Bluff, something said at a venture. *Faire à l'estomac*, to bluff.

**à l'impossible nul n'est tenu**
*(F)*. No one is bound by the impossible.

**allant (avoir de l')** *(F)*. To
have pep, " zip ".

**aller à la pêche** *(P)*. To be
jobless, out of work, unemployed, " on
the beach ".

**aller aux champs** *(Sl)*. To go to
the races, to gamble on the ponies.

**aller comme sur des roulettes** *(F)*. To go without a hitch, like
clockwork, smoothly.

**aller comme un gant** *(F)*. To
fit one like a glove.

**aller contre vent(s) et marée(s)** *(F)*. To go against wind and
tide, against strong opposition.

**aller en cabane** *(Sl)*. See :
*cabane*.

**aller fort** *(P)*. To exaggerate, to
pitch it strong.

**aller les pieds devant (s'en)**
*(P)*. To die, to " go home feet first ".

**aller mal** *(Sl)*. To exaggerate.
Ex. : *Tu vas mal, toi !* That's a bit
stiff !

**aller manger les pissenlits
par la racine** *(P)*. To die, to
" push up daisies ". See also : *manger
les pissenlits par la racine.*

**aller où le roi va à pied** *(P)*.
To go to the toilet, to " go see a
dog ", to " go see a man about a dog ".

**aller son petit bonhomme de
chemin** *(F)*. To jog along.

**aller son petit traintrain** *(P)*.
To follow one's daily routine, to be
jogging along.

**aller tout doux** *(Sl)*. To take
one's sweet time, to take it easy.

**allez vous coucher !** *(P)*. Pack
off !

**allez vous rhabiller!** *(P)*. Same
as : *allez vous coucher !*

**allonger** v. *(P)*. *Allonger une
gifle à q.*, to slap a person in the face.
*Les allonger*, to pay, to ante up.

**allonger (s')** *(P)*. To treat oneself to, to " land ". *Il s'est allongé un
bon déjeuner*, he treated himself to a
fine lunch.

**allons-y !** *(P)*. Let's begin ! Let's
start ! Let's go ! Let's have a shot at
it !

**allumage** sm. *(Sl)*. Light drunkenness.

**allumé (être)** *(Sl)*. To be drunk,
to be corked up, to be half seas over.

**allumer** v. *(Sl)*. To excite sexually,
to " sexcite ".

**allumeuse** sf. *(Sl)*. B-girl.

**à l'ombre** *(F)*. In jail, in " stir ".

**amener (s')** *(P)*. To come along,
to show up.

**amener comme une fleur (s')**
*(P)*. To drop in quite unceremoniously.

**\* amène ta viande !** *(Sl)*. Come
here ! Come along !

**Amerlo(ck)** sm. *(Sl)*. American,
Yankee, Yank. (Also : *Amerlot*).

**aminche** sm. *(Sl)*. Friend, pal,
bud.

**amis comme cochons** *(P)*.
Palsy-walsy, inseparable friends who

are always together, sworn friends. (Pop. phrase, often said jocularly).

**amocher** *v. (Sl)*. To spoil, to "louse up", to "ball up", to "muss" up.

**amourette** *sf. (F)*. Passing fancy.

**amphi** *sm. (P)*. Amphitheater.

**amuse-gueule** *sm. (P)*. Hors-d'œuvre, titbits that perk up the appetite, cocktail canapés, appetizer, "appe-teaser".

**amuser comme un rat mort (s')** *(P)*. To be bored to death. (See also : *ennuyer comme un rat mort (s')*.

**amuser le tapis** *(F)*. To keep the audience, the company, amused.

**amusette** *sf. (Sl)*. Little game of a small-time crook.

**anarcho** *sm. (Sl)*. Anarchist.

**Anastasie** *sf. (Sl)*. The censorship.

ANASTASIE.

**ancêtres** *sm. pl. (F)*. Parents, "old folks".

**andouille** *sf. (P)*. Very stupid person, dumbbell, chump, blockhead, lunkhead, chowderhead, noodlehead, fathead.

**âne bâté** *sm. (P)*. Silly ass, jackass, chump.

**âne de Buridan (l')** *(F)*. Person who constantly hesitates and cannot make up his mind.

**Anglais (les)** *(P)*. Menses, "visitors".

**Angliches (les)** *sm. pl. (P)*. The English, the Limies (Limey).

**anguille sous roche** *(F)*. See : *il y a anguille sous roche*.

**anicroche** *sf. (F)*. Hitch, "bug".

**animal** *sm. (Sl)*. Dumbbell, dope.

**antisèche** *sm. (Sl)*. Unfair aid at an exam, "pony", "crib", "cabbage".

**à Pâques ou à la Trinité** *(P)*. Never, when hell freezes over.

**apéro** *sm. (Sl)*. Appetizer.

**à perpète** *(P)*. For ever, perpetually.

**à perte de vue** *(F)*. As far as the eye can see (reach).

**aplatir q.** *v. (Sl)*. To astound, to astonish, to knock one in a heap, to bowl one over, to "knock for a loop", to beat one to a frazzle.

**à plat ventre devant q. (être)** *(P)*. To toady, to flatter, to kowtow.

**aplomb (avoir de l')** *(F)*. To have crust, cheek.

**à poil** *(P)*. Naked.

**appeler un chat un chat** *(F)*. To call a spade a spade.

**appuyer (s')** *(P)*. *Qu'est-ce qu'il s'est appuyé !* he had a heck of a time, a heck of a job. Same as : *se taper*.

**appuyer sur la chanterelle** *(F)*. To draw attention to, or lay stress on, the most important point.

**appuyer sur le champignon** *(P)*. To step on the gas (accelerator).

**après cela, il faut tirer l'échelle** *(P)*. Said of a top performance, 4-0, mighty good show. Sometimes, ironically, meaning : that's the limit !

**à qui dites-vous !** *(F)*. You are telling me !

**araignée dans le plafond (avoir une)** *(F)*. To be eccentric, to have bats in the belfry, to be a crackpot.

**archi** *(F)*. Prefix expressing a superlative. Ex. : *être archifauché*, to be stone-broke.

**archicube** *sm. (Sl)*. Student in the fourth year at the *Ecole Normale Supérieure*.

**ardoise** *sf. (P)*. *Avoir une ardoise chez le restaurateur,* to have meals on tick, to put it on the cuff, to chalk it up. *Laisser une ardoise,* to leave behind unpaid debts, unpaid bills.

**argent à la pelle (remuer de l')** *(P)*. To have money to burn.

**argenté comme une cuiller de bois** *(P)*. Penniless, stone-broke.

**aristo** *sm. (P)*. One of the Four Hundred, one of the Upper Crust, one of the Upper Ten, one of the " gilded roosters ".

**aristoche** *sm. (Sl)*. Same as : *aristo.*

**arlequins** *sm. pl. (P)*. Odds and ends of left-over food given away or sold at cut prices by large restaurants.

**arpète** *sf. (P)*. Apprentice girl, young girl employed mainly for errands in the dress-making business.

**arpions** *sm. pl. (Sl)*. Feet, "purps".

**arracher les côtes** *(P)*. Said of a cycler (in a bicycle race) who keeps speed up-hill, on a gradient.

**arranger** *v. (Sl)*. To beat up badly, to cook one's goose, to settle one's hash. To injure, to wound s.o., to infect with a venereal disease. Also derisively : to spoil, to impair, to " louse up ", to throw out of gear.

**arranger (s')** *v. (F)*. To cope with (or to find the way out of) a difficult situation, to " worry along ".

**arranger des chiffres, des statistiques, etc.** *(P)*. To cook up (to doctor) figures, statistics, etc.

**arrangeur** *sm. (Sl)*. Swindler, crook, chiseler, slicker, sharpie.

**arrangeuse** *sf. (Sl)*. Feminine form of *arrangeur.*

**arrêter les frais** *(F)*. To give in, to yield, to call off all bets, to give up as a bad job.

**arrêter pile (s')** *(P)*. To stop sharp on.

**arrière-train** *sm. (P)*. The human buttocks, posterior, fanny.

**arriver** *v. (P)*. *Tu y arrives ?* Can you manage it ? Can you get it ?

**arriver à point nommé** *(F)*. Same as : *tomber à pic.*

**arriver comme Mars (marée) en carême** *(F)*. To arrive in the very nick of time.

**arriver comme une flèche** *(F)*. To blow in.

**arriver comme une fleur** *(P)*. Same as : *amener comme une fleur (s').*

IL ARRIVE DANS UN FAUTEUIL.

**arriver dans un fauteuil** *(P)*. To win easily in a competition. Also said of a horse that wins easily at the races.

**arriver pile** *(P)*. To come in very punctually, in the very nick of time.

**arriviste** *sm. (F)*. Go-getter, hustler, careerist.

**arrondir (s')** *v. (P)*. To be pregnant, *enceinte*. To get drunk, to become tight.

**arrondir (se l')** *v. (Sl)*. Same as : *accrocher (se l')*. *Il peut se l'arrondir !* He can whistle for it !

**arroser** *v. (P)*. To confirm a deal, to celebrate victory, success, etc. with a drink. Ex. : *Arroser une affaire, un contrat, une victoire, etc.*, to wet a bargain, a deal, a victory, etc.

**arsouille** *sm. (P)*. Scoundrel, low-bred cad, hooligan.

**artiflot** *sm. (Sl)*. Artilleryman.

**as** *sm. (P)*. Ace, expert (mainly in aviation, but also in many other fields), "wiz", "whiz", "wizard", a cracker-jack.

**as de pique** *(P)*. See : *fichu comme l'as de pique.*

**à sec** *adv. (F)*. *Etre à sec*, to have no money, to be broke.

**asperge** *sf. (P)*. Tall and skinny person.

**asphyxier** *v. (Sl)*. To astound, to astonish, to flabbergast, to knock dead. To have strong halitosis.

**assaisonner** *v. (Sl)*. To beat up, to thrash, to dust one's jacket, to give the leather. To contaminate s.o. with V.D. To do up brown.

**assassiner** *v. (Sl)*. To ruin, to "ball up", to spoil, to "louse up".

**asseoir q.** *v. (P)*. To confuse, to strike pink, to flabbergast, to perplex, to floor one. Ex. : *Ça m'a assis,* that floored me.

**assiette** *sf. (F)*. See : *ne pas être dans son assiette.*

**assiette au beurre** *sf. (P)*. A fat government job, pie(-counter).

**assis** *(P)*. See : *en être assis.*

**assommer** *v. (F)*. To blackjack, to bore one to death.

**assommeur** *sm. (F)*. Ruffian, bully. Bore.

**asticot** *sm. (P)*. Guy, gazabo, gazook, geezer, punk.

**asticoter** *v. (P)*. To plague, to tease, to worry.

**à tire-larigot** *(F)*. In abundance, to one's heart's content. *Boire à tirelarigot,* to drink like a fish.

**à tout casser** *(F)*. Hell of a, "helluva". *Une histoire à tout casser,* a hell of a story.

**atouts dans son jeu (avoir tous les)** *(F)*. To hold all the winning cards.

**attaque (être d')** *(P)*. To be full of pep, full of beans.

**attendri (être)** *(Sl)*. To be slightly drunk, to be a bit boozy.

**attention aux épluchures !** *(Sl)*. Mind the risk! Mind the danger! Mind the consequences !

**attifer (s')** *v. (F)*. Same as : *accoutrer (s').*

**attiger** *v. (Sl)*. To exaggerate.

**attrape-pognon** *sm. (Sl)*. Game (cards, roulette, dice, etc.).

**attraper la crève** *(Sl)*. To catch a severe (fatal) cold, to catch one's death.

**attraper (se faire)** *(P)*. To get bawled out.

**à tu et à toi avec q. (être)** *(F)*. To be on very familiar terms with s.o.

**aubaine** *sf (F)*. An unexpected piece of good fortune, godsend, windfall.

**aubergine** *sf. (Sl)*. Red nose, full-blown nose.

**au bout de son rouleau (être)** *(F)*. To be near death.

**au bout du fil** *(F)* On the 'phone.

AU BOUT DU FIL.

**au clou** *(P)*. Pawned, in " hock ", " in lavender ".

**au-dessous de tout** *(P)*. Contemptible, despicable, ignominious, abominable.

**au diable au vert** *(P)*. Long way off, very far away.

**au doigt et à l'œil** *(P)*. See : *obéir au doigt et à l'œil.*

**au petit bonheur la chance** *(F)*. As chance directs, as chance will have it.

**au pied levé** *(F)*. At a moment's notice.

**au poil** *(P)*. Very accurate(ly), exact(ly), " on the nose ".

**autant en emporte le vent** *(F)*. Gone with the wind.

**autor (d')** *(Sl)*. Unhesitatingly.

**auto-stop** *sm. (P)*. Hitch-hiking.

**autre paire de manches (c'est une)** *(F)*. This is a different proposition, horse of another color.

**autres chats à fouetter (avoir d')** *(F)*. To have other things to do (or to worry about).

**autres chiens à peigner (avoir d'autres)** *(F)*. Same as : *autres chats à fouetter (avoir d').*

**aux abois (être)** *(F)*. To be in a desperate position, on one's last legs.

**aux anges (être)** *(F)*. To be delighted.

**aux petits oignons** *(P)*. See : *accommodé aux petits oignons.*

**aux trousses de q. (être)** *(F)*. To be on s.o.'s heels, to dog s.o.'s steps.

**avalé le pépin (avoir)** *(Sl)*. To be pregnant.

**avaler des couleuvres** *(P)*. To pocket a reprimand, to put up with an affront.

**avaler la consigne** *(P)*. To forget to carry out the instructions received, to forget to deliver a message.

**avaler la pilule** *(P)*. To take one's medicine, to swallow the pill.

**avaler sa chique** *(Sl)*. To die, to " kick the bucket ", to " cash in one's checks ".

**avaler sa langue** *(Sl)*. Same as : *avaler sa chique.*

**avaler son extrait de naissance** *(Sl)*. To die, to " kick the bucket ", to " step out of the picture ".

**avancer (s')** *(P)*. To make headway.

**avant-scène** *sf. (Sl)*. Breasts, " titties ".

**avaro** *sm. (Sl)*. Trouble, accident.

**avec des " si " et des " mais ", on mettrait Paris dans une bouteille** *(P)*. If wishes were horses, beggars would ride. If my aunt had been a man, she'd have been my uncle. If If's and And's were pots and pans, there'd be no work for tinker's hands.

**avec sa smalah** *(P)*. With all one's tribe, with the whole kit and caboodle.

**\* avoir chaud aux fesses** *(Sl)*. To be frightened, to get the jitters ; to be actively sought by police.

**avoir fini** *(F)*. To be through with.

**avoir gardé les cochons ensemble** *(P)*. Generally in the negative form : *Nous n'avons pas gardé les cochons ensemble !* Fling at one who gets too familiar with you.

**avoir le truc** *(P)*. To have the know-how, the knowledge, the expertness, the savvy.

**avoir l'œil et le bon** *(P)*. To be on the alert, to keep a weather-eye.

**avoir l'œil sur** *(F)*. To keep tabs on, watch systematically.

**avoir q.** *v. (P)*. To deceive, to fool, to " suck in ", to double-cross, to defeat. Ex. : *Ils m'ont eu,* they sucked me in, they double-crossed me.

**avoir vu le loup** *(P)*. (Of a girl) to have lost her virginity.

**à vous la balle !** *(F)*. It's your turn !

**à vue de nez** *(P)*. At a venture, estimated roughly, " guesstimated ".

# B

**baba** *adj. (P)*. Astonished, astounded, flabbergasted. Ex. : *J'en suis resté tout baba,* that took my breath, I was " flummergasted ", stunned.

**babillard** *sm. (Sl)*. Letter, paper, any written piece of news.

**babillarde** *sf. (Sl)*. Letter.

**babille** *sf. (Sl)*. Same as : *babillarde*.

**babiole** *sf. (P)*. Knicknack, doodad, what-not, doohickey.

**babouines** *sf. pl. (P)*. Ex. : *S'en lécher les babouines,* to smack one's lips (to express relish over something tasty), to lick one's chops. (Also spelt : *babines*).

**bac** *sm. (P)*. Baccalaureate. Baccarat.

**bacchanal** *sm. (P)*. Rumpus, hubbub, noisy disturbance, roughhouse.

**bacchantes** *sf. pl. (Sl)*. Moustache. *Bacchantes en guidon :* handlebar moustache.

**bâche** *sf. (Sl)*. Cap, bonnet. Bedsheet.

**bâcher (se)** *v. (Sl)*. To go to bed, to turn in.

**bachot** *sm. (P)*. Baccalaureate.

**bachotage** *sm. (P)*. Cramming (intense preparation for the " *bac* ").

**bâcler** *v. (F)*. To botch, to make a " quickie ".

**bada** *sm. (Sl)*. Hat.

**badaud** *sm.* (F). Jay-walker, " rubberneck ".

**badauder** *v. (F)*. To jay-walk, to " rubberneck ".

**baderne** *sf. (F)*. *Vieille baderne,* old dodo, old mossback, old fool, old foggy.

**badigoinces** *sf. pl. (Sl)*. Lips, mouth, cheeks. (Syn. : *babouines*).

**Badingue** *(P)*. Same as : *Badinguet*.

**Badinguet** *(P)*. Nickname for Napoleon III.

**baffre** *sf. (Sl)*. Slap in the face.

**bafouille** *sf. (Sl)*. Letter.

**bafouiller** *v. (P)*. To talk nonsense, to talk baloney.

**bâfrer** *v. (P)*. To eat hurriedly and greedily, to "load up", to "hog it down", to "cram".

**bagarre** *sf. (F)*. Brawl, scuffle, free-fight, confused struggle, fracas.

**bagarreur** *sm. (F)*. Individual who likes (or is always ready to start) a fight, a brawl.

**bagatelle (une)** *sf. (F)*. Trifle, unimportant and negligible amount or thing.

**bagatelle (la)** *sf. (P)*. Amour, love-affair. *Etre porté sur la bagatelle*, to be a fast man, a high-pressure papa, a bit of a Casanova. *Une femme très portée sur la bagatelle*, a hot mama. *Un homme porté sur la bagatelle*, a "fastie".

**bagatelles de la porte (les)** *(P)*. Petting, caressing (a woman), preliminaries to love.

**bagnole** *sf. (Sl)*. Any car. Old car, jalopy, geloppy. Une *vieille bagnole*, an old crate.

**bagouler** *v. (Sl)*. To talk, to speak, to yackety-yack.

**bagout** *sm. (P)*. Great facility of speech, gift of the gab, glibness of tongue. *Avoir du bagout*, to have the gift of the gab.

**baguenauder** *v. (Sl)*. To idle, to fool around, to louse around.

**bahut** *sm. (Sl)*. School. Taxicab, "crate".

**Baille (la)** *(Sl)*. Naval Academy in Lanvéoc-Poulmic (formerly in Brest) (School slang). Water, Davy Jones's locker.

**bain** *sm. (P)*. See : *dans le bain (être), envoyer au bain.*

**bain de pieds** *sm. (P)*. Coffee or tea slopped in the saucer. "Half and half" coffee : half in the cup and half in the saucer. Also : bad coffee.

**bain qui chauffe (c'est un)** *(P)*. Popular saying meaning : there will be another shower in a few minutes, although the sun is shining hot and hard.

**\* baisé (être)** *adj. (Sl)*. To be a victim of ; to be caught, "nabbed" ; to be cheated, to be swindled, to be "stung", to be "done".

**balade** *sf. (P)*. Walk, ride, stroll, joy-ride.

EN BALADE.

**balader (se)** *v. (P)*. To take a walk, to stroll, to traipse.

**balai** *sm. (Sl)*. Last train at night (at 1 a.m.) in the Paris *métro* (subway).

**balancer** *v. (Sl)*. To dismiss, to kick out, to fire, to give the gate, to boot out.

**balanstiquer** *v. (Sl)*. To throw, to toss, to dismiss, to fire one.

**bal des 4 z'arts** *(P)*. Art students' ball in Paris.

**balle** *sf. (P)*. Franc (usually from 10 on). Ex. : *dix balles, cent balles, mille balles, etc.*

**balle** *sf.* *(Sl)*. Face, " mug ", " pan ". Head, " bun ", " pate ", " nob ", " noodle ".

**ballon** *sm.* *(P)*. Glass having the shape of a small balloon.

*(Sl)*. Jail, prison, clink, " stir ", " college ", " booby hatch ".

**ballonner** *v.* *(Sl)*. To put in jail, to " run in ".

**ballot** *sm.* *(P)*. Stupid person, fool, dumbbell, chump, muff, fat-head.

**bal musette** *sm.* *(P)*. Popular, low-class dance-hall.

**balourdise** *sf.* *(P)*. Stupidity, blunder.

**baluchard** *sm.* *(Sl)*. Stupid person, fathead, dumbbell.

**baluchon** *sm.* *(P)*. Bundle of clothes.

*(Sl)*. Blockhead, dumbbell, dope.

**bambochard** *sm.* *(P)*. Hell-raiser, " high-stepper ", " cutup ".

**bamboche** *sf.* *(P)*. A drinking spree.

**bambocher** *v.* *(P)*. To " raise hell ", to " high-step ", to " hell around ".

**bambocheur** *sm.* *(P)*. Same as : *bambochard*.

**bambou** *sm.* *(Sl)*. Opium pipe, bamboo, hop stick.

**bamboula** *sm.* *(P)*. Nigger.

**bamboula** *sf.* *(Sl)*. Binge, bust, carousal. *Faire la bamboula,* to go on a bust, binge, to hit it up, to paint the town red.

**bande de vaches !** *(P)*. Insult for an individual or for a group of people.

**banlieusard(e)** *sm.* *sf.* *(P)*. Suburbanite.

**banquistes** *sm. pl.* *(Sl)*. Circus performers.

**baptiser du vin** *(P)*. To water down one's wine.

**baragouin** *sm.* *(F)*. Unintelligible speech, gibberish, " choctaw ".

**baragouiner** *v.* *(F)*. To talk gibberish, " choctaw ", double-Dutch.

**baraque** *sf.* *(P)*. House, joint, spot, shack, shebang. *Toute la baraque,* the whole shebang.

**baratin** *sm.* *(P)*. Clever sales talk, selling spiel, spiel, " build-up ", " line ", as in : the girl didn't fall for the four-flusher's line.

**baratin (faire du)** *(P)*. Same as : *boniment (faire du)*.

**baratiner** *v.* *(P)*. To high-pressure, to argue into ; to give a spiel, to hand a sweet line.

**baratineur** *sm.* *(P)*. " High-pressure " salesman with clever sales-talk, " builder-upper ", " line tosser ".

**barbant** *adj.* *(Sl)*. Boring, annoying, tiresome (thing or individual).

**barbaque** *sf.* *(Sl)*. Meat of inferior quality.

**barbe** *sf.* *(Sl)*. Bother, botheration. *La barbe !* Botheration ! (Excl. of an angry person).

**barbeau** *sm.* *(Sl)*. Procurer, " cadet ", man supported by a woman, pimp.

**barber** *v.* *(Sl)*. To bore, to pester, to bother, to weary.

**barbifiant** *adj.* *(Sl)*. Boring.

**barbillon** *sm.* *(Sl)*. Same as : *barbeau*.

**barbot** *sm.* *(Sl)*. Same as : *barbeau*.

**barbotage** *sm.* *(Sl)*. Theft, snitch, swipe, " lift ", stealing, lifting.

**barboter** *v.* *(Sl)*. To steal, to pinch, to swipe, to "lift", to "salvage".

**barboteur** *sm.* *(Sl)*. Thief, rustler.

**barda** *sm.* *(P)*. The kit, the whole kit, traps, luggage, personal belongings.

**barder** *v.* *(P)*. *Ça barde !* it's getting hot ! Things are humming now ! *Ça va barder !* Now for it ! Look out for squalls !

**baron** *sm.* *(Sl)*. Stooge, confederate.

**baroud** *sm.* *(P)*. Fighting, free-for-all.

**barouf** *sm.* *(Sl)*. Hell of a noise, rumpus, rookus, ruckus.

**barouf du diable (faire un)** *(Sl)*. To raise hell, to raise a rookus.

**barrer (se)** *v.* *(Sl)*. To go away hurriedly, to duck out, to scram.

**bas bleu** *sm.* *(F)*. Bluestocking, a pedantic girl or woman, affected feminine learning.

**bas de laine** *sm.* *(P)*. Savings put away in a stocking (like country folk used to do), "First National". *Un bas de laine bien garni*, a well-lined stocking.

BAS DE LAINE.

**bas de plafond** *(Sl)*. Stupid fellow, dead from the neck up.

* **bas-du-cul** *sm.* *(Sl)*. Sarcastic and vulgar word for a diminutive man.

**bas les pattes ! (à)** *(P)*. Hands down ! (See : *pattes*).

**basse pègre** *sf.* *(P)*. Thieves, roughs, of the lowest kind.

**bassinant** *adj.* *(Sl)*. Annoying, boring, tiresome (thing or individual).

**bassiner** *v.* *(Sl)*. To pester, to make one tired, to importune, to plague one. *Il me bassine avec sa musique*, he gives me a pain with his music.

**basta !** *adv.* *(P)*. Enough ! stop ! sign off !

**Bastoche (la)** *sf.* *(Sl)*. *La Bastille* and its district (in Paris).

**bastos** *sf.* *(Sl)*. Bullet, "pill", "Chicago pill", hot lead.

**bastringue** *sm.* *(Sl)*. Honky-tonk, cheap amusement joint or dance-hall.

**bataclan** *sm.* *(Sl)*. *Tout le bataclan*, the whole kit and caboodle, the whole shooting match.

**bat d'Af** *sm.* *(Sl)*. *Bataillon d'Afrique*, disciplinary battalion (in North Africa).

BATEAU-MOUCHE SUR LA SEINE.

**bateau** *sm.* *(P)*. Cheat, spoof, take-in, hoax, phoney boloney. *Monter un bateau à q.*, to hoax s.o.

**bateau-mouche** *sm.* *(F)*. Small passenger boat on the Seine (for tourists).

**bateaux** *sm. pl. (Sl)*. Unusually large feet or big size(d) shoes, " violin case ".

BATEAUX.

**bath** *adj. (Sl)*. First-rate, bang-up, swell, dandy, classy. *C'est bath !* that's tiptop !

\* **bâton merdeux** *sm. (Sl)*. Grouser, grumbler, griper.

**bâtons rompus (à)** *(F)*. By snatches, by fits and starts.

**battage** *sm. (P)*. Ballyhoo, boosting, publicity, " plugging ".

**batterie de cuisine** *sf. (P)*. Array of medals worn on a uniform, " fruit salad ".

**batteur** *sm. (Sl)*. Liar.

**battre à plate(s) couture(s)** *(F)*. To beat to a frazzle, to beat all to pieces, to knock for a loop, to slaughter.

**battre de l'aile** *(F)*. To be tired, to be near exhaustion.

**battre la breloque** *(F)*. To be off one's head, off one's bean.

**battre le fer pendant qu'il est chaud** *(F)*. To strike while the iron is hot.

**battre le pavé** *(F)*. To pound the sidewalk.

**battre q. comme plâtre** *(P)*. Same as : *battre q. à plates coutures*.

**battre sa flemme** *(P)*. A pop. variant of *tirer sa flemme*.

**battre son plein** *(F)*. To be in full swing, in full blast.

**bavard** *sm. (Sl)*. Lawyer, " mouthpiece ".

**bavard comme une pie (être)** *(F)*. To talk the hind leg off a donkey, to be a chatterbox.

**bavasser** *v. (P)*. To talk idly, to drool, to cackle, to chew the fat.

**baver (en)** *v. (Sl)*. *J'en bavais*, I was mad with rage, I suffered a lot from it. *Il n'a pas fini d'en baver !* his sufferings are not yet over ; the bitterest is yet to come !

FIER DE SA BATTERIE DE CUISINE.

**bazar** *sm. (P).* The whole kit and caboodle, one's personal belongings, traps.

**bazarder** *v. (P).* To sell off one's belongings, to sell something at any price in order to turn it quickly into money.

**beau, belle** *adj. (P).* In the pop. language often pej. : thorough, egregious, consummate, out and out, arch-, etc. Ex. : *un beau coquin,* a thorough scoundrel, *un beau menteur,* an out and out liar, *une belle fripouille,* an arrant cad.

**beau brin de fille (un)** *(F).* A well-built, beautiful girl, a chunk of a girl, a peach.

**beau châssis (un)** *sm. (Sl).* Well shaped feminine body, girl's perfect figure, million-dollar figure.

UN BEAU CHASSIS.

**beau mâle** *sm. (F).* He-man, pin-up boy, glamour boy.

**beauté du diable (la)** *(F).* Young girl's natural beauty.

**bébête** *adj. (P).* Silly, simple, goosey, " simpy ".

**bec** *sm. (P).* Mouth, " beak ".

**bécane** *sf. (P).* Bicycle, wheel, bike.

**bécasse** *sf. (P).* Gullible, unsophisticated girl, " goose ".

**bec et ongles (avoir)** *(F).* To be strong enough to defend oneself.

**bêcher** *v. (F).* To run one down, to " pull one to pieces ".

**bécot** *sm. (P).* Kiss, buss.

**bécoter** *v. (P).* To kiss, to neck.

**bécoteur** *sm. (P).* Man who likes kissing, necking.

**bécoteuse** *sf. (P).* Feminine form of : *bécoteur.*

**becquetance** *sf. (Sl).* Food, " grub ", " chow ", " chuck ".

**becqueter** *v. (Sl).* To eat.

**becqueter des briques** *(Sl).* To go without food.

**bec salé (avoir le)** *(P).* To be always ready for a drink.

**bectance** *sf. (Sl).* Same as : *becquetance.*

**bedaine** *sf. (F).* Belly, tummy, " corporation ".

**bedon** *sm. (P).* Same as : *bedaine.*

**bégueule** *sf. (F).* Prudish girl or woman.
*adj.* Prudish.

**béguin** *sm. (F).* Love, crush, fancy, craze, mad pash, amorous caprice.

**béguin** *sm. (Sl).* Fancy man.

**béguin pour (avoir le)** *(F).* To have a crush on, a pash for s.o., to be stuck on.

**beigne** *sf. (Sl).* Hard blow to the body (on the nose, in the face, etc.), punch, " biff ".

**belle étoile (coucher à la)**

*(F)*. To sleep in the open. (See also : *coucher à la belle étoile*).

**belle lurette (il y a)** *(F)*. Long time ago.

**bénard** *sm. (Sl)*. Trousers, pants.

**bénef** *sm. (Sl)*. Profit, " gravy ", cut.

**béni-oui-oui** *(P)*. Yes-man, a subordinate who agrees with everything his boss says.

**bergère** *sf. (Sl)*. Woman, girl, " broad ".

**berlingot** *sm. (Sl)*. Pimple, boil. Old or bad car. *Un drôle de berlingot,* an old " crate ".

**berlue (avoir la)** *(P)*. To be blind (fig.), not to see things in their proper light, to have hallucinations.

**bernique !** *(P)*. Excl. meaning : No go ! no soap ! no sale !

**bêta** *sm. adj. (P)*. Silly or stupid person. Saphead, bonehead, dope, chump, goofy.

**bêtasse** *sf. adj. (P)*. Stupid woman or girl. Saphead, bonehead, blockhead, " dumb Dora ".

**bête** *adj. (F)*. Silly, stupid. *Pas bête,* no dumbbell. *Bête à manger du foin,* a jackass.

**bête comme chou (c'est)** *(F)*. It's simple, simplicity itself, couldn't be simpler.

**bête comme ses pieds (être)** *(F)*. To be exceedingly stupid, to be a dumb ox.

**bête noire** *sf. (F)*. Anything one hates most.

**bêtises de Cambrai** *sf. pl. (P)*. Popular peppermint candy, a specialty in France.

**betterave** *sf. (Sl)*. Red nose, full-blown nose.

**beuglant** *sm. (Sl)*. Cheap amusement joint, honky-tonk.

**beurre** *sm. (Sl)*. See : *galette*.

**beurre (du)** *sm. (Sl)*. Easy job, " pushover ", " duck soup ".

**beurre dans les épinards (du)** *(P)*. Any increase in one's revenue that makes life easier or more comfortable.

**bibard** *sm. (Sl)*. Old drunkard.

**biberon** *sm. (Sl)*. Drunkard, booze-hitter, " stew ", " soak ", " booze-hound ", person addicted to drink.

**biberonner** *v. (Sl)*. To swizzle, to drink (wine, beer, liquor, etc.), to tipple, to booze. (Same as : *picoler*).

**bibi** *sm. (P)*. Woman's hat (usually a small one).

**bibl** *(Sl)*. Number one, oneself, the speaker, Uncle Dudley. Ex. : *C'est pour bibi,* it's for me.

**bibine** *sf. (Sl)*. Low-grade beer or liquor, " belly-wash ", " belch ".

**bicarré** *sm. (Sl)*. Senior (student in his fourth year).

**bicher** *v. (P)*. *Ça biche,* it's going well, it's all right, it's O.K., okey-dokey.

**bichonner (se)** *v. (F)*. To primp, to spruce up.

**bicoque** *sf. (P)*. Small house, coop, crib, shack, shebang.

**bicot** *sm. (P)*. Pej. for an Arab, a North African.

**bidard** *adj. (Sl)*. Lucky.

**bide** *sm. (Sl)*. Belly, tummy.

**bidoche** *sf. (Sl)*. Meat.

**bidon** *sm. (Sl)*. Trickery, deceit, swindling trick, con game, funny business, monkey business. *C'est du bidon,* that's all humbug, bluff, phoney-baloney.

*Adj.* : phon(e)y, fake, bogus. *F. i. un chèque bidon, un Picasso bidon, un médecin bidon, etc.*

**bidonnant** *adj. (P).* Too funny, amusing, funny as a barrel of monkeys.

**bidonner (se)** *v. (P).* To laugh oneself silly, to split one's sides with laughter.

**bidonville** *sm. (P).* Slum district, shantytown.

**bien balancée** *adj. (Sl).* Shapely. Said of a girl (or a woman) who has a graceful, pleasing figure, dream shape.

**bien ballottée** *adj. (Sl).* A less frequent variant of preceding entry.

**bien bas** *adv. (F).* At a low ebb.

**bien bonne (une)** *(F).* A good story, a good joke.

**bien fait de sa personne (être)** *(F).* To be good looking.

**\* bien foutue** *adj. (Sl).* Well shaped, million-dollar figure (of a girl or a woman). (Syn. : *bien fichue, bien roulée*).

**bien fringué** *adj. (Sl).* Well dressed.

**bien sonné** *adj. (F). Grand-père a 80 ans bien sonnés,* grand father is 80, if he is a day.

**bière** *sf. Ce n'est pas de la petite bière,* it's not to be sneezed at.

**bière du père Adam** *sf. (P).* Water, Adam's ale, Adam's wine.

**bière panachée** *sf. (F).* Half beer and half lemon soda.

**biffe** *sf. (Sl).* Junkman's business. Infantry (see : *biffin*).

**biffin** *sm. (Sl).* Ragman, junkman. Infantryman, footslogger.

**bigler** *v. (Sl).* To look, to get a load of, to take a gander at.

**bignolon** *sm. (Sl).* Prison guard, hack.

**bigorne** *sf. (Sl).* Fight(ing), blows.

**bigorner** *v. (Sl).* To beat.

**bigorner (se)** *(Sl).* To fight, to come to blows, to exchange blows.

**bigornette** *sf. (Sl).* Cocaine, coke, " white cross ".

**bigre !** *(P).* Gosh ! Gee !

**bigrement** *adv. (P).* Very, awfully, jolly, rattingly, deucedly.

**bikini** *sm. (P).* Bikini bathing suit.

**bile (se faire de la)** *(P).* To worry, to fret.

**biler (se)** *v. (P).* To worry. Ex. : *Ne te bile pas !* Don't worry ! Don't fret !

**bileux** *adj. (P).* Easily given to worrying, easily worried, fazed, worrisome. *Pas bileux,* not easily upset, insouciant.

BILLARD.

**billard** *sm.* *(P)*. Bald head, "billiard ball". Operating table.

**billard (du)** *(P)*. *C'est du billard,* something easy to do, a "push-over", "velvet", easy as pie.

**bille** *sf.* *(Sl)*. Stupid person, mutton-head, dumbbell. Face, "dial", "pan". Mug, head, "nut", "knob".

**bille de billard** *sf.* *(Sl)*. Bald head, "billiard ball".

**bille de clown** *sf.* *(Sl)*. Stupid guy, blockhead, dumbbell, muff.

**billet doux** *sm.* *(F)*. Love letter, valentine.

**binette** *sf.* *(Sl)*. Face, "mug".

**bique** *sf.* *(P)*. Goat, she-goat. Old, unpleasant woman, ill-natured old woman.
*(Sl)*. Old horse, jade.

**birbe** *sm.* *(P)*. Usually and popularly : *vieux birbe,* old man, dodo.

**biribi** *sm.* *(P)*. Disciplinary battalion in North Africa.

**bisbille** *sf.* *(P)*. Petty quarrel, dispute, bickering. Ex. : *Etre en bisbille avec q.,* to be at odds with s.o., disagreeing with s.o.

BISTROT PARISIEN.

**bise** *sf.* *(P)*. Kiss, buss.

**biseness** *sm.* *(Sl)*. Business, racket.

**bisenesseuse** *sf.* *(Sl)*. Harlot, prostitute, "hooker", "hustler".

**biser** *v.* *(P)*. To kiss, to buss.

**bisque** *sf.* *(P)*. Vexation.

**bisquer** *v.* *(P)*. To be riled, vexed.

**bistouille** *sm.* *(P)*. Coffee laced with liquor. Inferior drink or low quality liquor.

**bistro(t)** *sm.* *(P)*. Bar, tavern, lower-grade saloon, public house. Bar-keeper, wine seller.

**bistrote** *sf.* *(P)*. Feminine form of : *bistro(t)*.

**bitume** *sm.* *(Sl)*. Sidewalk, pavement. *Fouler le bitume,* to pound the sidewalk.

**bizness** *sm.* *(P)*. Business, racket, any shady means of livelihood.

**bizut** *sm.* *(Sl)*. Freshman, babe (student).

**bla-bla-bla** *sm.* *(P)*. Chitter-chatter, gassy talk, blah-blah, "chin music".

**blafarde** *sf.* *(P)*. Death. Moon.

**blague** *sf.* *(F)*. Joke, yarn, story. Nonsense, guff. *C'est de la blague !* That's bosh ! It's all applesauce ! It's all baloney ! Phoney baloney !

**blague à part!** *(P)*. No kidding, kidding apart !

**blague dans le coin!** *(P)*. Kidding apart, joking apart !

**blaguer** *v.* *(F)*. To joke, to tease, to jolly.
*(Sl)*. To talk, to "jaw".

**blagues à tabac** *sf. pl.* *(Sl)*. A woman's pendant breasts, "droopers".

**blagueur** *sm.* *(F)*. Liar, person not to be taken seriously.

**blair** *sm.* *(Sl)*. Nose, "conk", "beak".

**blaireau** *sm.* *(Sl)*. Nose, "horn", "schnozzle".

**blairer** *v.* *(Sl)*. Ne pouvoir blairer, not to be able to stand (a person). *Je ne peux pas le blairer*, I can't stand him. (Used mainly in the negative form).

**blanc (le)** *sm.* *(Sl)*. Cocaine, coke. White wine. Ex.: *Un petit blanc*, a glass of white wine.

**blanc (être)** *(Sl)*. To have a clean police record.

**blanc-bec** *sm.* *(F)*. Inexperienced youth, greener, greenie, little feller, little squirt.

**blanche** *sf.* *(Sl)*. Cocaine, "coke".

**blé** *sm.* *(Sl)*. See : *galette*.

**blèche** *adj.* *(Sl)*. Ugly, lousy, inferior (in quality).

**bled** *sm.* *(Sl)*. Country, region, out-of-the-way spot, jumping-off place.

**bleu** *sm.* *(P)*. Trace of physical injury, bruise, "mouse", "strawberry". Young soldier, recruit, rookie, Johnny Raw. Tyro, beginner. Worker's overall, jean.

**bleusaille** *sf.* *(P)*. Derisive term for : young soldier, rookie ; group of young soldiers, "awkward squad", novices, beginners.

**blindé** *adj.* *(Sl)*. Drunk, "blotto".

**bloc** *sm.* *(P)*. Jail, cooler, "stir", "booby-hatch", guardhouse, calaboose.

**bloquer** *v.* *(Sl)*. To jail, to "slap in", to toss in the can.

**blouser** *v.* *(Sl)*. To deceive.

**bluffeur** *sm.* *(F)*. Four-flusher.

**bobard** *sm.* *(P)*. Baloney, eyewash. Ex. : *C'est des bobards,* that's all baloney, false news, phonus bolonus.

**bobéchon** *sm.* *(Sl)*. Head, "bun".

**bobinard** *sm.* *(Sl)*. Brothel, "cathouse".

**bobine** *sf.* *(Sl)*. Face, "dial", "pan".

**bobinette** *sf.* *(Sl)*. Gambling game played with three dice.

**bobo** *sm.* *(P)*. A sore.

**bobonne** *sf.* *(F)*. Sweetie-pie.

**bocal** *sm.* *(Sl)*. Stomach.

**bocard** *sm.* *(Sl)*. Brothel, bordello, "pad".

**Boche** *sm.* *(Sl)*. German, Kraut, Jerry.

**Bochie** *sf.* *(Sl)*. Germany.

**bœuf** *adj.* *(P)*. Colossal, admirable, tremendous, a hell of a, helluva. Ex. : *un toupet bœuf,* a hell of a crust ; *un succès bœuf,* a tremendous success.

**B.O.F.** *(P)*. Abbr. *Beurre-Œufs-Fromages*. Big butter-and-egger, big ham-and-egger. Butter and eggdealer who got rich in the trade.

**boire** *v.* *(F)*. To drink intemperately, frequently ; to tipple, to souse. Also : *boire comme un Polonais, boire comme un tonneau, comme une éponge, comme un trou, comme un sonneur, comme un templier, etc.*

**boire à tire-larigot** *(F)*. To drink like fish.

**boire comme du petit lait (se)** *(P)*. Said of any drink that slips down easily.

**boire comme une éponge** *(P)*. See : *boire*.

**boire comme un Polonais** *(P)*. See : *boire*.

**boire comme un sonneur** *(P)*. See : *boire*.

**boire comme un templier** *(P)*. See : *boire*.

**boire comme un tonneau** *(P)*. See : *boire*.

**boire comme un trou** *(P)*. See : *boire*.

**boire du lait** *(P)*. To experience great delight or keen satisfaction, to be happy.

**boire (en) Suisse** *(P)*. To take a drink by oneself, without company.

**boire la goutte** *(P)*. To get (nearly) drowned.

**boire le calice jusqu'à la lie** *(F)*. To drink a bitter cup to its dregs.

**boire sec** *(P)*. To drink neat.

**boire tout son saoul** *(F)*. To drink oneself under the table.

**boire un bouillon** *(P)*. To sustain a heavy loss (in a business enterprise, in a venture).

**boire un coup** *(P)*. To have a drink, a "go".

**boire un coup de trop** *(P)*. To take a drop too much, to drink more than one can bear.

**bois** *sm. pl. (Sl)*. Furniture.

**boite** *sf. (P)*. Joint, dump, spot, disorderly or dishonest business establishment, gyp joint, clip joint.
*(Sl)*. Mouth, bazoo. Prison, hoosegow.

**boîte à cancans** *(P)*. Same as : *potinière*.

**boîte à sel** *sf. (P)*. Control counter (in a theater).

**boîtes à lait** *sf. pl. (Sl)*. A woman's breasts, "milk bottles".

**boîtes à lolo** *sf. pl. (Sl)*. A variation of *boîtes à lait*.

**boîte de nuit** *sf. (F)*. Night club, nitery.

**bombe** *sf. (P)*. Binge, bust, spree. *Faire la bombe,* to go on a binge, to go on a bust, on a bender, to paint the town red.

**bomber (se)** *v. (Sl)*. To go without food. *Tu peux te bomber !* You may wait, you will never get it ! (Same as : *fouiller (se)*).

**bon (être)** *(Sl)*. To be a victim, dupe, sucker. To be arrested, to be "nabbed", to be pinched. (See also : *fait (être)*.

**bon à tuer** *(P)*. Said jocularly of a bungler.

**bon boulot !** *(P)*. Good show !

**bon chat, bon rat (à)** *(P)*. Diamond cut diamond.

**bon coup de fourchette (avoir un)** *(P)*. To have a hearty appetite, to be a good trencherman.

**bondieusard** *sm. (P)*. Pej. for a shopkeeper who sells religious articles.

**bondieuseries** *sf. pl. (P)*. Pej. for religious articles sold by specialized shops around churches.

**bonhomme** *sm. (F)*. Individual, guy.

**boniche** *sf. (P)*. See : *bonniche*.

**boniment** *sm. (P)*. Baloney, phoney baloney, eyewash, claptrap, hoax, stuff, spiel, bally(hoo), patter, sales talk of a street-vendor.

**boniment (faire du)** *(P)*. To make love to, to hand a sweet line, to try to coax s.o.

**bonimenteur** *sm. (P)*. Spieler, ballyhooer, "barker".

**bonnard** *sm. (Sl)*. Victim, sucker.

**bonne (une bien)** *(F)*. See : *bien bonne (une)*.

**bonne femme** *sf. (F)*. Jane, female, woman, broad.

**bonne pâte** *sf. (P)*. Good-natured individual, " good egg ".

**bonne pondeuse** *sf. (Sl)*. Woman with many children.

**bonnet blanc et blanc bonnet (c'est)** *(P)*. It's six of one and half a dozen of the other.

**bonnet d'évêque** *sm. (P)*. Parson's nose, pope's nose, the rear end of a cooked fowl.

**bonniche** *sf. (P)*. Disparaging popular term for a young house-maid, a maid servant.

**bon prince (être)** *(F)*. To be good-natured, decent.

**bon sang !** *interj. (P)*. Heck !

**bon vivant** *sm. (F)*. Gay dog, gay bird.

**bonze** *sm. (P)*. *Vieux bonze,* old fuddy-duddy, a pompous old ass.

**bon zigue (un)** *sm. (Sl)*. Trustworthy individual, " good egg ", reg'lar guy, reg'lar fellow.

**book** *sm. (Sl)*. Bookmaker, bookie (turf).

**Borda (le)** *(P)*. Name of a former school-ship of the Naval Academy at Lanvéoc-Poulmic (formerly in Brest), hence the name of the Naval Academy. *Entrer au Borda* means : *être reçu à l'Ecole Navale.*

**bordache** *sm. (P)*. Naval Academy cadet.

**bordée (être en)** *(P)*. To be (to go) on a spree, on a binge, (mostly said of a sailor who overstays his leave and goes on a spree).

**bordel** *sm. (Sl)*. In slang use not only a brothel, but also : a very disorderly place, disorder, mess-up, bother, annoyance. *Quel bordel !* What an awful messy place ! What a mess ! *Tout le bordel !* The whole mess !

**bosco(te)** *adj. sm. sf. (Sl)*. Hunchback, " humpy ".

**bosse de (avoir la)** *(P)*. To be exceptionally gifted for.

**bosser** *v. (Sl)*. To work, to drudge, to toil.

**botte** *sf. (Sl)*. *Sortir dans la botte,* to graduate " *summa cum laude* ", to be classified among the best graduates at *Polytechnique.* (See also : *bottier*).

**botter** *v. (P)*. To kick s.o. in the pants. Also popularly : *Ça me botte,* it suits me down to the ground, that suits me to a T, it's " just what the doctor ordered ".

**botter le derrière à q.** *(P)*. To kick one's bottom, to boot one.

**bottier** *sm. (Sl)*. *Polytechnique* graduate " *summa cum laude* " who is classified in the so-called " *botte* ". Student who obtained excellent graduation notes from the school, top graduate. (See also : *botte*).

**bottin** *sm. (P)*. Directory.

**bottine** *sf. (Sl)*. The world of lesbians.

**bouboule** *(P)*. " Fatty ", " greaseball ".

**bouc** *sm. (P)*. Pointed beard on the chin, goatee.

**boucan** *sm. (Sl)*. Noise, rumpus, hullabaloo.

**bouché à l'émeri** *(Sl)*. Stupid, chump, dumbbell, dead from the neck up.

**bouche-trou** *sm. (P)*. Stop-gap, " filler-inner ".

**bouchon** *sm. (P)*. Small wineshop, small *bistro.* Baby, the youngest child of a family.

**bouclage** *sm. (Sl)*. Imprisonment.

**boucler** *v. (Sl)*. To close, to shut, *Boucle-la !* Shut up ! To put in jail, to throw " in the can ". (See also : *la boucler*).

**bouclette** *sf. (Sl)*. Lock.

**bouder** *v. (P)*. Not to sell well. Ex. : *Cet article boude*, this article doesn't sell, is difficult to sell (popular term among shopkeepers).

**boudin** *sm. (Sl)*. Prostitute, " hooker ", zook.

**boudins** *sm. pl. (Sl)*. Automobile tires, " hoops ", " doughnuts ".

**boueux** *sm. pl. (P)*. Garbage-man.

**bouffarde** *sf. (Sl)*. Pipe.

**bouffer** *v. (Sl)*. To eat.

**bouffer à s'en faire crever la peau du ventre** *(Sl)*. To eat a lavish meal.

**bouffer de la vache enragée** *(Sl)*. A slang variant of *manger de la vache enragée*.

**bouffer des briques** *(Sl)*. To go without food.

**bouffer des clarinettes** *(Sl)*. A joc. variant of *bouffer des briques*.

ILS N'ONT PAS FINI
DE SE BOUFFER LE NEZ.

**bouffer le nez (se)** *(Sl)*. To quarrel.

**bouge** *sm. (F)*. Dive, low-grade saloon or cheap restaurant.

**bougeotte (avoir la)** *(F)*. To have the fidgets. Said of a person who is constantly on the move, a restless traveler or one of a wandering disposition.

**bougie** *sf. (Sl)*. 5-franc coin. Face, " mug ", " pan ". Head, " knob ", " coconut ".

**bougnat(e)** *sm. sf. (P)*. Nickname for the coalman (retailer) in Paris.

BOUGNAT LIVRANT UN SAC
DE CHARBON.

**bougnoul** *sm. (Sl)*. Negro, nigger.

**bougre** *sm. (P)*. Individual, guy. Ex. : *Pauvre bougre*, poor guy ; *sale bougre*, ugly customer.

**bougre !** *interj. (P)*. Heck ! hell !

**bougrement** *adv. (P)*. Awfully, considerably, deucedly.

**bougresse** *sf. (P)*. Feminine form of *bougre*, female, mollie, jane.

**bouiboui** *sm. (P)*. Cheap restaurant, cheap bar, beanery, dive, "juice-joint", "dump", hovel, hole.

**bouif** *sm. (P)*. Pej. for a cobbler.

**bouillabaisse** *sf. (F)*. Name of a highly seasoned fish soup.

**bouille** *sf. (Sl)*. Face, "dial", "dish", "pan". Head, "knob".

**bouillon** *sm. (P)*. Water. Dirty water. Heavy shower. Cheap restaurant. Unsold newspapers (or books). (See also : *boire un bouillon*).

**bouillon d'onze heures** *(P)*. Poison.

**bouillonner** *v. (P)*. To be left unsold at the newsstands (newspapers, books, etc.).

**bouillotte** *sf. (Sl)*. Face, "mug". Head, "noodle".

**boulangère** *sf. (Sl)*. Woman who supports a fancy man, "meal ticket". *Ma boulangère*, my "meal ticket", my "sister-in-law". (Syn. : *marmite*).

**boule** *sf. (Sl)*. Head, "bun".

**boules de loto** *(P)*. Goggle eyes.

**boulette** *sf. (F)*. Mistake, error, "boo-boo", goofing.

**boulevardier** *sm. (F)*. Equivalent of "Broadway Johnny".

**Boul' Mich'** *(P)*. *Boulevard Saint-Michel* in the Latin Quarter, center of schools and student life in Paris.

**boulonner** *v. (Sl)*. To work hard.

**boulot** *sm. (P)*. Work, job. *Ce n'est pas mon boulot !* it's not my job ! *C'est ton boulot !* that's your baby ! *(Sl)*. Burglary, "crash".

**boulot(te)** *adj. (P)*. Pudgy, plump, fattish.

**boulotter** *v. (Sl)*. *Ça boulotte*, it's going well, all right (see also : *ça biche, ça colle, ça gaze*). To eat.

**bouquet** *sm. (F)*. Apex, "pay-off". *C'est le bouquet*, that crowns all.

**bouquin** *sm. (P)*. Book.

**bouquiner** *v. (P)*. To browse, to glance through books for pleasure, to "mouse" over books. To look up the bookstalls *(bouquinistes)* along the Seine embankments, to hunt after second-hand, old books.

**bourde** *sf. (P)*. Big mistake, big blunder, boner.

**bourdon** *sm. (Sl)*. Horse, old nag. The blues. *Avoir le bourdon*, to have the blues (same as : *avoir le cafard*).

**bourgeoise** *sf. (P)*. One's wife, the "missis".

**bourin** *sm. (Sl)*. Inferior horse (in a race), a nickel horse. (See : *bou(r)-rin*).

**bourlinguer** *v. (P)*. To toil and moil, to rough it, to lead a hard life.

**bourratif** *adj. (F)*. Filling at the price (joc.).

**bourre** *sm. (Sl)*. Police dick, plain-clothesman.

**bourrée** *sf. (Sl)*. Beating, licking, rubbing-down, hiding.

**bourrer le crâne** *(P)*. To fill one up with false stories, lies; to lay it on thick.

**bourreur de crâne** *sm. (P)*. Liar, one who fills people up with false news (especially during the war : person who dispenses false stories of victory).

**bourrichon** *sm.* See : *monter le bourrichon (se)*.

**bourricot** *sm. (P).* Donkey.

BOURRICOT.

**bou(r)rin** *sm. (Sl).* Old and inferior horse, jade, a palooka, a nickel horse. (Syn. : *carcan, canasson*).

**bourrique** *sf. (P).* Stupid person, dumbbell, chump, jackass.

**bourse plate (avoir la)** *(P).* To be penniless, broke.

**boursicoter** *v. (P).* To speculate on a small scale on the Stock Exchange, to " pike ".

**boursicoteur** *sm. (P).* Speculator on a small scale (Stock Exchange), piker.

LA BOUSCULETTE.

**bouscaille** *sf. (Sl).* Fix, sorry plight.

**bousculer le pot de fleurs** *(Sl).* To exaggerate.

**bousculette** *sf. (Sl).* Jostling and bustling crowd.

**bousillage** *sm. (Sl).* " Louse-up ", " killing ", " murder ". Bad play. Bungling. Inferior and careless work, mismanaged affair.

**bousiller** *v. (P).* To " ball up ", to bungle (up), to spoil, to " gum up ", to " jazz up ", to " louse up ", to " muff ".
*(Sl).* To kill, to slay, to " erase ", to " bump off ", to " blot out ".

**boussole** *sf. (Sl).* Head, " bean ", " knob ", " conk ".

**boustifaille** *sf. (Sl).* Food, " chow ", " grub ", " chuck ".

**boustifailler** *v. (Sl).* To eat, to " grub ".

**bouteille (avoir de la)** *(P).* To be old, ripe ; to be an old-timer (with experience).

**bouteille à l'encre (c'est la)** *(P).* Hopeless mess, clear as mud.

**bouteille de derrière les fagots** *(F).* Bottle of old wine.

**boutonnière** *sf. (P).* Corsage, orchid or small bouquet worn by a woman, at the waist or on the shoulder.

**bouzin** *sm. (Sl).* Big noise, uproar. *Faire du bouzin,* to raise a disturbance, to raise hell.

**boxon** *sm. (Sl).* Brothel, house in the red-light district.

**boyau** *sm. (P).* Communication trench.

**boyautant** *adj. (Sl).* Very funny,

comical, very amusing, funny as a barrel of monkeys.

**boyauter (se)** v. (Sl). To amuse oneself, to laugh oneself silly.

**brailler** v. (F). To shout, to holler, to yell.

**braise** sf. (Sl). Money, "moolah", "gravy".

**branche** sf. (P). See : *vieille branche*.

**branche (avoir de la)** (P). To have aristocratic manners.

**branler dans le manche** (F). To be shaky, unstable, insecure.

**branquignol** adj. (Sl). Crackpotty, eccentric, non-sensical.

**braquage** sm. (Sl). Hold-up, stick-up, "heist".

**braque** adj. (Sl). Crazy, cracked.

**braquer** v. (Sl). To hold up, to stick up.

**bras long (avoir le)** (F). To be influential, powerful (socially or in business).

**bras retournés (avoir les)** (P). To be lazy, to be a lazy dog, to be born tired.

**brasseur d'affaires** sm. (F). Businessman with interests in many companies.

**bredouille** (F). See : *rentrer bredouille*.

**brêmes** sf. pl. (Sl). Playing cards, (the) "books", "broads".

**bric et de broc (de)** (F). Here a little and there a little (See also : *de bric et de broc*).

**bricheton** sm. (Sl). Bread.

**bricolage** sm. (P). Boondoggling, pottering about, "do-it-yourselfing".

**bricole** sf. (P). Something worthless, small thing of no importance, odds and ends, trifle, buttons, "peanuts", "chicken feed".

**bricoler** v. (P). To engage in valueless or small, trifling, odd jobs, to putter, to tinker with.

**bricoleur** sm. (P). Boondoggler, "do-it-yourself" worker.

**briffe** sf. (Sl). Food, "chow", "grub".

**briffer** v. (Sl). To eat.

**briller par son absence** (F). To be conspicuous by one's absence. (Here is a fine example of antithesis in French).

**brindezingues (être dans les)** (Sl). To be drunk, blotto, full to the brim.

**bringue** sf. (Sl). Binge, hell-raising, time of your sweet life. *Faire la bringue,* to go on a drinking spree, to burn up the town, to paint the town red.

BRINGUE.

**bringue (faire la)** (Sl). See : *bringue*.

— 33 —

**brique** *sf.* (Sl). One million (francs). Gold bar, ingot.

**briscard** *sm.* (P). Old soldier, vet.

**briser (se la)** *v.* (Sl). To scram.

**bristol** *sm.* (P). Visiting card, calling card.

**broc** *sf.* (Sl). *Ne pas valoir une broc*, not worth a plugged nickel.

**brocante** *sf.* (P). Trade in second-hand goods.

**brochant sur le tout** (F). To crown all, as a pay-off.

**broquille** *sf.* (Sl). Minute.

**brossée** *sf.* (Sl). Beating, brushing, licking, shellacking.

**brosser (se)** *v.* (P). *Tu peux te brosser !* you can whistle for it !

**brosser le ventre (se)** (P). To go without food.

**brouillamini** *sm.* (P). Same as : *embrouillamini*.

**brouillard (être dans le)** (Sl). To be lost.

**brouillards (être dans les)** (Sl). To be boozy. Same as : *vignes du Seigneur (être dans les)*.

**brouille-ménage** *sm.* (P). Ordinary red wine.

BROUILLE-MÉNAGE.

**brousse** *sf.* (F). *Dans la brousse*, in the sticks.

**broutilles** *sf. pl.* (P). Things of insignificant value, " chicken feed ".

**broyer du noir** (F). To be gloomy, depressed, to have the blues, to have the pip.

**brûle-gueule** *sm.* (P). Short pipe, " nose warmer ".

**brûlé** *adj.* (Sl). Ruined, (a) gone coon, (one) whose goose is cooked.

**brûler** *v.* (Sl). To unmask. (See also : *griller*).

**brûler la politesse à q.** (F). To fail to keep an appointment with s.o., to leave one without saying good-by, to take French leave.

**brutal** *sm.* (Sl). Ordinary red wine.

**bu** *adj.* (Sl). Drunk, " plastered ".

**bûche** *sf.* (P). Stupid fellow, chump, dumbbell. *Ramasser une bûche*, to fall down, to take a header, to take a spill, to get a cropper, a flop.

**bûcher** *v.* (P). To work hard, to study hard, to plug, to grind, to keep one's nose to the grindstone.

**bûcheur** *sm.* (P). Hard worker, grind, greasy grind, plugger, hard working student.

**budgétivore** *sm.* (F). Said of government employees, jobholders, etc. whose salary is paid out of government funds.

**buffet** *sm.* (Sl). Belly, chest, lungs, stomach. *En avoir dans le buffet*, to be brave, tough, tenacious.

**burette** *sf.* (Sl). Head, " knob ". Face, " mug ".

**burlingue** *sm.* (Sl). Office, bureau.

**buse** *sf.* (P). Extremely stupid person, dope, chump, dumbbell.

**butor** *sm. (P).* Rough and stupid person, rough and crude guy, roughneck.

**Butte (la)** *(P). Montmartre* (hill in Paris).

**Buttes (les)** *(Sl). Les Buttes-Chaumont* (district in the north-eastern part of Paris).

**buvable** *adj. (Sl).* Usually in the negative : *pas buvable, imbuvable,* unpleasant, socially unacceptable (person).

**buveur d'encre** *sm. (Sl).* Newsman, newspaper man. Office worker, ink-splasher.

# C

**C (la)** *sf. (Sl)*. Cocaine, cee, C, "coke".

**ça alors !** Excl. of surprise or astonishment : Oh, my ! My word ! Can you beat that !

**cabane** *sf. (Sl)*. Bordello. Mean dwelling, "caboose". Jail, clink, pokey, jug. Ex. : *Tu iras en cabane,* you will go to jail.

**cabèche** *sf. (Sl)*. Head, "pate".

**caberlot** *sm. (Sl)*. Head, "knob", "pate".

**ça biche !** *(P)*. It's okie-dokie, it's going all right.

**cabochard** *sm. adj. (P)*. Bullhead, pig-headed, mulish (person).

**caboche** *sf. (Sl)*. Head, "nut", "pate", "knob".

**cabot** *sm. (P)*. Corporal. Dog, pooch. Short for *cabotin :* inferior actor, ham actor, bum actor.

**cabotin** *sm. (P)*. Inferior actor, ham actor.

**caboulot** *sm. (P)*. Cheap bar, low drinking place, barrel house, little rum-hole around the corner.

**cacafouiller** *v. (P)*. Humorous for *cafouiller.*

**cache-cache (jeu de)** *(F)*. Peek-a-boo.

**cache-misère** *sm. (F)*. Long overcoat hiding shabby clothes underneath.

**cacher son jeu** *(F)*. To hold out on.

**cachet (avoir du)** *(F)*. To have a distinctive air, style, appearance, etc.

**cachot** *sm. (P)*. Jail, prison, pokey.

**cachottier** *sm. (P)*. Person who keeps things of minor importance in a mysterious secrecy.

**cacique** *sm. (Sl)*. First of his class at the *Ecole Normale Supérieure.*

**ça colle !** *(P)*. It's O.K., it "clicks", it "jibes".

**cadavre** *sm. (P)*. Emptied wine or liquor bottle, "dead soldier", "dead man".

CADAVRES.

**cadet de ses soucis (être le)** *(F)*. The last thing to bother about, the least of one's worries or troubles.

**cadre** *sm. (Sl)*. Painting, picture, portrait.

**cafard** *sm. (P)*. Melancholy, humps, blues, low spirits, the pip. *Avoir le cafard,* to be depressed, to have the humps, to be browned off, to have the pip.

**cafard(eur)** *sm. (P)*. One who carries tales, one who tells on another, one who snitches.

**cafardant** *adj. (P)*. What gives you the blues, the humps.

**cafarder** *v. (P)*. To inform on, to "snitch".

**cafardeux** *adj. (P)*. *Etre cafardeux,* to be melancholy, to feel blue, to be browned off, sad and low spirited, down in the mouth.

**caf'-conc'** *sm. (P)*. Burlesque show, burleycue.

**café arrosé** *sm. (P)*. Laced coffee, coffee intermixed with rum.

**café Liégeois** *sm. (P)*. Soft ice-cream dessert with whipped cream (called *café Viennois* before World War I).

**cafetière** *sf. (Sl)*. Head, "knob", "pate".

**cafouiller** *v. (P)*. To act in a confused way, to muddle, to talk nonsense.

**cafouilleur** *sm. (P)*. A blundering person, mussy guy, muddler.

**ça gaze !** *(P)*. Excl. of approval : it's going all right, it's fine, okeydokey.

**cagibi** *sm. (F)*. Little poky hole, cubby-hole.

**cagna** *sf. (P)*. One's dwelling (place), one's shanty, "shebang". Dug-out (army).

**cagne** *sf. (Sl)*. Preparatory class in a "lycée" for *Ecole Normale Supérieure*.

**cagner** *v. (P)*. Same as : *caler.*

**cagneux** *sm. (Sl)*. Student in a "*cagne*". (See : *cagne*).

**cagnotte** *sf. (P)*. Kitty.

**caïd** *sm. (Sl)*. Topman.

**caillou** *sm. (P)*. Head (sometimes : bald head), "billiard ball". (Also : *caillou déplumé*).

**Caïphe à Pilate (renvoyer de)** *(F)*. To send from pillar to post.

**caisse** *sf. (Sl)*. Military jail, cooler, booby-hatch, clink. D.B., disciplinary barracks. Lungs.

**caisson** *sm. (P)*. See : *faire sauter le caisson (se)*.

**ça la fiche mal** *(Sl)*. That makes it look lousy.

**ça la fout mal** *(Sl)*. Same as : *ça la fiche mal,* but more vulgar.

**calancher** *v. (Sl)*. To die, to "kick the bucket", to "pass out", to "check out".

**calé** *adj.* *(F)*. Difficult, requiring a great deal of expert knowledge. Learned, capable. *Etre calé sur q. ch.,* to be hep to, to know all about, to know the " score ".

**caler** *v.* *(Sl)*. To be afraid, to be frightened, to get cold feet.

**caler (se les)** *(Sl)*. Same as : *caler les joues (se)*.

**caler les amygdales (se)** *(Sl)*. See : *caler les joues (se)*.

**caler les badigoinces (se)** *(Sl)*. See : *caler les joues (se)*.

**caler les joues (se)** *(Sl)*. To eat a good meal with appetite, to " feed one's face ".

**calibre** *sm.* *(Sl)*. Revolver, rod, shooting iron.

**calicot** *sm.* *(P)*. Salesclerk in a retail store, counterjumper.

**Calino** *(F)*. Personification of a sap, " simp ", Johnny Sap.

**calinotade** *sf.* *(F)*. Silly remark, silly action of a silly person.

**calotin** *sm.* *(P)*. Priest, holy Joe. *Les calotins,* over-zealous church-goers.

**calotte** *sf.* *(P)*. Clergy. Clericalism, clerical party. Slap in the face (see also : *calotter q.*).

**calotter q.** *v.* *(P)*. To box one's ears, to slap s.o. in the face.

**calter** *v.* *(Sl)*. To go away, to leave, to check out, to scram.

**calva** *sm.* *(Sl)*. *Calvados* (liquor).

**Camarde** *sf.* *(P)*. Death, " Old Floorer ".

**cambriole** *sf.* *(Sl)*. Burgling, burglary, " crack ".

**cambrioler** *v.* *(F)*. To commit burglary, to burglarize.

**cambrioleur** *sm.* *(F)*. Burglar, " cracksman ".

**Cambronne** *(P)*. See : *mot de Cambronne*.

**cambrousard** *sm.* *(Sl)*. Peasant, hick, hayseed.

**cambrous(s)e** *sf.* *(Sl)*. Country (as opposed to cities), back country, " sticks ".

**cambuse** *sf.* *(Sl)*. Dwelling, room.

**came** *sf.* *(Sl)*. Narcotics, drug, junk, cocaine.

**camelot** *sm.* *(P)*. Street vendor, street spieler, street peddler, pitchman.

**camelote** *sf.* *(P)*. Goods of inferior quality, junk. *C'est de la camelote,* that's junk.

*(Sl)*. Goods. *C'est de la bonne camelote,* that's good stuff, the real Mc Coy.

**camembert** *sm.* *(Sl)*. Traffic beacon or traffic policeman's raised platform.

FLIC SUR UN CAMEMBERT,
EN TRAIN DE RÉGLER
LA CIRCULATION.

**camouflet** *sm.* *(F)*. Insult.

**camplouse** *sf.* *(Sl)*. Same as : *cambrous(s)e*.

**canaille** *sf. (F).* Bad lot, roughs, riff-raff, rabble.

**ça n'a pas de nom !** *(P).* Said of s.th. unbelievable, unqualifiable, beyond words.

**ça n'a pas traîné !** *(P).* It didn't take long, no time was lost.

**canard** *sm. (P).* Newspaper, news-sheet. Hoax, false report, a " snake story ". Horse. Piece of sugar dipped in coffee or liquor.

**canarder** *v. (P).* To shoot from a hidden position, to snipe, to clobber.

**canasson** *sm. (P).* Horse, hack, old worn-out horse, jade.

**cancans** *sm. pl. (F).* Same as : *potins.*

**ça ne casse rien !** *(P).* It cuts no ice ! Nothing to write home about, no great shakes.

**ça ne prend pas !** *(P).* I don't believe you ! Nothing doing ! No go ! No sale !

**ça ne se trouve pas dans le pas d'un cheval** *(P).* That's not to be found every day (meaning anything rare).

**ça ne tourne pas rond** *(P).* Something is wrong, there is a bug somewhere. (See also : *ne pas tourner rond*).

**ça ne vaut pas chipette !** *(P).* See : *ne pas valoir chipette.*

**ça ne vaut pas les quatre fers d'un chien** *(P).* Not worth shucks, not worth a continental, not worth a plugged nickel.

**ça n'existe pas !** *(P).* Pop. excl. meaning categorical refusal or denial.

**canon** *sm. (Sl).* Glass.

**canulant** *adj. (Sl).* Tiresome, boring, plaguing.

**canular** *sm. (Sl).* Practical joke of older students at the expense of fresh-men. (Also : *canularium*).

**canularium** *sm. (Sl).* See : *canu-lar.*

**canule** *sf. (Sl).* Bother, bothera-tion, trouble ; bore, plague.

**canuler** *v. (Sl).* To pester, to bother, to make one tired, to bore, to plague.

**capiston** *sm. (Sl).* Captain.

**Capitaine Ronchonneau** *(P).* Old buzzard, old gripe, nickname for a griping army officer.

**caporal** *sm. (P).* Sort of cheap tobacco.

**carabin** *sm. (Sl).* Medical student.

**carabiné** *adj. (P).* Very strong, beefy, excessive, violent ; capital, first-rate, crack.

**carafe** *sf. (Sl).* Head, " knob ", " pate ".

**carafon** *sm. (Sl).* Same as : *carafe.*

**carambouillage** *sm. (Sl).* Swin-dle, racket, crooked deal perpetrated by a *carambouilleur.* (See : *carambouil-leur*).

**carambouille** *sf. (Sl).* Same as : *carambouillage.*

**carambouilleur** *sm. (Sl).* Crook who buys goods on credit and sells them at once for cash without paying the supplier's bill.

**carapater (se)** *v. (Sl).* To de-camp, to make oneself scarce, to scram.

**carat** *sm. (Sl).* Years (to deter-mine a person's age). *Quarante carats,* forty years (of age) ; *cinquante carats,* fifty years (of age), etc.

**carcan** *sm. (P).* Worn-out or infe-rior horse, jade.

*(Sl).* Tall and lean woman.

**carcasse** *sf. (P).* Body, carcass.

**carder le cuir** *(Sl)*. To thrash, to beat, to tan one's hide.

**cardinal** *sm. (Sl)*. A 1.000-franc bank-note, with Richelieu's effigy.

**caresser la bouteille** *(P)*. To tipple.

**carne** *sf. (Sl)*. Old horse, nag. Malicious, ill-natured, unkind individual. Insult for a disliked person.

**carogne** *sf. (Sl)*. Debauched woman, hag, bitch, slut.

**carottage** *sm. (P)*. Same as : *carotte*.

**carotte** *sf. (P)*. "Sell", trick, skin game, bunko game, racket.

**carotter** *v. (P)*. To gyp (out of), to swindle.

**carotteur** *sm. (P)*. Gypster, wangler, swindler.

**carottier** *sm. (P)*. Same as : *carotteur*.

**carouble** *sf. (Sl)*. Skeleton key.

**caroubleur** *sm. (Sl)*. Burglar.

**carré** *sm. (Sl)*. Sophomore (student in the second year). Landing (of stairs).
*adj. (P)*. Frank, loyal, straightforward, absolutely honest.

**carreau** *sm. (Sl)*. Monocle. (See also : *grand carreau, petit carreau*).

**carreaux** *sm. pl. (Sl)*. Eyes, "daylights", "windows".

**carrée** *sf. (Sl)*. Room.

**carrément** *adv. (F)*. Straightforwardly, honestly. Without hesitation or detours.

**carrosse** *sm. (Sl)*. Police bus.

**carte blanche** *(F)*. Unlimited powers (to give a free hand).

**carte grise** *sf. (P)*. Circulation license for a car.

**casbah** *sf. (Sl)*. One's dwelling, house, hang-out.

**case en moins (avoir une)** *(P)*. To be cracked, to be a crackpot.

**ça sent le roussi** *(Sl)*. Excl. of a person who feels that trouble is brewing, danger is nearing.

**ça sent mauvais** *(Sl)*. Same as : *ça sent le roussi*.

**caser** *v. (P)*. Etre casé(e), to be married.

**casque (avoir son)** *(Sl)*. Same as : *culotte (avoir sa)*.

**casque (la)** *sf. (Sl)*. Pay.

**casquer** *v. (Sl)*. To pay up, to "fork out", to "shell out", to "cough up".

**casquette** *sf. (Sl)*. Money lost in a gamble.

**cassage** *sm. (Sl)*. Burglary. (See : *fric-frac*).

**casse** *sf. (P)*. *Il y aura de la casse*, pop. saying meaning that trouble is ahead, there will be trouble.

*(Sl)*. Burglary, crack-in, crash.

**casse-cou** *sm. (P)*. Break-neck. Heller, daredevil.

\* **casse-couilles** *sm. (Sl)*. Awful bore, nuisance, "pain in the neck".

**casse-gueule** *sm. (Sl)*. Very strong liquor, "panther sweat". Low-class joint, dive, low-grade drinking place. Dump, hangout, cut-throat, inferior and dangerous dance hall.

**cassement** *sm. (Sl)*. Burglary. (See : *fric-frac*).

**casse-olives** *sm. (Sl)*. Same as : *casse-pieds*.

**casse-pattes** *sm. (Sl)*. Very strong spirit, strong liquor, "tanglefoot".

**casse-pieds** *sm. (P)*. Awful bore, nuisance, pesterer, pain in the neck.

**casse-pipe** *sm. (Sl)*. War, "fracas".

**casse-poitrine** *sm. (Sl)*. Same as : *casse-pattes*.

**casser du sucre sur le dos de q.** *(P)*. To run s.o. down, to speak ill of s.o.

**casser la croûte** *(Sl)*. To have a light meal, a snack.

**casser la gueule** *(Sl)*. To beat up, to thrash, to lick the stuffin' out of one.

**casser le cou (se)** *(P)*. To break one's neck, to kill oneself.

**casser le morceau** *(Sl)*. To confess, to betray, to "squeal", to report to police.

**casser le nez (se)** *(P)*. To find the door shut and nobody at home. *(Sl)*. To fail (in business), to get a cropper, to fall flat.

**casser les oreilles à q.** *(P)*. To make one sick with noise.

**casser les pieds** *(Sl)*. To importune, to tire, to pester, to plague s.o. *Dites-lui qu'il me casse les pieds*, tell him he gives me a pain in the neck (he gets in my hair).

**casser les vitres** *(P)*. To raise hell.

**casserole** *sf. (Sl)*. Derogatory for a low class woman, a prostitute, "zook". Informer, stool-pigeon, "squealer".

**casser sa pipe** *(P)*. To die, to "pass out", to "cash in one's checks".

**casser son verre de montre** *(P)*. To fall upon one's buttocks.

**cassis** *sm. (Sl)*. Head, "knob".

**castapiane** *sf. (Sl)*. V.D., venereal disease.

**cateau** *sf. (Sl)*. Same as : *catin*.

**catéchiser** *v. (F)*. To lecture one, to try to persuade one with reasoning to do something.

**ça te la coupe !** *(Sl)*. That bowls you over !

**catholique** *sm. (P)*. See : *pas très catholique*.

**catin** *sf. (F)*. Woman of easy morals, floozey.

**cato** *sf. (Sl)*. Same as : *catin*.

**cautère sur une jambe de bois (c'est un)** *(P)*. Like prescribing Scott's emulsion for a broken leg, (used to signify an inefficacious remedy or any ineffective effort, measure, deed, action, etc.).

**cavale** *sf. (Sl)*. Flight (from jail), escape. *Etre en cavale*, on the lam, in flight.

**cavaler** *v. (Sl)*. To make one tired, to importune s.o., to pester s.o. To run. To chase girls, women, to chase skirts.

**cavaler (se)** *v. (Sl)*. To go away, to leave, to make oneself scarce, to scram, to flee, to escape.

**cavalerie** *sf. (Sl)*. Loaded dice, crooked dice, "peeties".

**cavalerie de St-Georges** *(P)*. Symbol for the British gold sovereigns (that bore on their reverse side the figure of St-George on horseback slaying the dragon) especially with reference to large quantities thereof for bribing the enemy.

**cavaleur** *sm. (Sl)*. Same as : *coureur*.

**cavalier** *sm. (Sl)*. British gold coin, one pound sterling.

**cavalier seul** *(P)*. Loner. See also : *cavalier seul (faire)*.

**cavalier seul (faire)** *(F)*. To act alone, to go it alone.

**ça vaut 10** *(P)*. Something perfect, remarkable, something to write home about.

**cave** *sm. (Sl)*. Prostitute's paying guest.

**ça vient comme un cheveu sur la soupe** *(P)*. That has nothing to do with the matter we are talking about.

**ça vous tombe dessus comme la misère sur le pauvre monde** *(P)*. Popular saying denoting or stressing suddenness.

**ça y est !** *(P)*. Got it !

**cégétiste** *sm. sf. (P)*. Member of the *C.G.T. (Confédération Générale du Travail*, a Labor Union).

**cela me chiffonne !** *(F)*. It annoys me! it worries me! it's bugging me !

**ce ne sont pas mes oignons** *(P)*. See : *c'est pas mes oignons*.

**ce n'est pas (bien) sorcier** *(F)*. It's easy like taking candy from a baby, easy as pie.

**ce n'est pas de la petite bière !** *(P)*. For a person : he's a big shot, a VIP. For a thing : it's not to be sneezed at.

**ce n'est pas de la rigolade !** *(P)*. It's no laughing matter ! no joke ! It's a serious matter !

**ce n'est pas drôle !** *(P)*. Euphemism for a sad story or a sorry plight.

**ce n'est pas la mer à boire** *(P)*. Anything easily done, not difficult to do.

**cent coups (être aux)** *(F)*. To be terribly upset, in distress or in desperation.

**Centrale** *sf. (Sl)*. Abbr. for : *Ecole Centrale des Arts et Manufactures*, engineering school in Paris.

**centrouse** *sf. (Sl)*. Pen(itentiary), the big house, " Cooler College ".

**ce que femme veut, Dieu le veut !** *(P)*. Popular saying meaning that a woman must have her way.

**ce que je m'en fiche !** *(P)*. I couldn't care less ! I don't care a damn !

**c'est à se les mordre** *(Sl)*. Very funny, very amusing, killing.

**c'est clair comme de l'eau de roche** *(F)*. It's clear, plain.

**c'est comme si je flûtais** *(P)*. It's as if I preached in the wilderness, as if I preached to deaf ears.

**c'est couru !** *(Sl)*. It's a cinch ! Also : *c'est couru d'avance !* A lead-pipe cinch.

**c'est dans le sac** *(P)*. In the bag, a cinch, sure business.

**c'est de l'hébreu pour moi !** *(P)*. It's choctaw for me ! it's double Dutch for me !

**c'est la bouteille à l'encre** *(P)*. See : *bouteille à l'encre*.

**c'est la fin des haricots** *(P)*. That is the limit ! can you beat that !

**c'est pas mes oignons** *(P)*. Pop. and low for : It's none of my business, it's not my funeral !

**c'est pas tes oignons** *(P)* Slovenly pop. for : Mind your business ! Nonya business !

**c'est pas une paille !** *(P)*. That's not a trifle !

**c'est plus fort que de jouer aux bouchons** *(P)*. Pop. excl. for anything unbelievable : It beats the Dutch !

**c'est trop fort !** *(P)*. That's a bit thick ! (stiff, steep).

**c'est une pierre dans mon jardin** *(F)*. It's a dig at me.

**c'est un monde !** *(P)*. Excl. denoting something huge, something incredible, a whale of a.

**c'est un peu fort de café (de tabac) !** *(Sl)*. Same as : *c'est un peu raide* !

**c'est un peu raide !** *(Sl)*. It's a bit stiff ! (a bit thick !), that's a bit steep !

**chahut** *sm. (Sl)*. Horseplay, rumpus, big to-do. (See also : *en faire un chahut*).

**chahuter** *v. (Sl)*. To engage in horseplay, to horse around, to raise hell, to " rag ".

**chair de poule** *sf. (F)*. Gooseskin, goose-pimples.

**chair de poule (avoir la)** *(F)*. To feel one's flesh crawl. *Donner la chair de poule,* to give one the creeps.

**chambard** *sm. (Sl)*. Noise, rumpus. (See also : *faire du chambard*).

**chamberlain** *sm. (P)*. Umbrella, " brolly ".

CHAMBERLAIN.

**chambouler** *v. (P)*. To turn everything upside down, to disrupt.

**chambrer une bouteille (de vin)** *(F)*. To bring a bottle (of wine) up to the room's temperature.

**chameau** *sm. (Sl)*. Bastard, lousy dog, stinker. (Of a woman : bitch).

**champignon** *sm. (P)*. Accelerator (auto). Ex. : *Appuyer sur le champignon,* to step on the gas.

**champoreau** *sm. (Sl)*. Mixture of coffee and liquor, laced coffee.

**chançard** *adj. (P)*. Lucky.

**chand-de-vin** *sm. (Sl)*. Bistro, wine seller.

**changer de crémerie** *(Sl)*. To move over to new quarters, to change one's residence, one's activity, etc.

**changer de disque** *(Sl)*. To turn the conversation to another subject.

**change de disque ! (changez de disque !)** *(P)*. Fling at one who is always repeating the same old story.

**changer d'épicerie** *(Sl)*. Same as : *changer de crémerie.*

**changer son fusil d'épaule** *(F)*. To change one's opinion, one's conception, one's tactics.

**chansons que tout ça !** *(F)*. Exclamation signifying : That's all bunk, all applesauce, all baloney !

**chanter** *v. (P)*. *Ça me chante,* it pleases me.

**chanter comme une seringue** *(Sl)*. To be a bad singer, to sing out of tune, off-key.

**chaparder** *v. (P)*. To steal, to pinch, to swipe.

**chapardeur** *sm. (P)*. Thief.

**chapiteau** *sm. (P)*. Circus tent, " big top ", " white top ". Head, " bun ".

**charabia** *sm. (P).* Gibberish, double Dutch, choctaw.

**charcutage** *sm. (P).* Butchering, bungled operation.

**charcuter** *v. (P).* To butcher a patient (said of a bad surgeon).

**Charenton** *(P).* Bedlam, bughouse, loony bin, idiotarium.

**chargé (être)** *(Sl).* To go armed, rodded up, heeled, in possession of a fire-arm, to pack a gun. To be drunk, tight.

**charibotée** *sf. (Sl).* Great quantities of, oodles, scads of.

**charivari** *sm. (P).* Cats' concert, shivaree.

**charmeuses** *sf. pl. (Sl).* Moustache, " tickler(s) ".

**charognard** *sm. (Sl).* Abusive term : Varmint, rotten egg, measly guy, any contemptible person, heel(er).

**charogne** *sf. (Sl).* Same as : *carne.*

**charrier** *v. (Sl).* To exaggerate, to pitch it strong. Ex. : *Tu charries !* you come it rather strong !

**châsses** *sm. pl.* Eyes, " blinkers ", " oglers ".

**chasseur (d'hôtel)** *sm. (F).* Bellboy, bellhop.

**châtaigne** *sf. (Sl).* Blow with the bare fist, hit, punch, " biff ".

**chat dans la gorge** *(F).* Frog in one's throat, hoarseness.

**château branlant** *sm. (P).* Tottery, unsteady being (or thing), toddler.

**châteaubriant** *sm. (F).* Beefsteak of superior quality.

**château-la-pompe** *sm. (F).* Sobriquet for drinking water.

**châteaux en Espagne** *(F).* Castles in the air, imagination.

**chaud de la pince** *(Sl).* Said of a passionate lover, hot daddy, fastie.

**chauffard** *sm. (F).* Hit-and-run driver, hit-runner, reckless driver, a " cowboy ".

**chauffer** *v. (F).* To " cram " (for an exam.).

**chausson** *sm. (F). Chausson aux pommes,* sort of French apple cake.

**chef** *sm. (F).* Chief cook. Master-sergeant.

**cheminot** *sm. (P).* Railroad man.

**chercher chicane à q.** *(F).* To pick holes in one's coat.

**chercher à q. des poux dans la tête** *(Sl).* To look for lice in one's head, popular saying meaning : to try to pick a quarrel with a person.

**chercher la petite bête** *(F).* To be overcritical in trifles, to pick holes.

**chercher midi à quatorze heures** *(F).* To look for complications where there are none.

**chercher noise à** *(F).* To pick on one.

**chercher une aiguille dans une botte de foin** *(F).* To look for a pin in a haystack.

**chérot** *adj. (P).* Rather high price, a bit too expensive.

**cherrer** *v. (Sl).* To exaggerate, to pitch it strong. Ex. : *Tu cherres !* That's a bit stiff ! You exaggerate !

**cherrer dans les bégonias** *(Sl).* To exaggerate.

**cheval de bataille** *sm. (F). C'est son cheval de bataille,* it's his pet argument.

**cheval de retour** *sm. (Sl).* Jail bird, old offender, old lag.

**chevalier d'industrie** *sm.* *(F).* Crook, swindler, wangler, grifter.

**chevaliers de la lune** *sm. pl.* *(Sl).* Thieves, burglars, safecrackers, yeggmen and the like who "work" at night.

**cheval pour le travail (c'est un)** *(F).* He's a real wheel horse.

**cheval sur (être à)** *(F).* To insist on something unyieldingly, uncompromisingly. Ex. : *Il est à cheval sur la régularité,* he is a stickler for regularity.

**cheveu sur la soupe** *(F).* See : *ça vient comme un cheveu sur la soupe.*

**cheveux (se faire des)** *(P).* To worry oneself grey.

**cheveux carotte** *sm. pl.* *(P).* Red hair.

**cheville ouvrière** *sf.* *(F).* Kingpin, mastermind.

**chialer** *v.* *(Sl).* To weep, to cry. (See : *chialeur*).

**chialeur** *sm.* *(Sl).* Term of disparagement for an individual who cries often and without cause ; also a person who complains constantly ; a crybaby, a blubber-head.

* **chiasse** *sf.* *(Sl).* Fear, blue fear, funkiness.

* **chiasser** *v.* *(Sl).* To be awfully frightened, to get the wind up, to have the shakes, "creeps".

* **chiasseur** *sm.* *(Sl).* Coward, person easily frightened.

**chiche !** *interj.* *(P). Chiche que j'oserai !* I bet I dare ! *Chiche que tu n'oseras !* I bet you don't dare !

**chichi** *sm.* *(F). Faire du (des) chichi(s),* to kick up a fuss.

**chichite** *sf.* *(Sl).* Any undefined illness, sickness.

**chichiteux** *adj.* *(F).* Fussy, fussbudgety.

**chic pour (avoir le)** *(F).* To have the knack of, to get the hang of.

**chic type (un)** *sm.* *(F).* Nice guy, regular guy, good sport.

**chien** *adj.* *(Sl).* Close-fisted, "close", stingy.

**chien (avoir du)** *(P).* To have umph, mmph, to have s.a. (sex appeal).

**chienchien** *sm.* *(F).* Term of endearment for a little dog.

**chiendent** *sm.* *(Sl).* Difficulty, hitch, snag, "bug". *Voilà le chiendent !* There's the snag !

**chien de quartier** *sm.* *(Sl).* Master-seargeant.

**chien du commissaire** *(Sl).* (Man) secretary of a police commissioner, clerk of a police station in Paris.

**chiennerie** *sf.* *(F).* Sordidness, meanness, shameless act.

**chien regarde bien un évêque (un)** *(F).* Said to a person who dislikes being looked at and says so.

**(les) chiens aboient, la caravane passe** *(F).* Pop. saying connoting fatalism.

* **chierie** *sf.* *(Sl).* Annoyance, trouble ; boring, tedious, annoying thing.

**chiffe** *sf.* *(Sl).* Junk business, junkman's business. Weakling.

**chiffonner** *v.* *(F).* See : *cela me chiffonne.*

**chignole** *sf.* *(Sl).* Same as : *tacot, bagnole,* old, ramshackle car.

**chignon véreux** *sm.* *(P).* Insulting term for a woman.

**chiner** *v.* *(P).* To guy, to rib, to needle one.

**chinois** *adj.* *(F).* Double Dutch,

choctaw. Ex. : *C'est du chinois pour moi,* it's double Dutch for me.

**chinois de paravent** *(F).* Term of disparagement for an individual, foul ball, punk, Siwash.

**chinoiser** *v. (P).* To engage in unpleasant and boring " *chinoiseries* ". (See : *chinoiseries* ).

**chinoiseries** *sf. pl. (F).* Red tape. *Chinoiseries administratives,* official red tape or rigid application of regulations entailing long and unpleasant delay in getting business done.

**chiot** *sm. (F).* Pup(py).

**\* chiottes** *sf. pl. (Sl).* Toilet, W.C., Johnny, " can ".

**chiper** *v. (P).* To steal, to swipe. *(Sl).* Etre chipé, to be in love. Ex. : *Je suis chipé pour cette fille,* I am nuts on that girl.

**chipeur** *sm. (P).* Thief, petty thief. Also friendly coll. for one who steals another fellow's girl.

**chipie** *sf. (F).* Derisive term for a prudish, proud and disagreable woman, ill-natured, cantankerous woman, " hell-cat ".

**chipoter** *v. (P).* To trifle, to diddle. To gnaw at, to nibble.

**chique** *sf. (Sl).* See : *couper la chique à q.*

**chiqué** *sm. (P).* Fuss. *C'est du chiqué,* it's all sham, fake, phoney (anything but genuine).

**chiquer** *v. (Sl).* To sham, to feign, to pretend.

**chnouf** *sf. (Sl).* Heroin (powerful narcotic) ; cocaine, " happy dust " ; " nose powder " ; powdered narcotic.

**chochotte** *sf. (F). Ma chochotte,* darling. *Faire sa chochotte,* said of a woman who behaves as if butter wouldn't melt in her mouth.

**chocolat** *sm. (P). Etre chocolat,* to have been " taken in ", " sucked in ", cheated, deceived ; to be a victim, " bag holder ". *A la fin il est chocolat,* he is left " holding the bag ", " holding the baby ".

**chocottes** *sf. pl. (Sl).* Teeth. (See also : *chocottes (avoir les)*).

**chocottes (avoir les)** *(Sl).* To be afraid, to be terribly frightened, jittery.

**choléra** *sm. (Sl).* Insult for a bad individual or a disliked personne.

**choper** *v. (Sl).* To steal, to pinch, to swipe. To catch, as in : *choper un rhume,* to catch a bad cold.

**choper au tournant** *(Sl).* A variation, of *choper au virage.*

**choper au virage** *(Sl).* To arrest, to " nab ", to " pinch ", to capture.

**chopeur** *sm. (Sl).* Petty thief.

**chopin** *sm. (P).* Real bargain, windfall, " pie ", " soft sugar ". Love conquest, wealthy lover, " gold mine ", " sugar bowl ", good catch. Ex. : *Faire un beau chopin.*

**chopiner** *v. (Sl).* To tipple.

**chosette** *sf. (Sl).* Love, amour.

**chou blanc (faire)** *(F).* To fail.

**chouchou** *sm. (F).* Lamby pie, sweetie-pie, ducky, darling, pet, the fair-haired child of.

**chouchoute** *sf. (F).* Same as : *chouchou* in fem. form, darling, sweetie-pie, ducky, etc.

**chouchouter** *v. (F).* To favor, to spoil.

**chouette** *adj. (Sl).* Real fine, A Nº 1, corking, clipping, swell.

**chouette !** *interj. (Sl).* Swell !

**chouriner** *v.* (*Sl*). To knife, to stab one.

**chuter** *v.* (*Sl*). To fall, to come a cropper, to take a spill.

**cibiche** *sf.* (*Sl*). Cigarette, " pill ", ciggie.

**ciblot** *sm.* (*Sl*). Civilian, civvy.

**ciboulot** *sm.* (*Sl*). Head, "knob", brains, "upper story". Ex. : *Se creuser le ciboulot*, to twist one's brains, to pound one's brains.

**cigare** *sm.* (*Sl*). Head, "knob", "nut". Ex. : *Avoir mal au cigare*, to have a headache.

**cigue** *sm.* (*Sl*). 20-franc gold piece. Twenty francs (as a unit). Ex. : 50 *cigues* : 1000 francs.

**cinglé** *sm., adj.* (*Sl*). Crazy (person), crack-pot(ty), cracked, loony.

**cinq à sept** *sm.* (*F*). Lovers' tryst.

**cinq lettres (les)** (*Sl*). Four-letter word. (In French, euphemism for : *merde*).

**cinquante-pour-cent (son)** *sm.* (*Sl*). Wife, "ball and chain".

**cinquième roue d'un carrosse (être la)** (*F*). To be the fifth wheel of a coach, to be entirely useless.

**cipal** *sm.* (*Sl*). Soldier of the Paris military police.

**cipaux** *sm. pl.* (*P*). Military policemen in Paris. (Plural of : *cipal*).

**Cirque (le)** *sm.* (*Sl*). Chamber of Deputies (joc.).

**citron** *sm.* (*Sl*). Head, "pate", "knob".

**civelot** *sm.* (*Sl*). Civilian, civvy.

**clac** *sm.* (*Sl*). Same as : *claque*.

**clair comme de l'eau de roche** (*F*). Plain as a pikestaff, clear and obvious, crystal-clear.

**clair comme le jour** (*F*). Very clear and obvious, plain as a pikestaff, as clear as noonday.

**clam(e)cer** *v.* (*Sl*). To die, to "check out", to "cash one's checks".

**clamser** *v.* (*Sl*). Same as : *clam(e)cer*.

**clandé** *sm.* (*Sl*). Abbr. of : *tripot clandestin, bordel clandestin*, illicit gambling joint, illicit brothel.

**clapoter** *v.* (*Sl*). To die, "to pass out".

**clapser** *v.* (*Sl*). To die, "to kick the bucket".

**claque** *sf.* (*Sl*). Brothel.

**claqué** *adj.* (*P*). Exhausted, tired to death, bushed, fazzled ; worn-out.

**claque-dents** *sm.* (*Sl*). Brothel, drinking joint of the lowest class.

**claquer** *v.* (*Sl*). To die, to "check out", to "kick the bucket".

**claquer (se)** *v.* (*P*). To tire oneself to death.

**claquer du bec** (*Sl*). To be hungry, to be starving.

**clebs** *sm.* (*Sl*). Dog, pooch, poodle.

**client** *sm.* (*F*). To be hot on, to be interested in, to be a sucker about. Ex. : *Cent mille balles pour ne rien fiche ? J'suis client !* Hundred thousand francs for doing nothing ? With pleasure !

**cliques et ses claques (ses)** (*P*). One's personal effects. *Prendre ses cliques et ses claques*, to "clear out", to leave.

**cliquettes** *sf. pl.* (*Sl*). Ears, "flappers".

**clochard** *sm.* *(P)*. Hobo, bum.

CLOCHARD.

**Cloche (A la)** *(P)*. Name of a hobo joint on the left bank.

**cloche** *sf.* *(Sl)*. Pumkin head, big dummy, ignoramus.

**cloche (être de la)** *(Sl)*. To be a hobo, a tramp, a bum.

**clocher** *v.* *(P)*. *Il y a q. ch. qui cloche,* there is a hitch, a bug, there is a screw loose somewhere.

**clodo** *sm.* *(Sl)*. Hobo, bum.

**clopinettes** *sf. pl.* *(Sl)*. Nothing. *Des clopinettes !* No sale !

**clou** *sm.* *(P)*. Old typewriter, old motocycle, old clunker, jalopy, junk. Drawing card, high spot, glamor spot, chief attraction. Pawnshop, hock, my uncle's, uncle Benny.

**clouer le bec (à q.)** *(Sl)*. To compel silence, to hush one's mouth, to put a stopper on.

**clous (des)** *sm. pl.* *(Sl)*. Nothing. Ex. : *Il travaille pour des clous,* he works for practically nothing.

**cocarde (avoir sa)** *(Sl)*. Same as : *nez piqué (avoir le)*.

**cocardier** *sm.* *(F)*. Derisive term for a chauvinist.

**cochon (être)** *(Sl)*. *C'est cochon !* It's a dirty trick.

**cochon de payant** *(P)*. Sarcastic popular term for the client, customer, theater-goer, etc. who pays for his seat.

**cochonnaille** *sf.* *(Sl)*. Pork-butchers' prepared products as pies, sausages, roasted meat ham, cold cuts, etc.

**cochonner** *v.* *(P)*. To botch, to muff, to "louse up", to make a mess of. (Syn. : *savater*).

**coco** *sm.* *(P)*. Pej. term for an individual. Ex. : *joli coco, drôle de coco*.
*(Sl)*. Head, "pate", "nut", "top story". *Avoir le coco fêlé,* to be loony, loco, nutty, loose in the bean.
*sf.* *(Sl)*. Cocaine, "coke", "Cecil".

**Coco-Bel-Œil** *(P)*. Nickname for any liked or disliked individual.

**coco fêlé (avoir le)** *(Sl)*. To be a crackpot, crackpotty, to be a screwball.

**cocoter** *v.* *(Sl)*. To smell strongly, to stink, to "hum".

**cocu** *sm.* *(P)*. Cuckold.
*(Sl)*. Lucky man. Joc. excl. : *Tu es cocu !* to express admiration for one's extraordinary luck.

**cocufier** *v.* *(Sl)*. To cuckold (one's husband, one's wife, one's lover, etc.).

**cœur d'artichaut** *(P)*. One who can love several persons at the same time.

**cœur net (le)** *(F)*. See : *en avoir le cœur net.*

**coucher avec les poules** e) (F). To go to bed early, to n early.

**couci-couça** (F). So so.

**coucou** sm. (P). Joc. for : cocu. ). Airplane, "crate".

**ouic** adv. (Sl). Nothing. Ex. : 'y comprends que couic, I under- d nothing ! I don't get it, I don't it !

**ouillon** sm. (Sl). Silly guy, p, mug, dumbbell.

**ouillon comme la lune** (Sl). of a very stupid or silly person.

**uillonnade** sf. (Sl). Nonsense, lity, guff, baloney, "bull", bun- e, "boo-boo".

**uillonner** v. (Sl). To make a f, to "take in", to swindle, to in ".

**iner** v. (P). To weep, to cry, ine.

**lage** sm. (F). Wasting, ser- pilferings in a household. Ex. : du coulage, there is much waste.

**é** adj. (P). Ruined, busted, out.

**er q.** v. (P). To ruin one, to ne out, to put one out of busi- knock one out.

**er douce (se la)** (P). To ings easy, to have a soft time live the life of Riley.

**oirs (faire les)** (P). To n lobbying.

sm. (P). Crime, "job". Qui coup ? Who committed the

**(il a bu un)** (P). Snoot- Un coup de trop, one over

**coup bas** sm. (P). Blow below the belt, unfair blow, below-the-belter.

**coup de balai** (P). Clean sweep.

**coup de bambou** (P). See : recevoir un coup de bambou.

**coup de blanc** (P). Glass of white wine.

**coup de canif dans le contrat (donner un)** (P). To be unfaithful (joc. term for a man or a woman who commits adultery).

**coup de chien** sm. (P). Violent (and generally unexpected) scuffle, riot, fight, disorder, violent clash between crowd and police.

**coup de collier** (P). See : donner un coup de collier.

**coup de fion** (P). See : donner le coup de fion.

**coup de fil** (F). Phone call "buzz". Donner un coup de fil, to give a "buzz".

**coup de foudre** sm. (P). Love at first sight.

**coup de fusil** sm. (P). Heavy bill (especially one overcharged). (See : essuyer le coup de fusil).

**coup de grâce** (F). See : donner le coup de grâce.

**coup de main** sm. (F). Help, assistance. (See also : donner un coup de main).

**coup de massue** sm. (P). Heavy blow ; also fig. : staggering news, "floorer". A heavy hotel or restaurant bill, any overcharged bill (especially an unexpected one).

**coup d'épée dans l'eau** (F). Said of a useless, sterile, futile effort. Donner un coup d'épée dans l'eau, to beat the air, to waste one's effort.

**coup de pied de l'âne** (F). The kick of the ass (who is no longer

**cœur sur la main (avoir le)** (F). To be kind-hearted, generous.

**coffre** sm. (Sl). Chest, lungs.

**coffrer** v. (Sl). To arrest, to "nab", to put in jail, to slap in, to run in.

**cognard** sm. (Sl). Gendarme, policeman, cop, bull.

**cogne** sm. (Sl). Same as : cognard.

**cogner** v. (Sl). To stink, to " hum ", to smell. Ça cogne, it stinks.

**coiffé de q. (être)** (F). To be nutty about, nuts over s.o.

**coiffer Sainte Catherine** (F). Said of a girl who remains single after she is 25 years old.

**coincer la bulle** (Sl). To do nothing, to laze, to be idle.

**colifichet** sm. (F). Trinket, " doodad ".

**colique** sf. (Sl). Bore, "pain in the neck".

**collabo** sm. (P). Collaborator.

**collage** sm. (P). Concubinage. (See also : ménage à la colle).

**collant** adj. (P). Said of a person one cannot get rid of. (Syn. : crampon).

**collante** sf. (P). Summons to an exam. (College slang).

**colle** sf. (P). Question difficult to answer, quiz, "stumper", "getter". Person difficult to get rid of.

**collé** adj. (P). Flunked, plucked, " failed " in an examination. (Student's slang). Stuck for, brought to a halt.

**coller** v. (P). To give, to put, to place. To silence one. (See also : coller un pain, coller une gifle, ça colle).

**coller (se)** (Sl). To stand one-

self, to treat oneself to. To "shack up".

**coller une gifle** (P). To box one's ears, to slap one in the face.

**coller un pain** (Sl). To give a punch on the nose. (See : pain).

**colleter (se)** To fight, to have a fight. (Same as : coltiner (se).

**collet monté** adj. (F). Stiff, pedantic, severe in his (her) opinions.

**collignon** sm. (F). Cabby.

**colon** sm. (F). Colonel.

**colonel** sm. (P). 1000-franc banknote.

**coloquinte** sf. (Sl). Head, "nut", "upper story", "noggin".

**cols bleus** sm. pl. (P). Sailors, bluejackets, "gobs".

**coltiner (se)** v. To fight, to have a brawl, to exchange blows.

**combinard** sm. (P). Schemer, hep guy, one who knows the "system".

**combine** sf. (P). Tie-up, shady scheme, racket, the " system ". Je connais la combine, I know the racket.

**\* comme cul et chemise** (Sl). Said of two persons who are always together, who are inseparable.

**comme de juste** (P). Of course.

**comme dit l'autre** (P). As the fellow says.

**comme l'oiseau sur la branche** (F). In an insecure, unsettled position.

**comme un crin (être)** (P). To be very irritable.

**... comme un sou** (P). Cela vaut mille francs comme un sou, it's amply worth one thousand francs, it's worth one thousand francs if it's worth a penny.

**commis-voyageur** *sm.* *(F).* Drummer, commercial traveler.

**commode** *adj.* *(F).* *Pas commode,* not easy to get along with.

**compas** *sm. pl. (Sl).* Legs, "pins".

**compas dans l'œil (avoir le)** *(P).* To have a sure eye, to size up things accurately.

**compère** *sm. (P).* Confederate of a street-vendor, "shill".

**compère-loriot** *sm. (P).* Sty (on the eye).

**compotier** *sm. (Sl).* Head, "knob", "nut".

**comprenette** *sf. (P).* Intelligence, I.Q., brains. Ex. : *Elle n'a pas la comprenette facile,* she's slow-witted.

**comprenette dure (difficile) (avoir la)** *(P).* To be dull-witted, to be a moron. (See also : *comprenette).*

**compte (avoir son)** *(Sl).* Same as : *culotte (avoir sa).*

**compte d'apothicaire** *sm. (F).* Overcharged bill on which a reduction is to be expected.

**\* c.o.n.** *sm. adj. (Sl).* Silly, stupid person, dope, dumbbell. (Also : *con).*

**\* conard** *sm. (Sl).* Stupid person, dumbbell, dope.

**\* conasse** *sf. (Sl).* Very rude term for a woman, prostitute not registered by police.

**\* con comme la lune** *(Sl).* Silly, stupid, goofie, dopey.

**condamné à perpète (être)** *(Sl).* To get a life sentence, a lifer, to "do a bookful".

**conduite** *sf. (P).* See : *acheter une conduite.*

**conjungo** *sm. (Sl).* Marriage.

**connaissance** *sf. (F).* Boy friend, girl friend.

**connaître comme sa poche** *(F).* To know s. th. all to pieces.

**connaître la musique** *(P).* To be in the know, to be hep on (to), to know what's what, to know the "score".

**connaître son bonhomme** *(P).* To have one's number, to have one's wave length.

**connaître toutes les ficelles** *(P).* To know the ropes, to be up to snuff.

**\* connerie** *sf. (Sl).* Nonsense, stupidity, baloney, tommyrot, poppycock, booshwah.

**connu comme le loup blanc (être)** *(F).* To be known to everybody.

**constipé** *adj. (Sl).* Sourpuss.

**conter fleurette à q.** *(F).* To court, to make love, to flirt.

**contredanse** *sf. (Sl).* Police ticket.

**contre mauvaise fortune bon cœur (faire)** *(F).* To grin and bear it.

**contre-petterie** *sf. (P).* Spoonerism.

**contrer** *v. (P).* To stymie.

**contre vent(s) et marée(s)** *(P).* See : *aller contre vent(s) et marée(s).*

**convalo** *sm. (Sl).* Convalescence.

**copain** *sm. (P).* Pal, mate, "pard.", buddy, crony. (Also : *copin).*

**copeaux (des)** *(Sl).* Nothing. (Syn. : *des clous, des prunes).*

**copin** *sm. (P).* Same as : *copain.*

**copine** *sf. (P).* Girl friend.

**coq** *sm. (Sl).* French *louis d'or.*

**coq en pâte (être comme un)** *(F).* To be spoiled, to live in clover.

**coquard** *sm. (Sl).* Blackened eye (following a hard hit), a "shiner".

COQUARD.

**coquelicot** *sm. (Sl).* Blackened eye, a "shiner".

**coqueluche** *sf. (F).* Ladies' man.

**coquillard** *sm. (Sl).* Eye. (See also : *s'en battre le coquillard).*

**coquin** *sm. (Sl).* Fancy man.

**coquin de sort !** *(F).* What a life ! Tough luck ! (Mild expletive).

**coquin fini** *(P).* See : *fini.*

**corbeau** *sm. (P).* Anonymous letter writer, "poison pen".

**cordon bleu** *(F).* Excellent cook.

**cornard** *sm. (P).* Deceived husband, cuckold.

**corniaud** *sm. (Sl).* Same as : *cornichon.*

**cornichon** *sm. (P).* Sap, palooka, dumbbell, chump, fathead, blubberhead, doughderhead.

**corrida** *sf. (Sl).* Freelent free-fight, scrap.

**cossard** *sm. (Sl).* Lazbones, "chair warmer".

**cosse** *sf. (Sl).* Lazine

**cosse (avoir la)** to be too lazy to work.

**costaud** *adj. (P).* hefty.

**cote (avoir la)** great (high) esteem.

**cote d'amour** *sf.*

**cote d'amour (a** To be in great favor.

**côtes en long** *(Sl).* Said of a lazy bu

**couche** *sf. (P).* S *couche.*

**coucher** *sm.* vants customer who spend her.

**coucher à la b** To sleep in the open pitch", to roost out the stars.

SANS FOY
A LA B

afraid of the sick and dying lion. Popular and semi-proverbial saying, after a well-known fable by Phaedrus, symbolizing the violence of a coward against an enemy who can no longer defend himself. A variant of " Hares may pull dead lions by the beard ").

**coup de pied de Vénus** *(P)*. V. D., venereal disease.

**coup-de-poing américain** *sm. (P)*. Knuckle-duster, brass knuckles, " iron mike ".

**coup de pompe** *(Sl)*. *Avoir reçu le coup de pompe*, to be run ragged, completely exhausted after a big physical effort.

**coup de pot** *(Sl)*. Fluke, lucky break.

**coup de pouce** *(P)*. *Donner un coup de pouce*, to aid, to assist, to lend a hand.
*(Sl)*. See : *Donner le coup de pouce.*

**coup de rouge (un)** *(P)*. Glass of red wine, a shot of red wine.

**coup de sens unique (un)** *(Sl)*. Glass of red wine, a shot of red wine.

**coup de torchon** *(P)*. Violent scuffle, violent clash.

**coup de Trafalgar** *(P)*. Unpleasant, startling and unexpected event (or act) that changes the situation, catastrophe.

**coup de veine** *(P)*. Fluke, a lucky stroke, lucky break.

**coup de vieux (avoir un)** *(P)*. Sudden aging.

**coup du lapin** *(Sl)*. *Faire le coup du lapin*, to murder, to knock out with a treacherous blow.

**coup du Père François** *(P)*. Treacherous blow or attack from behind. Originally : garroting, named

after a hoodlum called *le Père François* who was notorious for attacks of this kind.

**coupe-file** *sm. (P)*. Courtesy card, police pass for a privileged category of people : diplomats, newspapermen, etc.

**couper (se)** *(P)*. To give oneself away, to " spill the beans ".

**couper à** *v. (P)*. To avoid, to dodge. Ex. : *Vous n'y couperez pas*, you won't avoid it, you are sure to get it. *Ceux qui essaient de couper à la conscription*, draft dodgers.

**couper dedans** *(P)*. To fall into the trap.

**couper la chique à q.** *(P)*. To cut another short, to interrupt another suddenly, to hinder another from expressing himself, to cramp one's style.

**couper la poire en deux** *(F)*. To compromise, to meet one half-way, to split the difference.

**couper le sifflet** *(P)*. To reduce one to silence, to silence one, to put a crimp in one's style.

**couper les vivres** *(F)*. To stop the supplies, to cut one's allowance.

**couper l'herbe sous le pied de q.** *(F)*. To cut the ground from under a person.

**couper un cheveu en quatre** *(F)*. To split hairs.

**coupes sombres (faire des)** *(F)*. To make drastic cuts, to chop.

**coupe-tiffes** *sm. (Sl)*. Hairdresser.

**coupeur de cheveux en quatre** *(F)*. Hair-splitter.

**coup monté** *(F)*. Got-up job.

**cour (faire la)** *(F)*. To make love.

**courailler** *v. (Sl)*. Same as : *courir.*

**courante** *sf.* *(Sl)*. Diarrhoea, "trots", "summer complaint".

**coureur** *sm.* *(P)*. Unsteady lover, "wolf", "fastie".

**coureuse** *sf.* *(P)*. Woman (or girl) of loose morals, fast girl.

**courir** *v.* *(P)*. To chase girls, women, to gallivant. (See also : *courailler, courir la prétentaine*).
*(Sl)*. To pester, to bother, to be a nuisance to s.o. (See : *courir sur l'haricot*).

**courir comme un dératé** *(P)*. To run very fast, to run like mad.

**courir la poste** *(P)*. To go post-haste, to "high-tail it".

**courir la prétentaine** *(P)*. To go the (merry) pace, to "hit it up", to gallivant.

**courir sur l'haricot** *(Sl)*. To weary s.o., to irritate, to bother, to plague s.o. *Tu me cours sur l'haricot*, you get on my nerves.

**court-circuiter** *v.* *(P)*. To "short-circuit", to shorten, to hasten, process by taking direct and unofficial action.

**courtier marron** *sm.* *(P)*. Unlicensed broker, gutter snipe.

**Courtille (la).** Old name of *Belleville*, a district of Paris.

**courtines** *sf. pl.* *(Sl)*. Race track, horse-race.

**couru d'avance** *(P)*. Fire-sure. *C'est couru d'avance !* It's a cinch, pipe cinch, lead-pipe cinch. Sure bet.

**cousette** *sf.* *(P)*. Apprentice in the couture business. Pocket sewing outfit, "hussy".

**cousin à la mode de Bretagne** *(P)*. Distant relation, "button-hole relation".

**cousu de fil blanc** *(F)*. *Finesses cousues de fil blanc*, tricks easily seen through.

**cousu d'or (être)** *(F)*. To be very wealthy, in the big money, well-heeled.

**cousue** *sf.* *(Sl)*. Factory-made cigarette, "tailor-made" (as opposed to "handmades").

**cousu-main** *adj.* *(Sl)*. *C'est du cousu-main*, it's a cinch.

**couteau dans la plaie (remuer ou retourner)** *(F)*. To rub it in.

**couteau sur la gorge (avoir le)** *(F)*. To be under violent threat, coercion, shot-gun business.

**couteaux tirés (à)** *(F)*. Hostile attitude between two parties.

**coûter les yeux de la tête** *(P)*. To make a hole in one's pocket, to be extremely expensive.

**coûter une peur et une envie de courir** *(Sl)*. Said of stolen goods. Ex. : *Ça m'a coûté une peur et une envie de courir*.

**couvert** *sm.* *(F)*. Minor charge in a restaurant (intended to cover bread served with the meal).

**couverture** *sf.* *(Sl)*. Front, "blind", as in : his profession was only a front, a "blind".

**craché** *adj.* *(P)*. Very much like. *C'est son père tout craché*, he's the very picture of his father, he is a chip of the old block, he is the spit and image of his father.

**cracher** *v.* *(Sl)*. To give money, to shell out, to fork out, to come down with, to pony up. To confess, to "sing", to "spit up the guts".

**cracher le feu** *(Sl)*. To be energetic, full of pep, to be on one's toes, to be a hustler.

**crachoir** *sm. (P)*. See : *tenir le crachoir*.

**crack** *sm. (P)*. Superior horse (turf).

**cracra** *adj. (Sl)*. Dirty, crummy.

**crampon** *sm. adj. (P)*. Tenacious individual one cannot get rid of.

**cramponnant** *adj. (P)*. Pestering, boring.

**cramponner** *v. (P)*. To weary, to pester, to plague, to bore s.o.

**cramser** *v. (Sl)*. To die, to "cash in one's checks".

**cran** *sm. (Sl)*. Day spent as punishment in the guardhouse, in military jail. Ex. : *Trois crans,* three days in the guardhouse.

**cran (avoir du)** *(P)*. To have plenty of guts (sand, grit). Ex. : *C'était un lutteur qui avait du cran,* he was a fighter, a man of grit, a man who got plenty of sand.

**cran (être à)** *(P)*. To be in a very ugly mood, in a nasty temper, ready to blow up.

**crâner** *v. (P)*. To show off, to make a splash, to throw one's weight about, to swank it, to put on the ritz.

**crâneur** *sm. (P)*. Swaggerer.

**crapaud** *sm. (P)*. Baby grand (piano).

**crapouillot** *sm. (Sl)*. Trench-mortar shell (army slang).

**Crapule et C$^{ie}$** *(P)*. The "fast-buck" set.

**crapulos** *sm. (P)*. Cheap cigar, stogy.

**craque** *sf. (P)*. Lie, fib, yarn, fish story.

**craspec** *adj. (Sl)*. Dirty, lousy, crumby.

**crasse** *sf. (Sl)*. Dirty trick, dirty play. *Faire une crasse à q.,* to play a nasty trick on s.o.

**cravate** *sf. Sl. C'est de la cravate,* it's mere showing off, it's just splash.

**cravater (se faire)** *(Sl)*. To get arrested, to get "nabbed".

**crème (la)** *sf. (P)*. The "(whipped-)cream", upper ten, upper crust, the "top", the upper classes.

**crème Chantilly** *sf. (P)*. Whipped cream.

**crêper le chignon (se)** *(P)*. Said of two women engaged in a violent fight and tearing each other's hair.

DEUX POULICHES
SE CRÊPANT LE CHIGNON.

**crêpe Suzette** *sf. (P)*. Pancake with *cognac* and *cointreau*.

**cresson** *sm. (Sl)*. Hair, "moss".

**cresson sur la cafetière** *(Sl)*. Hair on one's head.

**crétin** *sm. (F)*. Dumbbell, chump.

**creuser le ciboulot (se)** *(Sl)*. To twist one's brains, to pound one's brains, to rack one's brains, to bat one's brains out.

**creuser le citron (se)** *(Sl)*. A variation of *creuser le ciboulot (se)*.

**creuser les méninges (se)** *(P)*. A pop. variant of *creuser le ciboulot (se)*.

**crevant** *adj. (Sl)*. Too tiring, killing. Very amusing.

**crève** *sf. (Sl)*. See : *attraper la crève*.

**crevé** *adj. (Sl)*. Dog-tired, exhausted, bushed.

**crève-la-faim (un)** *(Sl)*. A poverty-stricken individual, starveling.

**crever** *v. (Sl)*. To kill, to bump off. To arrest, to " nab ", to knock off. To die.

**crever de faim** *(Sl)*. To be utterly destitute, to live in half starvation and privations.

**crever les yeux** *(P)*. *Ça vous crève les yeux*, it's under your very nose.

**cri-cri** *sm. (P)*. Popular name for a chirping cricket (leaping insect). *(Sl)*. Epithet for a skinny little woman (or girl).

**crier par-dessus les toits** *(P)*. To proclaim loudly, to noise abroad.

**crincrin** *sm. (P)*. Fiddle.

**criquet** *sm. (Sl)*. Puny, sickly individual, weakling. Ex. : *un petit criquet*.

**croche-pied** *sm. (P)*. *Faire un croche-pied à q.*, to trip one up.

**crochet** *sm. (P)*. Amateur night (radio).

**crochets (avoir les)** *(Sl)*. To be hungry, to be dog-hungry.

**crocs (avoir les)** *(Sl)*. Same as : *crochets (avoir les)*.

**croire au Père Noël** *(P)*. To believe in Father Christmas, to deceive oneself with illusions. Ex. : *Tu crois encore au Père Noël !* So you believe in Father Christmas ! (Fling at a naive person).

**croire dur comme fer à** *(P)*. To be a staunch, strong believer in.

**croire que c'est arrivé** *(P)*. To engage in wishful thinking. *Il croit que c'est arrivé*, he takes it all for a cinch, he thinks there's nobody like him.

**croire qu'on est sorti de la cuisse de Jupiter** *(F)*. To imagine oneself to be of exalted birth, to think no small beer of oneself.

**croix** *sf. (Sl)*. Swiss 20-franc gold coin.

**croix des vaches** *(Sl)*. A knife scar or razor cut on the face, " stoolmark ", " rat-mark ".

**croix et la bannière (c'est la)** *(F)*. A helluva time, a hell of a job. Ex. : *C'est la croix et la bannière pour le faire obéir*, it's a hell of a job to make him obey.

**croquant** *sm. (Sl)*. Peasant, " hayseed ", rube, yokel.

**croque-mitaine** *sm. (F)*. Bogey, Frankenstein.

**croque-monsieur** *sm. (P)*. Fried cheese *(gruyère)* and ham sandwich.

**croquenots** *sm. pl. (Sl)*. Shoes, " kicks ".

**croquer** *v. (Sl)*. To arrest, to capture, to grab, to " nab ". To eat.

**croquer le marmot** *(P)*. To be kept waiting, to cool one's heels, to dance attendance.

**croqueuse de diamants** *sf. (P)*. " Gold digger ", woman who uses her feminine charm to extract profit from men.

**croquignolet** *adj. (Sl)*. Nice (looking).

**crosseur** *sm.* *(Sl)*. A quarreler.

**crotte** *sf.* *(Sl)*. Mud.

**crotte !** *interj.* *(Sl)*. Euphemism for *merde !*

**crottes de bique** *sf. pl.* Trifles, hogwash, worthless (or insignificant) things or individuals, shucks, " chicken feed ", small fry.

**croulant** *sm.* *(Sl)*. Teenager's satirical term for a middle-aged man.

**croûte** *sf.* *(P)*. Bad painting, " pot-boiler ", daub. *(Sl)*. Food, " grub ", " chow ".

**croûter** *v.* *(Sl)*. To eat, to cheer the inner man.

**cruche** *sf.* *(P)*. Silly person, dumbbell, muff, chump, dope.

**cruchon** *sm.* *(P)*. A variant of *cruche*.

**cube** *sm.* *(Sl)*. Junior (student in the third year).

**cucu(l)** *adj.* *(Sl)*. Silly, stupid, chumpish.

**cueillir** *v.* *(P)*. To arrest, to capture, to pick up, to " nab ".

**cuiller** *sf.* *(Sl)*. Hand, " fin ". *Serrer la cuiller,* to shake hands, to flip a fin.

**cuir** *sm.* *(P)*. *Faire un cuir,* to make an incorrect " *liaison* " (in speaking French. F. i. *trop aimable,* pronounced : *trop-z-aimable*). Fluff.

**cuisiner q.** *(P)*. To " grill ", to put on the grill, to put the screws on, to " sweat ".

**cuisse hospitalière (avoir la)** *(P)*. Said of a woman of easy morals, a " round-heeler ".

**cuistance** *sf.* *(Sl)*. Food, " eats ".

**cuistot** *sm.* *(Sl)*. Cook, " kitchen mechanic ", K.P.

**cuit (être)** *(Sl)*. Same as : *fichu.*

**cuite** *sf.* *(Sl)*. Drunkenness, " soak ", *Prendre une cuite,* to get dead-drunk.

**cuite (avoir sa)** *(Sl)*. Same as : *culotte (avoir sa).*

**cuiter (se)** *v.* *(P)*. To get drunk, " cooked ", " soaked ".

* **cul** *sm.* *(Sl)*. Very silly, stupid person, dope, dumbbell, " saperoo ".

**cul de poule** *sm.* *(P)*. Pout, pouting of the lips. Ex. : *Faire sa bouche en cul de poule.*

**culot** *sm.* *(Sl)*. Impudence, crust, gall, cheek, sassiness. *Quel culot !* Some cheek ! *Avoir du culot,* to have a crust.

**culotte** *sf.* *(P)*. See : *prendre une culotte.*

**culotte (avoir sa)** *(Sl)*. To be thoroughly drunk, " cooked ", " blotto ", " full to the brim ".

**culotté** *adj.* *(Sl)*. Impudent, cocky, cheeky, saucy, sassy, crusty. *Un type culotté,* an impudent, brazen-faced individual.

* **cul par-dessus tête** *(Sl)*. Neck and crop.

**cul-sec** *(Sl)*. See : *faire cul-sec.*

**cul-terreux** *sm.* *(Sl)*. Peasant, rube, hayseed, hick, man from the country.

**curieux** *sm.* *(Sl)*. Judge, examining magistrate, hizzoner.

**cuver sa cuite** *(Sl)*. To sleep off one's booze.

**cuver son vin** *(F)*. To sleep off the effects of a heavy drink, of a spree.

**cyclo** *sm.* *(Sl)*. Policeman, cop on wheels.

# D

**dabe** *sm. (Sl)*. Father, boss, the old man.

**dabesse** *sf. (Sl)*. Mother, the old lady.

**dabs** *sm. pl. (Sl)*. Parents, old folks.

**d'ac** *(Sl)*. Excl. denoting approval : O.K., okey-dokey, hunky-dory.

**dada** *sm. (P)*. Hobby, fad, pet subject, pet idea.

**dadais** *sm. (P)*. A clumsy and stupid fellow, lout, goofie, gawk, goop, big lug. *Grand dadais,* big lummox.

**dalle (que)** *adv. (Sl)*. Nothing. Ex. : *Je ne comprends que dalle (= je ne comprends rien),* I don't understand, "I don't compree", I don't get it.

**dalle** *sf. (Sl)*. Mouth, "gin trap", throat, "gargler".

**dalle en pente (avoir la)** *(Sl)*. Said of a tippler, of a "booze-hound".

**dame !** *interj. (F)*. Sure! You bet!

**damer le pion à q.** *(F)*. To outdo s.o., to surpass s.o., to outbeat s.o., to lick s.o., to beat hollow.

**dans de beaux draps (être)** *(F)*. To be in a nice fix, in hot water.

**danse** *sf. (Sl)*. Beating, thrashing, shellacking.

**danser devant le buffet** *(F)*. To go without food ; to have a bare cupboard and have nothing to eat.

**dans la bouscaille (être)** *(Sl)*. To be in a sorry plight, in a fix, in a pretty mess.

**dans la course (être)** *(P)*. To be in the business, in the lot, to take part in.

**dans la dèche (être)** *(F)*. To be broke, to be in a tight hole.

**dans la lune (être)** *(P)*. To daydream, to be absent-minded.

**dans la marmelade (être)** *(Sl)*. Same as : *dans la mélasse (être)*.

**dans la mélasse (être)** *(Sl)*. To be in a fix.

**dans la mouscaille (être)** *(Sl)*. To be in a sorry plight, in a fix, in a pretty mess.

**dans le bain (être)** *(P)*. To be in a fix, in trouble, in hot water, in a hot box. To be in the very heart of a business, to be " in " on, and responsible for, things.

**dans le lac** *(P)*. Lost, busted. " Failed out ".

**dans le nez (avoir q.)** *(Sl)*. To have a strong dislike for one.

**dans le panneau** *(F)*. See : *donner dans le panneau.*

**dans le pastis(se) (être)** *(Sl)*. See : *pastis(se).*

**dans le sac** *(P)*. In the bag safely secured. Cinch, anything held safely.

**dans les bonnes grâces de q. (être)** *(F)*. To be in one's good graces.

**dans les bras de Morphée (être)** *(F)*. To be asleep, to be in the arms of Morpheus.

**dans les grandes largeurs** *(P)*. Amply, utterly, totally, completely, entirely, extremely, with a vengeance.

**dans les petits papiers de q. (être)** *(F)*. To be in one's good graces.

**dans les vignes du Seigneur (être)** *(P)*. To be drunk, to be boozy.

**dans le ventre (avoir q. ch.)** *(P)*. To have dexterity, some special talent, knowledge or ability ; to have something on the ball.

**dans ses bois (être)** *(P)*. To have a flat furnished with one's own furniture.

**dans ses cordes** *(F)*. Down (up) one's alley.

**dans ses petits souliers (être)** *(F)*. To be in a very embarrassing position, in a fix. Ex. : *J'étais dans mes petits souliers,* I was on pins and needles.

**dans une situation intéressante (être)** *(F)*. To be pregnant, to be expecting, infanticipating.

**dans un fauteuil** *(P)*. Easily, hands down, in a canter. (Said of an easily won victory).

**dare-dare** *(P)*. Very quickly, in a jiffy, post-haste, p.d.q., pretty damn quick.

ALLONS-Y DARE-DARE !

**daron** *sm. (Sl)*. Father.

**daronne** *sf. (Sl)*. Mother.

**dattes (des)** *sf. pl. (Sl)*. Nothing (at all), nope.

**déballage** *sm. (Sl)*. Said of a woman who in going to bed takes off her artificial charms.

**déballer ses outils** *(Sl)*. Same as : *déballonner (se).*

**déballonner (se)** *v. (Sl)*. To confess.

**débarbouiller** *v. (P). Laisser q. se débarbouiller,* to let one shift for himself.

**débarquer** *v. (P).* Said of an unsophisticated country boy (or girl) who comes to town. (A hick comes to town). To remove one from office, to sack, to fire one. Ex. : *Ils ont été débarqués,* they have been fired, removed from office.

**débarrasser de q. (se)** *(P).* To kill s.o., to " erase " s.o., to take s.o. for a ride.

**débarrasser le plancher** *(Sl).* To go away, to leave, to pull out, to clear out, to " light out ", to " bug out ".

**débecter** *v. (Sl).* To vomit, to " shoot the cat ". (Also : *débecqueter*).

**débinage** *sm. (Sl).* Disparagement, " knocking ", running down.

**débine** *sf. (Sl).* Distress, extreme poverty. Ex. : *Etre dans la débine,* to be down at the heel, to be in the pinches, to be on the hog.

**débiner** *v. (Sl).* To run down a person, to talk disparagingly of one, to pull one to pieces.

**débiner (se)** *v. (Sl).* To fly the coop, to flee, to beat it, to scram.

**débloquer** *v. (Sl).* To talk nonsense, to talk baloney, to goof off. (Syn. : *dérailler, déménager, perdre la boule).*

**déboucher** *v. (Sl).* To open, to break open (safe, till, door, etc.).

**déboulonner** *v. (Sl).* To remove s.o. from office, to dismiss.

**déboutonner (se)** *v. (Sl).* To unbosom oneself, to get s. th. off one's chest, to confess. (Same as : *déballonner (se).*

**débrayer** *v. (P).* To strike, to

knock off, to cease work (for a strike), to walk out.

**de bric et de broc** *(F).* From various sources, from various sides, from here and from there, a little here and a little there.

**débringué** *adj. (Sl).* Slovenly, negligent.

**débrouillard** *sm. adj. (F).* Resourceful person, smart individual, slick guy, able to handle any tricky situation.

**débrouillardise** *sf. (P).* Resourcefulness.

**débrouiller (se)** *v. (F).* To get over difficulties, to shift for oneself, to be able to deal with any tricky or difficult situation, to " get along ".

**décamper** *v. (F).* To flee, to beat it, to scram.

**décaniller** *v. (Sl).* To get out of bed.

**décapant** *sm. (Sl).* Low quality wine, inferior booze, hog-wash.

**décarcasser (se)** *(P).* To work like a slave, to toil, to drudge.

**décatir (se)** *(P).* To lose one's freshness.

**décavé** *adj. (Sl).* Financially ruined, broke.

**déchanter** *v. (F).* To come down a peg or two. Ex. : *Vous allez déchanter bientôt !* Soon you will sing a different tune.

**déchard** *sm. (Sl).* Bum (who is always on the rocks, always broke).

**dèche** *sf. (F).* See : *dans la dèche (être).*

**décoction** *sf. (Sl).* Beating, thrashing, lambasting, shellacking.

**décollage** *sm. (P).* Take-off ('plane).

**décoller (se)** v. (Sl). To weaken, to ail, to be in a bad way, to go to pieces, to deteriorate completely.

* **déconner** v. (Sl). To talk nonsense, to talk hot air, to talk baloney, to goof off.

**découcher** v. (F). To sleep out, to stay out all night, to spend the night away from home.

**découvrir le pot aux roses** (F). To find out the mystery of a secret affair.

**décrasser** v. (F). To polish up one's manners.

**décrocher la timbale** (F). To hit the jackpot, to win the first prize.

**décrochez-moi ça** sm. (P). Cheap ready-made clothes shop, hand-me-down, reach-me-down.

**décrotter** v. (Sl). To round up one's rough manners, to improve one's manners.

**décuiter (se)** v. (Sl). To get over one's drink.

DÉGELÉE BIEN MÉRITÉE.

**dedans** (Sl). See : mettre dedans.

**dédouaner** v. (Sl). To give a clean bill of health, to clear on a charge.

**défendre (se)** v. (P). To earn fairly well, to get along fairly well. Il se défend, he's holding his own, he is getting along.

**défiler (se)** v. (P). To escape, to run off, to flee, to scram, to duck out. To dodge s.th. unpleasant.

**dégaine** sf. (F). Awkward gait.

**dégelée** sf. (Sl). Beating, licking, shellacking.

**dégingandé** adj. (F). Clumsy, akward, ungainly.

**déglingué** adj. (P). Utterly ruined, completely out of order, on the bum, out of kilter.

**dégobiller** v. (P). To vomit, to " shoot the cat ".

**dégoiser** v. (Sl). To palaver, to talk a blue streak.

**dégommer** v. (P). To remove one from office.
(Sl). To kill, to murder, to " erase ", to " blot out ", to " liquidate ".

**dégonflade** sf. (P). Exhibiting cowardice, backing down (out), climbing down, " crawling out ".

**dégonflage** sm. (P). Same as : dégonflade.

**dégonfler (se)** v. (P). To back out, to crawl out, to climb down, to backtrack (through fear), to go back on, to " cop out ", to " dog it ", to " chicken out ", to " punk out ".

**dégonfleur** sm. (P). Coward who " climbs down ", who " cops out ", who " punks out ".

**dégoter** v. (P). To find, to hit

upon, to discover accidentally, to spot, to unearth, to dig up.

**dégoulinage** *sm. (P)*. Rolling, falling down, dripping.

**dégoulinante** *sf. (Sl)*. Clock, timepiece.

**dégouliner** *v. (P)*. To drip, to trickle (slowly or drop by drop).

**dégourdi** *adj. (F)*. Wide-awake, " hep ", " hip ".

**dégourdi sans malice** *(P)*. Said of a stupid person.

**dégourdir** *v. (F)*. Same as : *décrasser*.

**dégringolade** *sf. (P)*. Fall, tumble, collapse, downfall.

**dégringoler** *v. (P)*. To tumble down, to kerplonk down. *Dégringoler l'escalier,* to come rushing down the stairs.

EN DÉGRINGOLANT L'ESCALIER.

**dégueulasse** *adj. (Sl)*. Disgusting, offensive, repulsive. *C'est dégueulasse !* It's disgusting, sickening !

**dégueuler** *v. (Sl)*. To vomit, to " shoot the cat ", to puke, to cough up one's cookies.

**déguiser en courant d'air (se)** *(P)*. To flee, to scram, to do a Houdini.

**déjeté** *adj. (P)*. Lopsided.

**déjeuner de soleil (un)** *sm. (F)*. Fragile or shoddy material whose color will fade easily in the sun. Fig. : Anything that does not last.

**de la classe (être)** *(Sl)*. Said of a soldier whose military service is drawing to its end and who therefore doesn't care much any longer.

**demain on rasera gratis** *(P)*. Joc. phrase implying an everlasting promise that will never be fulfilled.

**démancher (se)** *v. (Sl)*. To take pains to do s. th. (Similar term : *décarcasser (se)*.

**démantibuler** *v. (P)*. To put out of joint.

**démarrage** *sm. (P)*. Kick-off, start.

**démarrer** *v. (P)*. To start (off).

**de mèche avec q. (être)** *(F)*. To be in cahoots with s.o.

JE DÉMÉNAGE A LA
CLOCHE DE BOIS.

**de même farine** (F). Of the same stripe, of the same nature.

**de mémoire d'homme** (F). Within men's memory.

**déménager** v. (P). To be off one's head, to be wacky.

**déménager à la cloche de bois** (F). To leave without paying rent, to "shoot the moon", to "hang the landlady", to move one's belonging at night to avoid seizure for rent.

\* **démerdard** sm. adj. (Sl). Resourceful (person), person who knows how to get out of a fix or how to tackle any difficult or tricky situation.

\* **démerder (se)** v. (Sl). To get out of a fix (out of a mess). To be able to deal with a tricky situation.

\* **démerdeur** sm. (Sl). Same as : démerdard.

**demi-portion** sf. (P). Undersized, puny man or woman, "half pint". adj. "Sawed off".

**demi-sac** sm. (Sl). Five hundred francs.

**demi-tour !** interj. (P). Scram !

**démolir** v. (Sl). To kill, to murder, to bump off.

**démouscailler (se)** v. (Sl). To get out of a predicament. (Same as : démerder (se).

**démurger (se)** v. (Sl). To leave hurriedly, to scram.

**dénicher** v. (F). To spot, to discover, to unearth, to dig up.

**denier à Dieu** sm. (F). Key money.

**dent (avoir la)** (Sl). To be hungry as a dog.

**dent contre q. (avoir une)** (F). To have a grudge, to harbor resentment against one.

**dents longues (avoir les)** (P). To be overambitious.

**dépagnoter (se)** v. (Sl). Same as : dépieuter (se).

**dépanner** v. (P). To help out, to lend s.o. money in an emergency case, to tide one over.

**dépatouiller (se)** v. To wriggle out of a fix, a difficulty, to extricate oneself.

**dépenaillé** adj. (P). Slatternly, loosely dressed, ragged.

**dépiauter** v. (Sl). To dissecate.

**dépiauter (se)** v. (Sl). To undress, to peel.

**de pied en cap** (F). From top to toe.

**dépieuter (se)** v. (Sl). To get out of bed, to "show a leg".

**déplumé** adj. (P). Bald.

**déplumer (se)** v. (P). To loose one's hair.

**déposer son bilan** (Sl). To die, to "kick the bucket", to "peg out".

**dépotoir** sm. (F). Junk heap.

**de première main** (F). At first hand.

**depuis A jusqu'à Z** (F). From A to izzard, from beginning to end.

**de quoi** (P). Money, dough, "what it takes".

**de quoi (avoir)** (F). To have plenty. Il y a de quoi rire, enough to make a cat laugh.

**de quoi croûter** (Sl). Something to eat, a bite.

**de quoi je me mêle !** (P). Fling at a troublesome meddler.

**der** sf. (Sl). Abbr. la dernière guerre, the last one.

**dérailler** *v. (P)*. To goof (off), to go off the trolley, off the beam.

**der des der** *sf.* Abbr. *la dernière des dernières (guerres)*, the very last one, absolutely the last one.

**dérouillée** *sf. (Sl)*. Beating, shellacking, lambasting.

**dérouiller** *v. (Sl)*. To get punishment, to take the rap. In streetwalkers slang : to get the first client of the day.

**dérouiller les jambes (se)** *(F)*. To stretch one's legs.

**derrière** *sm. (P)*. The part on which we sit, seat of the pants, sitter(s).

**derrière à terre entre deux selles (tomber le)** *(Sl)*. To fall between two stools.

**derrière la cravate (s'en jeter une)** *(Sl)*. To drink, to have a drink, to down another slug of, to put one down one's neck, to sink a pint down one's hatch.

**descendre** *v. (Sl)*. To murder, to kill, to "rub out", to "erase", to knock off, to "blot out". To take one for a (buggy) ride.

**descendre dans la rue** *(P)*. To go out for a mass demonstration.

**des clous !** *interj. (P)*. Nonsense ! balls ! baloney ! Nuts !

**désopilant** *adj. (F)*. Very funny, side-splitting, too funny for words.

**désordre** *adj. (F)*. Disorderly, messy, mussy. Ex. : *Il est très désordre,* he's a mussy guy.

**désossé** *adj. (Sl)*. Flexible, supple (person).

**dés pipés** *sm. pl. (P)*. Crooked, loaded dice which always turn up high, "peeties", "shapes".

**dès potron-minet** *(F)*. At daybreak.

**dessalé** *adj. (Sl)*. Wised-up, who knows all the tricks, who has been through the mill, who has been around. Ex. : *Une fille dessalée,* a wised-up baby, a hard(-boiled) baby.

**dessaler** *v. (Sl)*. To wise up, to make a smart guy (smart baby) of.

**dessaler (se)** *(Sl)*. To get wise, wordly-wise, to get experience, to wise up, to smart up, to get hep.

**dessoûler (se)** *(Sl)*. To sober off.

**dessous** *sm. pl. (F)*. Lingerie, women's underwear. *Dessous froufroutants,* pretty and delicate feminine underwear.

**dessous de table** *sm. (P)*. An underhand commission, "kickback".

**dessus du panier** *sm. (F)*. Same as : *crème*.

**dételer** *v. (Sl)*. To knock off, to interrupt work. Also jocularly said of an aging Lothario (a libertine who "eases off" after fast living).

**de toutes les couleurs** *(P)*. See : *en faire voir de toutes les couleurs, en voir de toutes les couleurs*.

**détraqué** *adj. (P)*. Mentally unbalanced, crazy, crackpot(ty).

**détraquer** *v. (P)*. To put out of order, out of business, to bugger up, to bust up.

**deux doigts de (à)** *(F)*. On the brink of.

**deux doigts de la mort (à)** *(F)*. At death's door.

**deux poids et deux mesures (avoir)** *(F)*. Symbol for unjustice, to have two laws (to be applied according to your preference or your interest).

**deux ronds de flan** *(P)*. See : *en être comme deux ronds de flan, en rester comme deux ronds de flan*.

**deux ronds de frites** *(P)*. See : *en rester comme deux ronds de frites.*

**deux sous de frites** *(P)*. See : *en être comme deux sous de frites, en rester comme deux sous de frites.*

**déveine** *sf. (P)*. Tough luck, a lousy break. *Avoir de la déveine,* to be unlucky, to have tough luck.

**dévider** *v. (Sl)*. To talk, to jazz, to "sling the lingo".

**dévider le jars** *(Sl)*. To use underworld lingo, to "sling the lingo".

**dévisser son billard** *(Sl)*. To die, to "cash in one's checks", to "kick the bucket".

**devoir une fière chandelle à q.** *(F)*. To be greatly obliged to s.o.

**dévoreuse** *sf. (Sl)*. Hot girl, "hot mama".

**diable à confesser (c'est le)** *(F)*. It's the devil to pay, hell of a job.

**diable à quatre (faire le)** *(F)*. To kick up a rumpus, to raise hell, to raise a hullabaloo.

**diable au corps (avoir le)** *(F)*. To be full of dash, of wild, restless, youthful passion, to be as if possessed by the devil.

**diable au vert (au)** *(P)*. *C'est au diable au vert (c'est au diable Vauvert),* very far, hell of a long way to get there, a distant point.

**diable bat sa femme et marie sa fille (le)** *(P)*. Rain and sunshine together, the "devil's smile".

**didis** *sm. pl. (Sl)*. Fingers, digits, "pickers".

**digue-digue** *sm. (Sl)*. Epilepsy. See also : *tomber en digue-digue.*

**dilater la rate (se)** *(F)*. To have a hearty laugh.

**dinde** *(sf). (P)*. Silly, stupid person, dumb-bunny, dumb Dora, dope.

**dindon** *sm. (F)*. Victim, sucker ; fall guy.

**dindon de la farce** *sm. (F)*. Victim, "goat", bag holder.

**dindonner** *v. (P)*. To fool, to cheat, to victimize one. (Syn. : *pigeonner*).

**dîner à la fortune du pot** *(F)*. To get pot-luck.

**dîner en ville** *(F)*. To dine out.

**dîner par cœur** *(F)*. To be deprived of dinner, to have an Irishman's dinner.

**dinette** *sf. (F)*. Doll's dinner, small and intimate meal of two persons. Ex. : *Une dinette d'amoureux.*

**dingo** *sm. adj. (Sl)*. Crackpot, screwball, crazy, loony dippy, batty, screwy, loco, cuckoo.

**dingue** *sm. adj. (Sl)*. Goof(y), daffy. Same as : *dingo.*

**dire à q. ses quatre vérités** *(F)*. To give s.o. a piece of one's mind, to tell a thing or two, to give one a lick with the rough side of the tongue.

**dire pis que pendre de q.** *(F)*. To say most discreditable things about s.o.

**dire son fait à q.** *(F)*. To give s.o. a piece of one's mind.

**discuter le coup** *(P)*. To have a lively discussion, to get down to brass tacks.

**disparaître dans la nature** *(P)*. To vanish into thin air.

**disparaitre de la circulation** *(P)*. Same as : *disparaître dans la nature.*

**distribution** *sf.* *(Sl)*. Beating, licking, thrashing.

**dites toujours !** Fire away ! Say it !

**dix sur dix** *(P)*. Excellent, A N° 1.

**dodo** *sm.* *(F)*. Bed. Sleep. Ex. : *Aller au dodo*, to go to bed, to turn in. *Faire dodo*, to sleep.

**doigts dans le nez (les)** *(Sl)*. Very easily, without the least effort.

**dondon** *sf.* *(P)*. Derisive term for a fat woman (generally : *une grosse dondon*, a large fleshy woman).

**donnant donnant** *(F)*. Tit for tat, cash down.

**donner (un)** *sm.* *(Sl)*. Anything easy to do, a " push-over ".

**donner** *v.* *(Sl)*. To inform on, reveal a secret, particularly give information to the police, to turn informer, to " stool on ".

**donner à pleins tubes** *(Sl)*. To drive or to go at full speed, to step on the gas, to give 'er the gun.

**donner carte blanche à** *(F)*. To give a free hand to.

**donner dans le panneau** *(F)*. To fall into the trap.

**donner de l'air (se)** *v.* *(Sl)*. To go away, to leave, to take the air, to take an airing, to escape, to scram.

**donner des airs (se)** *(F)*. To give onself airs, to put on (the) dog, to put on lugs.

**donner des coups d'encensoir** *(F)*. To flatter fulsomely, to butter up.

**donner des coups d'épée dans l'eau** *(F)*. To denote a wasted effort or a totally useless action.

**donner des gants (se)** *(P)*. To brag, to boast.

**donner du fil à retordre (à)** *(F)*. To give one trouble, to create difficulties, to involve one in much inconvenience, to lead one a pretty dance.

**donner la chair de poule** *(F)*. To make one's flesh crawl.

**donner la pièce** *(P)*. To give a small present, particularly a small bribe.

**donner le change** *(F)*. To hoodwink. Fig. : To put one on the wrong scent, to bring into a controversy an irrelevant matter to confuse the issue (a " red herring ").

**donner le coup de fion** *(F)*. To give the finishing touch.

**donner le coup de grâce** *(F)*. To give the finishing stroke.

**donner le coup de pouce** *(Sl)*. To strangle. (See also : *coup de pouce, filer le coup de pouce*).

**donner plein gaz** *(F)*. To give it the gun, to step on the gas.

**donner sa langue au chat** *(F)*. To give up guessing, to give up. (Said by one who is unable to give the right answer to a " poser ").

**donner sur les doigts** *(P)*. To rap one on the knuckles.

**donner un coup de balai** *(P)*. To make a clean sweep of.

**donner un coup de collier** *(F)*. To make an extra effort, to turn on the heat.

**donner un coup de main à q.** *(F)*. To give a helping hand.

**donner un œuf pour avoir un bœuf** *(P)*. To throw a sprat to catch a herring.

**donneur** *sm.* *(Sl)*. Informer, stool pigeon.

**donzelle** *sf. (F)*. Damsel, missy.

**doper** *v. (P)*. To give a stimulant, drug, to "soup up". To dope a horse to increase his speed. (Turf slang).

**dorer la pilule** *(F)*. To gild the pill.

**dormir à la belle étoile** *(F)*. More often : *coucher à la belle étoile* (which see).

**dormir à poings fermés** *(F)*. To sleep like a log.

**dormir sur ses deux oreilles** *(F)*. Not to lose sleep over. Ex. : *Tu peux dormir sur tes deux oreilles*, you needn't feel uneasy, you needn't lose sleep over that matter.

**doryphore** *sm. (Sl)*. Nickname for a German, "Kraut", Jerry (during the occupation years 1940-1944).

**dos-vert** *sm. (Sl)*. Euphemistic variant of *maquereau*, a man supported by a woman.

**doublage** *sm. (Sl)*. Cheating, double-crossing.

**doubler** *v. (Sl)*. To cheat, to double-cross.

**doublure** *sf. (F)*. Understudy, stand-in.

**douche écossaise** *sf. (P)*. Shower-bath with alternating warm and cold streams of water. Fig. : effect achieved by alternating good and bad news, good and bad treatment.

**doucher** *v. (Sl)*. *Il a été douché,* he's been seriously shaken, fleeced, he suffered a loss, he burnt his fingers, etc.

**doudounes** *sf. pl. (Sl)*. Girl's exciting fleshy charms.

**douilles** *sf. pl. (Sl)*. Hair, "thatch".

**douloureuse** *sf. (P)*. Joc. term for : bill, check, especially a heavy one, (restaurant, hotel, rent, etc.).

LA DOULOUREUSE.

**dragée** *sf. (Sl)*. Pistol bullet.

**dragon** *sm. (P)*. Termagant, a violent, brawling woman, shrew.

**dresser sur ses ergots (se)** *(F)*. To get on one's high horse.

**droguer** *v. (Sl)*. To wait, to be left to cool one's heels.

**drogués (les)** *sm. pl. (Sl)* Drug addicts, dope fiends, "junkers", "gow-heads".

**drôle de coco (un)** *sm. (P)*. Contemptible person, a lousy bum, queer guy.

**drôle de mec (un)** *sm. (Sl)*. Queer customer. Sometimes : ace, remarkable person, lollapaloosa.

**drôle de paroissien (un)** *sm. (P)*. Odd fellow, disliked person, gazabo.

**drôle de pierrot (un)** *sm. (P)*. Same as : *drôle de type*.

**drôle de pistolet (un)** *sm. (Sl)*. Odd fellow, queer guy.

**drôle de sieur (un)** *(P)*. Same as : *drôle de paroissien*.

**drôle de touche (une)** *sf. (P)*. Queer looks.

**drôle de type (un)** *sm. (P)*. Queer customer. Sometimes : ace, remarkable person.

**drôle de zèbre (un)** *sm. (Sl)*. Same as : *drôle de paroissien*.

**drôlichon** *adj. (P)*. Funny, rather funny.

**dross** *sm. (Sl)*. Residue left in an opium pipe, " green mud ".

**duch(e)nock** *sm. (Sl)*. Stupid person, dope, dumbbell.

\* **duconnard** *sm. (Sl)*. A variant of *duconneau*.

\* **duconneau** *sm. (Sl)*. Silly person, chump, dumbbell, goofie.

**dulcinée** *sf. (F)*. One's inamorata, one's flame, O.A.O. (one and only).

**du même bord (être)** *(F)*. To be in the same party as.

**du monde au balcon** *(Sl)*. Said of a woman's profuse breasts.

**du pareil au même** *(F)*. Equal, identical, one and the same.

**Dupont-Durand** *(P)*. Man in the street, the average Frenchman, " Pierre Q. Frenchman ", French equivalent of Joe Doakes, John Q. Public.

**dur (le)** *sm. (Sl)*. Gold, gold dollar (Stock Exchange slang).

**dur (un)** *sm. (Sl)*. Tough (guy), rough guy, roughneck. Ex. : *C'est un dur*, he's a tough one.

**dur** *adj. (P)*. Difficult, tough.

**dur à cuire** *(P)*. Hard-shell.

**dur à la détente** *(F)*. Stingy, cheap skate, pinchpenny, nickel pincher.

**dur à les lâcher** *(Sl)*. Stingy, close-fisted.

**dur de dur (un)** *(Sl)*. A rough guy, convict, " lag ", " bully ".

**dur de la feuille (être)** *(Sl)*. To be hard of hearing.

DUR DE LA FEUILLE.

**durs (les)** *sm. pl. (Sl)*. Hard labor.

# E

**eau dans le gaz (de l')** *(Sl)*. Trouble, "bug". Ex. : *il y a de l'eau dans le gaz,* there is some difficulty, some trouble, there is a bug in the deal.

**eau de bidet** *sf. (Sl)*. Something contemptible, of no value, mean, cheap, "tinhorn", baloney.

**eau de boudin** *(P)*. Hogwash. *S'en aller en eau de boudin,* to fail, to flivver out, to fizz out, to end in smoke, to melt into thin air.

**eau de rose (à l')** *(F)*. Watered down.

**ébréché** *adj. (Sl)*. Slightly drunk, a "bit on".

**échalas** *sm. (P)*. Great, lanky fellow.
*sm. pl. (Sl)*. Very long and skinny legs, broomsticks, spindle-shanks.

**échasses** *sf. pl. (P)*. Spindle-shanks, "toothpicks".

**échigner (s')** *v. (P)*. To exert oneself, to toil hard, to worry oneself.

**éclairer la lanterne de q.** *(F)*. To explain.

**éclipser (s')** *(F)*. To take French leave, to depart on the q. t., without saying good-by, to decamp, to scram.

**école buissonnière (faire l')** *(F)*. To skip school, to play hooky.

**économies de bouts de chandelles** *(F)*. Stingy, cheeseparing savings.

**écoper** *v. (P)*. To take the blame, to take the rap, to get it in the neck.

**écorcher un pou pour en avoir la peau** *(P)*. To skin (flay) a flint.

**écrabouiller** *(P)*. To bruise, to crush, to smash.

**écrase !** *(Sl)*. Shut up ! Dry up !

**écrire comme un chat** *(F)*. To write illegibly.

**écureuil** *sm. (P)*. Cycler riding in circle in a velodrome.

— 69 —

**éducation anglaise** *sf. (Sl)*. Flagellation.

**effronté comme un page** *(F)*. Impudent, saucy.

**elle est (vraiment) raide, celle-là !** *(P)*. That's a bit thick !

**emballé** *adj. (P)*. Very enthusiastic, very keen on, keenly interested in.

**emballer** *v. (P)*. To scold strongly, to bawl out, to dress down. *(Sl)*. To arrest, to pull in, to haul in, to send up the river.

**emballer (s')** *v. (P)*. To flare up, to lose one's temper, to get excited, to " go ape " over.

**embarquer** *v. (P)*. To arrest, to " haul in ".

**emberlificoter** *v. (F)*. To involve one in difficulties, to get round s.o., to wheedle.

**emberlificoteur** *sm. (P)*. Wheedler, coaxer.

**embêtant** *adj. (P)*. Tiresome, boring, annoying (thing or individual), to be a nuisance.

**embêter** *v. (P)*. To bother, to tire, to make one tired.

**embistrouiller** *v. (Sl)*. Same as : *emberlificoter.*

**embobiner** *v. (P)*. To cajole one into, to get round a person, to " rope in ".

**emboîter le pas à q.** *(F)*. To follow on one's heels, to follow the lead.

**emboucaner** *v. (Sl)*. To stink, to smell (up).

**embrouillamini** *sm. (P)*. Pretty mess, mess-up, hell of a mess.

**embusqué** *adj. (P)*. Soldier who has a cushy job in the military administration (and doesn't do active service).

**éméché (être)** *(P)*. To be slightly drunk, a " bit high ", " lit a bit ".

\* **emmerdement** *sm. (Sl)*. Trouble, annoyance, worriment, headache.

\* **emmerder** *v. (Sl)*. To bother, to make one tired, to annoy, to weary, to bore s.o. (In writing : em(m)...) : *Je l'emm... !* he can go to hell ! *Tu m'emm... !* what a pest you are ! Stop annoying me ! *Je m'emm....* I am terribly bored.

\* **emmerdeur** *sm. (Sl)*. Bothersome, quarrelsome individual, man who creates trouble, difficulties; a real nuisance.

**emmiellement** *sm. (Sl)*. Euphemistic variation of *emmerdement.*

**emmieller** *v. (Sl)*. To annoy, to bother, to sicken, to plague s.o. Euphemism for : *emmerder.*

**emmouscaillement** *sm. (Sl)*. Euphemistic variant of *emmerdement.*

**emmouscailler** *v. (Sl)*. Euphemistic variation of *emmerder :* to annoy, to pester, to sicken, to plague s.o.

**empaillé** *adj. (Sl)*. Silly, stupid, dopey, dumbbell.

**empaumer** *v. (Sl)*. To dupe, to take in, to " suck in ".

**empêcheur de danser en rond** *sm. (F)*. Wet blanket, sourmouth, spoil-sport.

**empiffrer (s')** *v. (Sl)*. To eat food greedily, to throw it down, to wolf it.

**empiler** *v. (P)*. To swindle, to take in, to " suck in ", to defraud, to gyp, to flimflam, to " sting ", to " sell a gold brick ", to pull the wool over one's eyes.

**empileur** *sm. (P)*. Swindler, crook, chiseler, slicker.

**emplâtre** *sm.* *(P).* Zombie, chicken, weakling.

**employer le système D** *(P).* To be unscrupulously resourceful. Said of an unscrupulous wangler; what an unscrupulous wangler does to reach his aim. (Here the letter D stands for: *débrouillard*).

**empoisonner** *v. (Sl).* To smell (up), to stink. To sicken, to annoy, to pester, to make one tired, to be a nuisance to s.o.

**empoivrer (s')** *v. (Sl).* To get drunk.

**emporter la gueule** *(Sl).* To burn the throat (said of strong drinks or of heavily spiced food). Ex. : *Ça emporte la gueule,* it's too spicy.

**emporter le morceau** *(P).* To win out (in a discussion).

**empoté** *adj.* *(P).* Silly, stupid, dimwit, dopey.

**ému** *adj. (P).* Slightly drunk.

**en abattre** *v. (P).* To have a fast tempo at work, to do a lot of work in a fast tempo.

**en avoir classe** *(Sl).* To be fed up on, to be tired of.

**en avoir épais** *(Sl).* Same as : *en avoir classe.*

**en avoir gros sur la patate** *(Sl).* To have good reason to be sad at heart.

**en avoir le cœur net** *(P).* To get to the very bottom of a thing in order to clear it up. To get the five w's of a thing (who ? what ? when ? where ? why ?).

**en avoir marre** *(Sl).* To be fed up, to be sick and tired of.

**en avoir par-dessus la tête** *(F).* Same as : *en avoir marre.*

**en avoir plein le dos** *(P).* Same as : *en avoir marre.*

**en avoir plein ses bottes** *(Sl).* Same as : *en avoir marre.*

**en avoir pour son compte** *(P).* To get bawled out, to get a thrashing.

**en avoir sa claque** *(Sl).* Same as : *en avoir marre.*

**en avoir soupé** *(P).* Same as : *en avoir marre.*

**en avoir une couche** *(P).* To be hopelessly dumb.

**en avoir une santé** *(P).* To be impudent, cheeky, crusty. Ex. : *Vous en avez une santé !* I like your nerve !

**en avril ne te découvre pas d'un fil, en mai fais ce qui te plaît** *(F).* Popular saying : never cast a clout till May is out.

**en baver** *v. (Sl).* To have to suffer a lot.

**en boucher un coin** *(P).* To astonish, to knock one off his pins, to knock for a loop.

**en boucher une surface** *(Sl).* Same as : *en boucher un coin.*

**en bourgeois (les)** *sm. pl. (Sl).* Policemen of the vice squad.

**encaisser** *v. (P).* To stand the gaff. Ex. : *Il est incapable d'encaisser,* he can't take it. (See also : *ne pas pouvoir encaisser q.).*

**en camp volant** *(P).* In temporary quarters.

**en carte (être)** *(P).* To be registered as prostitute by Police.

**en chair (bien)** *(P).* Fat, cornfed, buxom.

**enchifrené** *adj. (P).* Having a slight cold.

**en cinq sec(s)** *(P).* Very quickly, in a crack, in a jiffy, in a kick, before you can say " knife ",

before you can say " Jack Robinson ",
in two shakes of a lamb's tail.

**\* en cloque (être)** *(Sl)*. To be
pregnant, " knocked up ".

**en coller plein la lampe (s')**
*(Sl)*. To have a tuck-in, a blow-out.
(Same as : *s'en mettre plein la lampe*).

**encroûter (s')** *v.* (P). To sink
into a routine.

**en cuire** *(P)*. *Il t'en cuira !* You
will be sorry for it !

**en délicatesse avec q. (être)**
*(F)*. To be in strained relations with.

**en deux temps et trois mou-
vements** *(P)*. Very quickly, pretty
damn quick.

**endéver** *v.* *(P)*. To be mad,
furious.

**endimanché** *adj. (F)*. In one's
best bib and tucker, Sunday best.

ENDIMANCHÉ.

**en dire de vertes et de pas
mûres** *(P)*. Same as : *en raconter de
vertes et de pas mûres.*

**endormeur** *sm. (P)*. Bore, " flat-
tire ", " bromide ".

**en douce** *(P)*. Silently, on the
quiet, on the q.t., on the mum.

**en écraser** *v. (Sl)*. To be fast
asleep, to sleep like a top.

IL EN ÉCRASE !

**en étouffer un** *(Sl)*. To have a
drink.

**en être assis** *(P)*. To be amazed,
to be dumb-founded.

**en être comme deux ronds
de flan** *(Sl)*. Same as : *en rester
comme deux ronds de flan.*

**en être comme deux ronds
de frites** *(Sl)*. Same as : *en rester
comme deux ronds de frites.*

**en être comme deux sous de
frites** *(Sl)*. Same as : *en rester
comme deux sous de frites.*

**en être pour ses frais** *(F)*.
To have spent one's efforts, time,
money, etc. in vain.

**en être quitte pour la peur**
*(F)*. To come off (to get off) with a
fright.

**en faire baver à q.** *(Sl)*. To give one a harsh treatment.

**en faire de belles** *(P)*. *Elle en a fait de belles !* Nice things she's been up to !

**en faire tout un plat** *(P)*. To make a long rigmarole.

**en faire un chahut** *(P)*. To kick up a row, a shindy, a racket, a dust.

**en faire une tartine** *(P)*. To make a long rigmarole, to exaggerate in speech or in writing, to make a fuss.

**en faire voir à q.** *(P)*. To involve one in much trouble and inconvenience, to treat one or to behave towards one roughly, abominably ; to lead one a pretty dance.

**en faire voir de toutes les couleurs** *(P)*. To lead one a pretty dance. See also : *en faire voir à q.*

**enfant de chœur** *sm. (P)*. Derisive for an innocent, naive soul.

**enfant de la balle** *(F)*. Child who follows his father's trade. Actor brought up on the boards.

**enfant de l'amour** *(F)*. Illegitimate child, bastard.

**enfiler (s')** *(Sl)*. To treat oneself to. (Same as : *envoyer (s')*.

**enfiler des perles** *(P)*. To idle away time, to loaf.

**enflé** *adj. (Sl)*. Stupid person, dumbbell, dope, fathead.

**enfoncer** *v. (Sl). Nous les avons enfoncés,* we got the better of them, we beat them, we defeated them.

**enfonceur de portes ouvertes** *(P)*. Fling at a noisy braggart, braggadocio.

**en froid avec q. (être)** *(F)*. To be cold towards one, to give the cold shoulder.

**en griller une** *(P)*. To smoke a cigarette, to take a gasper.

**engueulade** *sf. (Sl)*. Bawling-out, going-over. Ex. : *Recevoir une engueulade,* to be bawled out, to get hell.

ENGUEULADE.

**engueulade-maison** *sf. (Sl)*. A severe bawling-out.

**engueuler** *v. (Sl)*. To bawl out, to " dress down ". *Engueuler comme du poisson pourri,* to bawl hell out of, to give hell, to give one hail Columbia.

**enguirlander q. (comme du poisson pourri)** *(P)*. Euphemism for : *engueuler q. (comme du poisson pourri)*.

**enlever** *v. (P)*. Same as : *barboter*.

**enlever (s') comme des petits pains** *(P)*. To sell like hot cakes, to sell briskly and easily.

**en mettre à gauche** *(P)*. To stash away money, to put one's savings in a safe place.

**en mettre plein la vue à q.** *(F)*. To hoodwink, to deceive s.o.

**en mettre plein les yeux à q.** *(F)*. Same as preceding entry.

**en mettre sa main au feu** *(F). J'en mettrais ma main au feu,* I should stake my life on it.

**en mettre un coup** *(P)*. To work hard, to "shoot the works".

**en moins de deux** *(P)*. Very quickly, in a crack, in a jiffy.

**ennuyer q.** *v. (F)*. To bother one.

**ennuyer comme un rat mort (s')** To be bored to death, to yawn oneself to death.

**ennuyer comme un vieux croûton (s')** *(P)*. Same as : *ennuyer comme un rat mort (s')*.

**en pénard** *(Sl)*. On the quiet, on the sly, on the shush, on the q. t.

**en père peinard** *(Sl)*. Quietly. (Same as : *en pénard*).

**en pincer pour** *(P)*. To have a crush, to be gone (on a person).

**en plein cirage (être)** *(Sl)*. To be dead-drunk.

**en prendre de la graine** *(F)*. Take a leaf from one's book, to follow one's example.

**en prendre pour son grade** *(P)*. To get a raking over the coals, a severe bawling out.

**en pure perte** *(F)*. To no avail.

**enquiquiner** *v. (Sl)*. To pester, to annoy, to weary, to vex, to get in one's hair.

**enquiquiner (s')** *(Sl)*. To be bored, to be fed up.

**enquiquineur** *sm. (Sl)*. A variant of *emmerdeur* (but a shade less vulgar).

**en rabattre** *v. (F)*. To get less exacting.

**en raconter de vertes (et de pas mûres)** *(P)*. To tell racy (spicy) stories.

**en rang d'oignons** *(P)*. In a perfect row.

**en rester baba** *(P)*. To be astonished, to be flabbergasted.

**en rester comme deux ronds de flan** *(Sl)*. To be astounded, to be struck all of a heap.

**en rester comme deux ronds de frites** *(Sl)*. Same as : *en rester comme deux ronds de flan*.

**en rester comme deux sous de frites** *(Sl)*. Same as : *en rester comme deux ronds de flan*.

**en rester comme une tomate** *(Sl)*. Same as : *en rester comme deux ronds de flan*.

**en rester comme une tourte** *(Sl)*. Same as : *en rester comme deux ronds de flan*.

**en rogne (être)** *(Sl)*. To be mad.

**en roter** *v. (Sl)*. Same as : *en baver*.

**en roter (des ronds de chapeau)** *(Sl)*. To be utterly disconcerted, astounded, bewildered, to be struck dumbfounded.

**en rouler une** *(P)*. To hand-roll a cigarette.

**\* en suer une** *(Sl)*. To have a dance.

**entendre comme larrons en foire (s')** *(F)*. To be as thick as thieves.

**en tenir pour q.** *(P)*. Same as : *en pincer pour*.

**en tenir une dose** *(P)*. A variation of *en avoir une couche*.

**en tenir une pochetée** *(Sl)*. Another variant of *en avoir une couche*.

**enterrer sa vie de garçon** *(P)*. To throw a farewell bachelor's party.

**entiché de q . (être)** *(F)*. To be nuts on, mad on, to be nutty over.

**enticher de (s')** *(F)*. To take a fancy to, to go crazy on, to "go ape" over.

**entôler** *v. (Sl)*. To inveigle and rob, to fleece.

**entôleur** *sm. (Sl)*. Robber, thief, inveigler.

**entôleuse** *sf. (Sl)*. Girl who robs a victim after luring him to room, "panel worker".

**entonnoir** *sm. (Sl)*. Throat, "funnel".

**entortiller** *v. (P)*. To coax, to wheedle, to rope in, to come round s.o.

**entourlouper** *v. (P)*. To play a trick, to play hob with.

**entourloupette** *sf. (P)*. Trick to achieve one's aim.

**en train (être)** *(Sl)*. To be slightly drunk.

**entraîneuse** *sf. (P)*. B-girl.

**entre chien et loup** *(P)*. In the twilight.

**entre deux vins (être)** *(F)*. To be slightly drunk, tipsy, to be a bit "on", a bit "high". (Other French slang words : *éméché, allumé, gai, lancé, parti, gris, pompette,* all meaning : slightly drunk).

**entre la poire et le fromage** *(F)*. After dinner, at the end of the meal, over the walnuts and wine (time for storytelling).

**entre l'enclume et le marteau** *(F)*. To be between the anvil and the hammer, to be between the devil and the deep sea.

**entre le zist et le zest (être)** *(F)*. To be undecided. Neither good nor bad.

**entre quat'z-yeux** *(P)*. Between you'n'me (and the lamp post), between us.

**entrer dans le chou** *(P)*. To "light into", to "pitch into", to attack.

**entuber** *v. (Sl)*. To take in, to "suck in", to swindle, to "horn-swoggle".

**en valoir le coup** *(P)*. To be worth-while.

**envelopper q.** *(Sl)*. To dupe, to swindle, to victimize.

**en venir à bout** *(F)*. To lick s.o. or s.th.

**en venir aux coups** *(F)*. Same as : *en venir aux mains.*

**en venir aux mains** *(F)*. To come to fight.

**en voilà du propre !** *(P)*. Fine things ! (Sarcastic excl.).

**en voir de dures** *(F)*. To have a bad time of it.

**en voir de raides** *(P)*. Same as : *en voir de dures.*

**en voir de toutes les couleurs** *(F)*. Same as : *en voir de dures.*

**en voir trente-six chandelles** *(F)*. To see the stars by daylight, to be stunned (following a heavy blow on one's head), "cutting paper dolls".

**envoyé** *adj. (P)*. Well-delivered, well-told. Ex. : *un coup envoyé,* a hard hit, a haymaker ; *une réplique envoyée,* a squelch, a clincher.

**envoyer (s')** *(P)*. To treat oneself, to blow oneself to, to stand oneself. (See : *taper (se)*).

**envoyer à tous les diables** *(F)*. To send to hell, to send packing, to send to the right-about.

**envoyer au bain** *(Sl).* To send one packing, to dismiss one brusquely and in anger.

IL L'ENVOIE AU BAIN.

**envoyer au diable** *(F).* A coll. variant of *envoyer au bain.*

**envoyer aux pelotes** *(Sl).* A slang variation of *envoyer au bain.*

**envoyer baller** *(Sl).* Another slang variation of *envoyer au bain.*

**envoyer bouler** *(Sl).* Still another slang variant of *envoyer au bain.*

**envoyer des bobards** *(Sl).* To make disparaging remarks, to make a dirty crack about.

**envoyer des postillons** *(P).* To splutter when speaking.

**envoyer dinguer** *(Sl).* To dismiss brusquely, to fire, to turn out neck and crop, to kick out, to send packing, to send to hell.

**envoyer en l'air** *(Sl).* To kill, to murder, to bump off, to "wipe out".

**envoyer faire fiche** *(Sl).* To turn out neck and heels, to send packing.

**\* envoyer faire foutre** *(Sl).* Same as : *envoyer faire fiche* (but more vulgar).

**envoyer paître** *(P).* A variant of *envoyer au bain.*

**envoyer péter** *(Sl).* A variant of *envoyer dinguer.*

**envoyer suer** *(Sl).* Same as : *envoyer faire fiche.*

**envoyer sur les roses** *(Sl).* A variation of *envoyer au bain, envoyer aux pelotes.*

**envoyer un pot (s')** *(Sl).* To treat oneself to a drink.

**épastrouillant** *adj. (Sl).* Amazing, astounding.

**épastrouiller** *v. (Sl).* To amaze, to astonish, to strike all of a heap.

**épatant** *adj. (F).* Cute, dandy, swell, great.

**épate (faire de l')** *(F).* To splash (it), to show off, to make a splurge, a big splash.

**épater** *v. (F).* To astound, to flabbergast.

**épauler** *v. (P).* To back up.

**épouser la grosse galette** *(P).* To marry a wealthy girl.

**épouser le gros sac** *(P).* Same as : *épouser la grosse galette.*

**épouser un gros magot** *(P).* Same as : *épouser la grosse galette.*

**époustouflé** *adj. (Sl).* Flabbergasted, knocked all of a heap.

**épouvantail** *sm. (P).* Grotesque person, a " fright ". Booger.

**éreintant** *adj. (P).* Too tiring, exhausting.

**éreinter** *v. (P).* To tire out, to poop out. To put one down hard, to run down, to criticize severely, to " knock ".

**éreinté** *adj. (P).* Pooped (out), dead-beat, bushed.

**esbigner (s')** *v. (Sl).* To pull out, to scram, to decamp.

**esbrouffe (faire de l')** *(P)*. To show off, to splash it, to splurge.

**esbrouffeur** *sm.* *(P)*. Swashbuckler, swaggerer.

**escogriffe** *sm.* *(P)*. Chiefly used with an adj. as in : *un grand escogriffe,* a great lanky fellow, a great lout of a fellow.

**esgourdes** *sf. pl.* *(Sl)*. Ears, " flappers ".

**esquintant** *adj.* *(P)*. Too tiring, killing.

**esquinter** *v.* *(Sl)*. To pull to pieces, to run down, to " knock ". To spoil, to " ball up ", to " louse up ", to " jazz up ", to mess up. To exhaust, to fag out, to wash up.

**essuyer le coup de fusil** *(P)*. To pay an overcharged restaurant (or hotel) bill.

**essuyer les plâtres** *(F)*. To occupy a home before the paint is dry, to be the first tenant of a newly built house.

**estampe** *sf.* *(Sl)*. Swindle, crooked deal, racket.

**estamper** *v.* *(Sl)*. To swindle, to gyp, to chisel, to " suck in ", to " trim ".

**estampeur** *sm.* *(Sl)*. Swindler, crook, chiseler, phon(e)y.

**estomac (à l')** *(Sl)*. Bluff. *Faire à l'estomac,* to bluff.

**estomac (avoir de l')** *(Sl)*. To have plenty of reserves and strong nerves to stand financial losses without batting an eyelash (at card games, races, Stock Exchange, etc.).

**estomac creux (avoir l')** *(F)*. Same as : *estomac dans les talons (avoir l').*

**estomac dans les talons (avoir l')** *(F)*. To be very hungry.

**estomac d'autruche (avoir un)** *(F)*. To have a cast-iron stomach that can digest anything.

**estomaquer** *v.* *(P)*. To flabbergast, to astound, to astonish, to knock s.o. silly, to strike s.o. pink, to faze.

**estourbir** *v.* *(Sl)*. To kill, to murder, to " blot out ", to bump off, to " erase ", to " liquidate ".

**étaler (s')** *v.* *(P)*. To fall, to take a spill, to come a cropper.

**et comment !** *(P)*. And how ! For sure ! You bet !

**éteignoir** *sm.* *(Sl)*. Humorous slang term for a big nose, schnozzo, " foghorn ".

**éteindre son gaz** *(Sl)*. To die, to " turn the lights off. " (Same as : *souffler sa veilleuse*).

**éternel triangle** *sm.* *(P)*. Cynical term implying the " triangle " of husband, wife and her lover.

**... et le pouce !** *(P)*. Popular phrase meaning : this...and a good deal more, or : this...plus a bit, or : this and a bit on top !

**et mon œil !** *interj.* *(Sl)*. Nothing doing ! baloney ! my eye ! (See : *mon œil !*).

**et ta sœur ?** *(Sl)*. Jocular but rude remark to silence one : silence ! knock it off ! pipe down ! cut it out ! Also scornful retort to one who is pestering you.

**étoffe (avoir de l')** *(F)*. To have the goods, the makings.

**et que ça saute !** *(Si)*. P.D.Q. ! rush ! make it snappy !

**étrenne de (avoir l')** *(F)*. To have the first use of.

**éventer la mèche** *(F)*. To spill a secret, to " spill the beans ".

**expédier** *v.* *(F)*. To whisk off. To " dispatch ", to eat up.

# F

**fabriqué (être)** *(Sl)*. To be arrested, to be "nabbed", to be "pulled in", to "get a number".

**fabriquer** *v. (P)*. To do. Ex. : *Qu'est-ce que tu fabriques ?* What are you doing ?
*(Sl)*. To arrest, to "nab". To steal, to pinch, to swipe.

**Fac** *sf. (P)*. University.

**façade** *sf. (P)*. A "blind", a pretence, something ostensible to conceal a covert design or trade.

**face de rat** *sf. (Sl)*. Ugly face, "mug".

**fâcher tout rouge (se)** *(F)*. To fly into a rage, into a fit of anger, to hit the ceiling, to "make the fur fly".

**façonné sur commande (sur mesure)** *(F)*. Tailor-made.

**fada** *adj. (P)*. Crazy, cracked, dopey, screwy.

**fadasse** *adj. (P)*. Tasteless.

**fadé (être)** *(Sl)*. To have got more than one bargained for.

**fafiots** *sm. pl. (Sl)*. Bank notes, greenbacks.

**fagoté** *adj. (F)*. Badly dressed.

**fagoter (se)** *(F)*. To dress badly, in bad taste.

**faiblard** *sm. adj. (Sl)*. Weakish, weakling, softie, sissy.

**faire** *v. (Sl)*. To steal, to swipe, to bum.

**faire arranger (se)** *(Sl)*. To get duped, fooled, victimized ; to get wounded or injured in a fight ; to get infected with V.D.

**\* faire baiser (se)** *(P)*. To get caught, arrested, "nabbed". To get duped.

**faire ballon** *(Sl)*. To go without food.

**faire bouillir la marmite** *(P)*. To keep the pot boiling.

**faire chanter** *(F)*. To blackmail one, to extort money from, to shake one down.

**faire coller (se)** *(P)*. To flunk, to fail.

**faire contre mauvaise fortune bon cœur** *(F)*. To stand the gaff, to keep up one's spirits, to bear up against bad fortune.

**faire cracher q.** *(Sl)*. To make one cough up (the money), to "put the shake" on s.o.

**faire cul-sec** *(Sl)*. To drink "bottoms-up".

**faire danser l'anse du panier** *(P)*. Said of a servant girl who "pads" the bills of her purchases for her masters.

**faire de chic** *(P)*. Said of an artist who works without a model.

**faire de l'œil à q.** *(F)*. To ogle, to try to attract the amorous attention of a person of the opposite sex.

**\* faire des conneries** *(Sl)*. To goof (off), to make bad mistakes.

**faire des épates** *(Sl)*. To be fussy, to kick up fuss (same as : *faire des manières*).

**faire des histoires** *(P)*. To kick up a fuss, to make a big to-do, to holler.

**faire des mamours** *(F)*. To canoodle.

**faire des paillons** *(Sl)*. A variation of *faire des queues*.

**faire des queues** *(Sl)*. To philander, to step out on one's husband, to be unfaithful, to cheat in love.

**faire des siennes** *(F)*. To play tricks, to be up to one's old tricks.

**faire des traits** *(Sl)*. Another variant of *faire des queues*.

**faire des yeux de merlan frit** *(Sl)*. To gaze, to look at s.o. with a blank stare.

**faire droguer** *(Sl)*. To keep waiting.

**faire du chambard** *(Sl)*. Same as : *faire du pétard*.

**faire du genou** *(P)*. To play footsies (under-the-table flirtation).

**faire du lard (se)** *(P)*. To grow fat (through idleness).

**faire d'une mouche un éléphant** *(F)*. To make a mountain out of a mole hill, to make a difficulty of trifles.

**faire d'une pierre deux coups** *(F)*. To kill two birds with one stone.

**faire du pétard** *(P)*. To raise hell, to raise a hullabaloo, to raise the roof, to kick up a ruckus, to "make the fur fly".

**faire du plat** *(Sl)*. To make love to.

**faire du zèle** *(F)*. To be over-zealous (what an eager-beaver is usually doing).

**faire fabriquer (se)** *(Sl)*. To get caught, arrested, "nabbed", discovered. To get cheated, duped, fooled, victimized, "sucked in".

**faire faire marron (se)** *(Sl)*. To get arrested, "nabbed".

**faire figaro** *(Sl)*. Among waiters : to get no tip.

**faire flèche de tout bois** *(F)*. To resort to any trick (to any shift).

**faire four** *(F)*. To fail utterly, to go to the dogs, to fall flat.

**faire gauler (se)** *(Sl)*. To get arrested, "nabbed".

**faire grise mine** *(F)*. To give the cold shoulder.

**faire la bringue** *(Sl)*. To go on a binge, to kick up one's heels, to carouse, to have a hot time.

**faire la main (se)** *(F)*. To do s. th. for exercise in order to get the knack of a thing.

**faire l'âne pour avoir du son** *(F)*. To pretend ignorance in order to get information and thus to attain one's end.

**faire la paire (se)** *(Sl)*. To escape, to decamp, to scram, to run hard.

**faire la pige à** *(P)*. To surpass, to outdo s.o.

**faire la pluie et le beau temps** *(F)*. To be all powerful.

**faire la queue** *(P)*. To line up.

**faire la retape** *(Sl)*. Same as : *faire le tapin*.

**faire la tête** *(F)*. To be sulky.

**faire la vie** *(P)*. To lead a dissolute life.

**faire le coup** *(P)*. *C'est lui qui a fait le coup*, it's his deed, he did it.

**faire le grand voyage** *(Sl)*. To die, " to take off for eternity ", to " join the great majority ".

**faire le macadam** *(Sl)*. A variation of *faire le tapin*.

**faire le mariolle** *(Sl)*. To act in a conceited manner, to play the smart-aleck.

**faire le point** *(F)*. To determine the exact position.

**faire le quart** *(Sl)*. To be on the " turf ". Said of a prostitute who walks on her " beat " in the street.

**faire le raccroc** *(Sl)*. To " hook ", to solicit, to accost men in the street.

**faire le rodomont** *(P)*. To be a blusterer, a braggart, a " horn tooter ".

**faire les quatre volontés de q.** *(F)*. To be at one's beck and call.

**faire les yeux doux à q.** *(F)*. To ogle, to make eyes at, to look invitingly or amorously at.

**faire le tapin** *(Sl)*. To solicit men in the street (said of a prostitute).

**faire le truc** *(Sl)*. To live on, to engage in, prostitution. (See also : *truqueuse*).

**faire main basse sur q. ch.** *(F)*. To steal, to grab.

**faire marcher** *(F)*. To bamboozle, to make a fool of.

**faire marron** *(Sl)*. To arrest, to capture, to " nail ".

**faire monter à l'échelle** *(Sl)*. To make one angry, to get one's monkey up.

**faire moucher (se)** *(P)*. To get a good hiding, a severe beating, thrashing.

**faire mousser** *(P)*. To crack up.

**faire mousser (se)** *(P)*. To make oneself important.

**faire passer le goût du pain à q.** *(P)*. To kill, to murder one, to " erase ", to " rub out ".

**faire piper (se)** *(Sl)*. To get arrested, to get " nabbed ".

**faire piquer (se)** *(Sl)*. To get arrested, to get " nabbed ".

**faire porter pâle (se)** *(Sl)*. To report illness.

**faire prendre des vessies pour des lanternes** *(F)*. To have one believe the moon is made of green cheese. *Tu veux me faire prendre des* *vessies pour des lanternes !* You want to prove to me that black is white !

**faire ramasser (se)** *(P)*. To get arrested, " nabbed ", by police. To get bawled out.

**faire recaler (se)** *(P)*. Same as : *faire coller (se)*.

**faire rétamer (se)** *(Sl)*. To get drunk.

**faire rincer (se)** *(P)*. To get wet in the rain.
*(Sl)*. To sponge on one for a drink. To suffer a heavy beating ; to sustain a heavy loss.

**faire ripaille** *(F)*. To have a blowout, to feast.

**faire risette** *(F)*. To crack a smile.

**faire sa pelote** *(P)*. To become prosperous, to make one's pile, to make money, to make a bankroll.

**faire sa Sophie** *(F)*. To affect prudishness.

**faire sauter le caisson (se)** *(P)*. To blow one's brains out, to commit suicide.

IL VA SE FAIRE SAUTER
LE CAISSON.

**faire ses quatre volontés** *(F)*. To do just as one pleases, to act at one's own sweet will.

**faire son affaire à q.** *(F)*. To settle one's hash, to cook one's goose, to make it hot for one.

**faire son baluchon** *(P)*. To pack up and go, to leave.

**faire son beurre** *(Sl)*. To get rich, to be prosperous, to amass a fortune.

**faire son deuil de q. ch.** *(F)*. To kiss good-by (joc.).

**faire sonner les cloches (se)** *(F)*. To get a severe reprimand, to get bawled out, to get it good and hot.

**faire suer** *(Sl)*. To pester, to annoy, to make one sick and tired.

**faire suer le burnous** *(P)*. To drive slaves, to slave-drive, to sweat (cheap labor).

**faire suisse** *(Sl)*. To have a drink alone, all by oneself.

**faire tapisserie** *(F)*. To be a wallflower.

**faire tirer la langue à q.** *(F)*. To keep a person waiting indefinitely (for something he wants eagerly).

**faire tourner q. en bourrique** *(F)*. To worry one out of his mind. To drive one crazy, mad.

**faire tout un plat de q. ch** *(P)*. To make a great fuss about s. th.

**faire un (beau) chopin** *(P)*. To make a real bargain, to win the heart of a wealthy lover, to find a gold mine, a sugar honey.

**faire un costume de bois (se faire)** *(Sl)*. To die, to " put on a wooden suit ".

**faire une belle jambe** *(P)*. *Ça me fait une belle jambe !* Ironical expression meaning : A lot of good that will do me ! What does that buy me ?

**faire une boulette** *(P)*. To goof, to make a " boo-boo ", to pull a bloomer.

**faire une fin** *(F)*. Said of a young man who gets married, settles down.

**faire une gaffe** *(F)*. To put one's foot into it, to make a blunder, a " boo-boo ".

**faire un levage** *(Sl)*. To secure a girl's (woman's) love, to make a big hit, to make a " pick-up ".

**faire un nez** *(P)*. To make a long face, a gloomy face, to look unhappy, to show depression.

**faire valser les écus** *(F)*. To " shoot the works ", to spend money recklessly.

**faire venir l'eau à la bouche** *(F)*. To make one's mouth water.

**faire vieux (se)** *(Sl)*. To be bored.

**faire volte-face** *(F)*. To do an about-face.

**faisander** *v.* *(Sl)*. To cheat, to swindle, to flimflam, to gouge, to trick, to victimize, to make a sucker out of. (Syn. : *pigeonner, dindonner*).

**faisan(dier)** *sm.* *(Sl)*. Crook, clip artist, flimflammer, fast-buck boy.

**faiseur** *sm.* *(P)*. Swindler, phoney, crook, clip artist, sharpshooter, sharpie.

**faiseur d'embarras** *sm.* *(F)*. Fusstail, fussbudget.

**fait (être)** *(Sl)*. To be arrested, " nabbed ", pinched, caught.

**fait comme un rat (être)** *(Sl)*. To be fooled, " spoofed ", victimized by one.

**fait du prince (le)** *(F)*. Arbitrary.

**faites chauffer la colle !** *(P)*. Joc. fling at one who dropped and broke a glass, a cup or the like.

**falzar** *sm.* *(Sl)*. Trousers, slacks.

**fameux** *adj.* *(F)*. First-rate, excellent, dandy, dingdong. *Pas fameux,* nothing to wire home about.

**fameux lapin (un)** *(P)*. *C'est un fameux lapin,* he's quite a guy, a spunky customer, a hotshot.

**\* famille tuyau de poêle (la)** *(Sl)*. Liaison of two homosexual males.

**fanfaron** *(F)*. Blowhard, bouncer, braggart.

**fantaisie** *sf.* *(F)*. Fancy, craze.

**faquin** *sm.* *(P)*. Disparaging term for an individual. Gazook, gink, cad, skunk, kike, gazabo.

**faramineux** *adj.* Stunning, astounding, big-time.

**faraud** *adj.* *(F)*. Snobbish, vain. *Faire le faraud,* to put on side.

**farfouiller** *v.* *(F)*. To rummage, to search. Ex. : *Les douaniers farfouillaient dans ses bagages,* the custom officials rummaged all through his baggage.

**farfouillette** *(P)*. Rummaging. Used humorously or affectionately especially in reference to : *Galeries-Farfouillette,* a pop. nickname for the department store *Galeries Lafayette* in Paris (where, traditionally, girls, women customers and other confirmed bargain hunters love to rummage among the many attractive articles sold in the various departments and bargain basements).

**fariboler** v. (P). To talk idly, chitter and chatter.

**faribole** sf. (P). Idle talk, " ya-ta-ta ya-ta-ta ".

**faridon** sf. (Sl). Binge, high-jinks. Faire la faridon, to go on a drinking bout, to go on a bust, on a binge.

**farine** sf. (F). De même farine, tarred with the same brush.

**fatiguer les oreilles à q.** (F). Same as : casser les oreilles à q.

**fatras** sm. (P). Jumbled mixture, mess.

**fauche** sf. (Sl). Theft, grab, pinch, swipe, " souvenir ".

**fauché** adj. (P). Broke, busted in the pocketbook. Un type fauché, a penniless person, a " broker ".

**faucher** v. (Sl). To steal, to pinch, to swipe, to walk off with, to " salvage ", to " win ", to " liberate ".

**faucheur** sm. (Sl). Thief.

**fausser compagnie à q.** (F). To give one the slip, to disappear.

**faute de grives on mange des merles** (F). Half a loaf is better than no bread at all.

**faut pas s'en faire !** (P). Loosely constructed pop. catch phrase : Take it easy ! Don't worry !

**faute d'un point Martin perdit son âne** (F). A familiar saying : A miss is as good as a mile.

**faux-col** sm. (P). Froth on a glass of beer.

**faux-col à manger de la tarte** (P). Joc. for an old-fashioned stand-up collar.

FAUX-COL A MANGER
DE LA TARTE.

**faux comme un jeton** (P). Sly dog, false and untrustworthy through and through.

**fayot** sm. (P). Bean.

**fée blanche (la)** (Sl). Cocaine, " coke ", " cee " ; morphine.

**fée brune (la)** (Sl). Opium, " pop ", " poppy ".

FAUX-COL SUR UNE CHOPE.

**fée Carabosse** *sf. (P).* Old, ugly hag ; derisive term for any old and ugly woman. Name of an evil fairy.

**feignant** *sm. (P).* Lazybones.

**feignasse** *sm. (Sl).* Lazy bum.

**feignasser** *v. (Sl).* To laze, to spend one's time lazily, to do nothing, to idle away one's time.

**feignasson** *sm. (Sl).* Another slang variant of *feignant (fainéant).*

**feinter** *v. (Sl).* To hornswoggle, to fool one, to take one in. Ex. : *Ces deux gamins m'ont joliment feinté,* these two little buggers took me in all right !

**fêlé** *adj. (Sl).* Crazy, cracked, loony, crackpot.

**femelle** *sf. (Sl).* Derogatory for : woman, moll, " broad ".

**femme à passions** *sf. (Sl).* Sexual pervert.

**femme en carte** *sf. (Sl).* Registered prostitute.

**femmelette** *sf. (F).* Effeminate man, " panty waist ", " tender foot ".

**fendre (se)** *v. (P).* To be generous, to spend money contrary to one's habit. Ex. : *Il s'est fendu de 100 francs,* he came down with 100 francs.

**fendre la pipe (se)** *(Sl).* To laugh heartily.

**ferme ça (ferme ta gueule) !** *(Sl).* Shut up ! button up your face ! button your lip !

**ferme-la !** *(Sl).* Same as : *ferme ça !*

**fermer boutique** *(P).* To fold (up), to wind up business, to liquidate.

**fermer les châssis** *(Sl).* To sleep, to " caulk off ".

**fermer les yeux (sur)** *(F).* To wink at.

**ferme ton bec !** *(Sl).* Shut up ! button up your lip !

**ferraille** *sf. (P).* Small coins, " chicken feed ".

**ferré** *adj. (P).* Learned, capable, able.

**feu de paille** *sm. (F).* A flash in the pan.

**feuille de chou** *sf. (P).* Small (provincial) newspaper.

**feuille de vigne** *sf. (P).* Figleaf, G-string.

**feuilles** *sf. pl. (Sl).* Ears, " flappers ", " taps ". *Dur de la feuille, constipé des feuilles,* to be hard of hearing.

**feuilles de chou** *sf. pl. (P).* Big ears, " taps ", " sails ".

**ficelé** *adj. (P).* Badly dressed.

**ficelle** *sf. (F).* Trickster, slicker. *Une vieille ficelle,* an old trickster. *(Sl).* Stripe, gold braid, bar worn on the sleeves, " hershey bar " (military slang). *adj. (F).* Tricky, slick.

**fichaise** *sf. (P).* Anything worthless, " poppycock ", " fudge ", shucks, " peanuts ", stuff and nonsense.

**fiche de consolation** *sf. (F).* Booby prize.

**ficher** *v. (F).* To do. To put. To give. To throw, to pitch, to chuck.

**ficher dedans** *(Sl).* To imprison s.o., to put s.o. in jug, to " slop in ", to " run in ".

**ficher dedans (se)** *(Sl).* To make a mistake, to make a bad break, to goof.

**ficher en l'air** *(P).* To throw away, to chuck up. *(Sl).* To murder, to kill, to " bump off ".

**ficher la frousse** *(Sl)*. To frighten.

**ficher la gueule par terre (se)** *(Sl)*. To fall, to take a flop, to take a spill.

**ficher la paix** *(Sl)*. To leave one alone. *Fiche-moi la paix !* Leave me alone !

**ficher la trouille** *(Sl)*. More vulgar for : *ficher la frousse.*

**ficher le camp** *(Sl)*. To leave hurriedly, to absquatulate, to scram. *Fiche le camp !* Scram !

**ficher son billet** *(Sl)*. Pop. excl. for reinforcing a statement : *Je ne céderai jamais, je vous en fiche mon billet !* I'll never give in, you can take it from me !

**ficher sur la gueule (se)** *(Sl)*. To fight, to have a fight, a " rookus ", to beat up one another.

**fichtre !** *interj.* *(P)*. Heck ! dash it all !

**fichu** *adj. (F)*. Done for, cooked, gone to hell, kaput, worthless. *Il est fichu,* his goose is cooked.

**fichu comme l'as de pique** *(F)*. Said of a sloppily dressed individual, tacky.

**fichu quart d'heure** *(F)*. Heck of a time.

**fière chandelle** *(F)*. See : *devoir une fière chandelle à q.*

**fifrelin** *sm. (F)*. See : *ne pas avoir un fifrelin.*

**figaro** *sm. (P)*. Hair-dresser, barber.

**fignoler** *v. (F)*. To do with meticulous care.

**figure d'enterrement** *(F)*. Gloomy face, a pessimist's doleful face, " sourpuss ", woe-begone look.

**figure de papier mâché (avoir une)** *(F)*. To have a very pale face.

**fil** *sm. (F)*. See : *au bout du fil.*

**fil à la patte** *(P)*. To be married, " hitched ".

**fil en aiguille (de)** *(F)*. From one subject to another, step by step, gradually.

**filer** *v. (P)*. To scram, to leg it. *Filez !* Cheese it !
*(Sl)*. To give, to pass.

**filer à l'anglaise** *(F)*. To take French leave, to depart unceremoniously.

**filer comme un zèbre** *(P)*. To go lickety-split, to run like mad, to hightail it.

**filer doux** *(F)*. To become docile, submissive, to pull in one's horns.

**filer le coup de pouce** *(Sl)*. Said of a shopkeeper trying to correct short weight in tipping the scale with a finger.

**filer le parfait amour** *(F)*. To be a sentimental lover. Bill and coo (said only jocularly).

**filer q.** *v. (F)*. To shadow s.o.

**filer une beigne** *(Sl)*. A variant of *filer une raclée.*

**filer une danse** *(Sl)*. Another variant of *filer une raclée.*

**filer une purge** *(Sl)*. Still another variant of *filer une raclée.*

**filer une raclée** *(Sl)*. To beat up, to shellac, to lick, to lambaste, to dust off, to give a " dose of strap oil ".

**filer une tisane** *(Sl)*. A frequent variant of *filer une raclée.*

**filer une tourlouzine** *(Sl)*. A variation of *filer une raclée.*

**filer une triquée** *(Sl)*. Same as : preceding entries.

**filer un mauvais coton** *(P)*. To be badly off (health).

**fille** *sf. (F)*. Prostitute, " hooker ", " hustler ".

**fillette** *sf. (F)*. Half-bottle (wine).

**filon** *sm. (F)*. Bonanza, fat job, cushy job, " gravy train ", any easy job with good pay.

**filou** *sm. (F)*. Swindler, gyp(ster), skinner, chiseler, yentzer, bunco artist, deadheat, finagler, flim-flammer.

**filouter** *v. (F)*. To finagle, to " hornswoggle ", to " flim-flam ".

**filouterie** *sf. (F)*. Swindle, cheat, fakement, spoof, con game, racket.

**fils à papa** *(F)*. Boy with a wealthy father.

**fils de pute !** *(Sl)*. Son of a bitch ! Son of a " bee " !

**fin des haricots (la)** *(P)*. This is the very end, the last of it.

**fine gueule** *sf. (Sl)*. Gourmet.

**fine mouche** *sf. (F)*. Cunning person, " shrewdie ", " smart apple ".

**fini** *adj. (F)*. *Un homme fini*, a goner ; *un coquin fini*, an arrant rogue.

**finir en eau de boudin** *(Sl)*. To fail, to end in smoke. (See also : *finir en queue de poisson*).

**finir en queue de poisson** *(F)*. To fail (generally after a promising start), to fizzle out, to tail off, to come to nothing.

**fin matois** *sm. (F)*. Sly fellow, sly dog, old file.

**finocher** *v. (F)*. An incorrect variant of *fignoler*.

**fiole** *sf. (Sl)*. Head, face, " mug ".

**fiston** *sm. (F)*. Son, sonny, sonny-boy.

**fistot** *sm. (Sl)*. Freshman at the Naval Academy in Lanvéoc-Poulmic (school slang).

**flafla** *sm. (F)*. Show-off, splurge, ostentation. Ex. : *Faire du fla-fla*, to cut a splurge.

**flambard (faire le)** *(Sl)*. To be conceited, to play the smartalec.

**flambé** *adj. (Sl)*. " Sunk ", ruined, done for. Same as : *foutu*.

**flancher** *v. (P)*. To lose courage, to weaken, to back down.

**flandrin** *sm. (F)*. *Un grand flandrin*, a great lanky fellow.

**flânocher** *v. (P)*. To loiter, to bum around, to mooch around, to monkey around.

**flanquer** *v. (P)*. To throw, to sling, to give, to pass. (Same as : *filer*).

LE VOILA FLANQUÉ
A LA PORTE.

**flanquer dedans** v. (P). To imprison s.o., to put s.o. in quod, to " run in ".

**flanquer q. à la porte** (P). To kick one out neck and crop, to hand one the can, to fire one, to give the boot.

**flanquer une pile à q.** (P). To give one a thorough hiding, beating, shellacking.

**flapi** adj. (Sl). Exhausted. bushed, dead-tired, done to a frazzle, run ragged, tuckered out.

**flaupée** sf. (P). Great quantity of, scads of, rafts of, oodles of.

**flèche de tout bois** (F). See : faire flèche de tout bois.

**flemmard** sm. (P). Lazy individual, an " afternoon farmer ", weary Willie.

**flemmarder** v. (P). To laze.

**flemme** sf. (P). Laziness (see also : tirer sa flemme).

**fleur (être)** (Sl). To be broke, stony-broke, on the hog, " clean wiped out ".

**fleur de nave** sf. (Sl). Silly individual, dumbbell, chump.

**fleur des pois (la)** (F). The very best, tops, the cream of, the " whipped-cream " of, the pick of the bunch.

**flic** sm. (Sl). Policeman, cop (in uniform), bull, man in blue, blue boy.

**flingot** sm. (Sl). Gun, shotgun, rifle, rod.

**fliquaille** sf. (Sl). Derogatory term for police, cops.

**flop(p)ée** sf. (P). Great quantity of, oodles of. Thrashing, lambasting, hiding. Ex. : Recevoir une floppée, to get shellacked, to get a panning.

**flotte** sf. (Sl). Water, rain.

**flotter** v. (Sl). To rain.

**flûte !** interj. (P). Darnation ! Dash it all !

**flûtes** sf. pl. (P). Long and skinny legs, " toothpicks ".

**foies (avoir les)** (Sl). (To be) white livered, in a funk.

**foin** sm. (Sl). Noise, din. Ex. : Faire du foin, to raise a stink.

**foin dans ses bottes (avoir du)** (F). Same as : pain sur la planche (avoir du).

**foin de** (F). Phooey on. Ex. : Foin des pique-niques ! Phooey on picnics !

**foire** sf. (Sl). Binge, bust, orgy, whoopee. Faire la foire, to paint the town red, to go on a bust, to go on a binge, to raise hell.

**foire (faire la)** (Sl). See : foire.

**foire aux croûtes** (P). Exhibition of cheap and bad paintings (turned out in quantities by daubers), cheap outdoor art show.

**foire d'empoigne** (P). See : acheter à la foire d'empoigne.

**\* foirer** v. (Sl). To have diarrhoea, to be terribly scared, frightened.

**foireux** adj. (Sl). Coward, funky, " yellowbelly ", " doormat ".

**folichon** adj. (F). Frolicky, frolicsome, merry (generally in the negative form : pas folichon, not merry, rather sad).

**foncer** v. (P). To dash, to proceed full steam ahead.

**foncer dans le brouillard** (Sl). To decamp, to scram.

**forçats de la route** *(P)*. Facetious epithet for racers in the traditional *Tour de France* bicycle race.

**forcer la main à q.** *(F)*. To force one into s. th.

**forcir** *v. (F)*. To get stronger, to put on flesh.

**formidable** *adj. (F)*. Something to write home about, remarkable, swell. (Often used in popular French, not only to express something tremendous, astonishing or startling, but as a simple exclamation of surprise in face of something excellent, or for emphasis : *Formidable !* What a beaut !).

**fort de café** *(Sl)*. See : *c'est un peu fort de café, c'est un peu raide*.

**fort des Halles** *sm*. Central market's burly meat carrier in Paris.

FORT DES HALLES.

**fort en gueule** *sm. (Sl)*. Swashbuckler.

**fort-en-thème** *sm. (P)*. Diligent student (but lacking originality).

**fort en X** *sm. (P)*. Student at the *Ecole Polytechnique*.

**fortiche** *adj. (Sl)*. Strong, hefty ; capable.

**fortifs** *sm. pl. (Sl)*. Short for : fortifications (especially the old defense works around Paris).

**fortune du pot (à la)** *(F)*. Pot luck.

**fouchtra !** *interj. (F)*. Dammit ! gee ! holy heck !

**fouetter** *v. (Sl)*. To stink, to smell strongly. *Ça fouette*, it stinks horribly.

**fouiller (se)** *v. (P)*. *Tu peux te fouiller !* You can whistle for it, boy ! (=you may try hard to get it, nothing doing !).

**fouiner** *v. (F)*. Same as : *fourrer son nez*.

**fouler (se)** *(P)*. *Ne pas se fouler*, not to be overzealous at work, to take it easy.

**foultitude** *sf. (P)*. Large amount of, great quantity of, scads, rafts of.

**four** *sm. (F)*. Failure, unsuccessful show, frost, " floppo ", " floppola ", fold-up. (See : *faire four*).

**fourbi** *sm. (F)*. Gadget, contraption, whatchamacallit. *Tout le fourbi*, the whole caboodle, the whole kit and caboodle, the whole shooting match.

**fourbu (être)** *(F)*. Same as : *flapi*.

**fourchette** *sf. (Sl)*. Pickpocket, " diver ", " whiz ", " gun ".

**fourchette du père Adam** *(F)*. Fingers.

**fourmis dans les jambes (avoir des)** (F). Prickling or tingling feeling in one's legs.

**fourneau** sm. (Sl). Stupid person, blockhead, chump, dumbbell, dumb cluck.

**fourrer au bloc** (P). To put in jail, to "run in", to clap one in quod.

**fourrer dans un guêpier (se)** (F). To fall into a hornets' nest.

**fourrer dedans** (Sl). To put s.o. in prison, to put in soak. To deceive, to cheat, to gyp.

**fourrer le doigt dans l'œil (se)** (F). To make a mistake, to be wrong, to be mistaken.

**fourrer son nez** (F). To poke one's nose into.

**fous le camp !** Scram ! Scram out of here !

**\* foutaise** sf. (P). Nonsense, baloney, applesauce, bushwah, "fudge". Also an exclamation signifying nonsense : hogwash !

**\* foutoir** sm. (Sl). House (or room) in disorder, messy (bed-)room.

**\* foutre !** interj. (Sl). Same meaning as : *fichtre !* (but much stronger and lower).

**foutre** v. (Sl). To do. Ex. : *Qu'est-ce qu'elle fout là ?* What is she doing there ? To give, to put, to throw, to chuck.

**\* foutre dedans** (Sl). To put s.o. in prison, in clink.

**foutre la paix à q.** (Sl). Same as : *ficher la paix à q.*

**foutre le camp** (Sl). To leave hurriedly, to scram, to take it on the lam.

**\* foutre sur la gueule à q.** (Sl). To hit one hard, to beat up, to "put the slug" on one.

**foutriquet** sm. (Sl). Chump, punk.

**foutu** adj. (Sl). Lost, ruined, done for. *C'est foutu !* It's done for, gone to hell, it's cooked, kaput ! *Il est foutu,* he's a dead pigeon, a gone coon.

**\* foutu comme l'as de pique** (Sl). Botched, bungled, "mussed up". Poor figure, poorly or sloppily dressed, thrown together.

**fracasseur** sm. (Sl). Burglar, "cracksman", "yegg".

**frais (être)** (P). To be in a holy mess, in a nice fix. *Nous sommes frais ! Nous voilà frais !* Here we are in a nice mess !

**frais comme l'œil** (P). Fresh as a daisy.

**frais comme une rose** (F). Fresh as a daisy.

**frais de la princesse (aux)** (P). On the house, at the expense of a firm, a company, or the Government, etc. (Money spent and charged to the firm, the company or the Government, etc.).

**fraise** sf. (Sl). Face, "dish", "mug", "pan".

**frangin** sm. (Sl). Brother.

**frangine** sf. (Sl). Sister.

**franquette** sf. (F). See : *à la bonne franquette.*

**frapper à tours de bras** (P). To hit with one's full strength.

**freluquet** sm. (F). Prig, "puppy", silly, conceited young man.

**frère** sm. (Sl). Pal, comrade, "pard".

**frère trois points** *(P)*. Free-mason.

**fric** *sm. (Sl)*. Money, dough, dust, cabbage(s), moolah.

**fricassée** *sf. (Sl)*. Beating, licking, lambasting, shellacking.

**fricassée de museaux** *sf. (Sl)*. Kissing, embraces.

**fric-frac** *sm. (Sl)*. Burglar, "cracks-man". Burglary, "(crib-)crack", "pete-job".

FRIC-FRAC RÉUSSI.

**frichti** *sm. (P)*. Food, "chow".

**fricot** *sm. (F)*. Food, mulligan.

**fricotage** *sm. (P)*. Wangling, wire pulling, juice (in politics).

**fricoter** *v. (P)*. To wangle.

**fricoter des comptes** *(P)*. To doctor, to cook accounts.

**fricoteur** *sm. (P)*. Wangler, wire-puller (in politics).

**frictionnée** *sf. (Sl)*. Beating, shellacking, "dose of strap oil".

**Fridolin** *sm. (Sl)*. Nickname for a German soldier or civilian during the occupation (1940-1944), Kraut, Jerry. (See also : *Fritz*).

**frigo** *sm. (P)*. Frozen meat.

**frigo (être)** *(Sl)*. To be cold.

**frime** *sf. (P)*. Make-believe, sham, feigning, pretense. *C'est pour la frime,* that's all buncombe, all bunk, all sham.

**fringale (avoir la)** *(F)*. Fit of hunger.

**fringue** *sf. (Sl)*. Dress, clothes.

**fringuer** *v. (Sl)*. To dress. *Bien fringué,* well dressed.

**fripouillard** *sm. (Sl)*. Same as : *fripouille.*

**fripouille** *sf. (F)*. Bad lot, cad, scalawag, heeler.

**frisquet** *adj. (P)*. Fresh, cool.

**frit (être)** *(Sl)*. To be lost, ruined, done for. (Same as : *flambé, fichu, foutu, grillé (être)*).

**frites** *sf. pl. (P)*. Popular for : *pommes frites,* French fries. (See also : *en rester comme deux ronds de frites*).

**friture** *sf. (P)*. Frying, crackling sound on the telephone, strays, static, mush.

**Fritz** *sm. (Sl)*. Nickname for a German, Kraut, Jerry. (See also : *Fridolin*).

FRITZ.

**froc** *sm. (Sl)*. Trousers, pants.

**froid de canard** *(F)*. Very cold (weather), cold enough to freeze the tail off a brass monkey.

**froid de loup** *(F)*. Same as : *froid de canard*.

**froides mains, chaudes amours** *(F)*. Cold hands, warm heart.

**fromage** *sm. (P)*. Easy job, easy source of revenue, "lining one's pockets". In politics : juice, plums, "pie".

**fromegi** *sm. (Sl)*. Cheese.

**frometon** *sm. (Sl)*. Same as : *fromegi*.

**frotte** *sf. (Sl)*. Itch, scabies, scotch fiddle.

**frottée** *sf. (Sl)*. Beating, licking, strapping.

**frotter l'échine à q.** *(Sl)*. To beat up, to give it to, to settle one's hash.

**frottin** *sm. (Sl)*. Game of billiards.

**froussard** *sm. (F)*. Coward, chicken-heart, "jitterbug".

**frousse** *sf. (F)*. Intense fear, blue fear, the "wimmies", jitters. *Ça me fiche la frousse*, it gives me the wimmies.

**frousse (avoir la)** *(F)*. To be frightened.

**fruits de mer** *sm. pl. (F)*. Seafood.

**fruit sec** *(F)*. Unsuccessful student, a failure, wash-out.

**frusques** *sf. pl. (F)*. Clothes, duds.

**fuir q. comme la peste** *(F)*. To give one a wide berth.

**fumer** *v. (P)*. To fulminate, to be very angry, mad, to make the fur fly.

**fumer comme une locomotive** *(F)*. To be a heavy smoker, to smoke like a chimney.

**fumerie** *sf. (F)*. Dope den, hop joint, pop-joint.

**fumeron** *sm. (P)*. Chain smoker.

**\* fumier** *sm. (Sl)*. Dunghill (very strong and vulgar term of abuse).

**fumiste** *sm. (F)*. Humbug, windbag. Ex. : *C'est un fumiste*, he's a fraud, an individual who is not what he pretends to be.

**fumisterie** *sf. (F)*. Hoax, "spoof", hornswoggle, "phonus bolonus".

**furibard** *adj. (Sl)*. Furious, mad.

FURIBARD.

**fusil** *sm. (Sl)*. Throat, stomach.

**fusiller** *v. (Sl)*. To spend freely, foolishly (particularly a big amount), to shoot the bucks, to "shoot the works". To spoil, to mess up, to "louse up", to "jazz up".

# G

**gabelou** *sm. (P).* Nickname for a custom-house officer, or a custom-house employee.

**gadoue** *sf. (P).* Slush, dirt.
*(Sl).* Term of contempt for a prostitute, low class streetwalker.

VIEUX GAGA.

**gadzart** *sm. (P).* Student at the technical school *Ecole des Arts et Métiers.*

**gaffe** *sf. (F).* Blunder.

**gaffer** *v. (F).* To make a mistake, a blunder, to goof off, to "boob" it, to put one's foot in it.
*(Sl).* To look, to observe.

**gaffeur** *sm. (F).* Blunderer.

**gaga** *sm. adj. (P).* Old dodo, old dotard.

**gagner le large** *(F).* To clear out, to pull up one's anchor, to scram.

**gagner sa matérielle** *(Sl).* To make a living, to earn a livelihood.

**gai (être)** *(Sl).* To be slightly drunk. (Syn. : *attendri*).

**gai comme un pinson** *(F).* Gay as a cricket, gay as a lark.

**gai luron** *(F).* Good-time Charley.

**galéjade** *sf. (F).* Tall story, tall talk, whopper, "strapper".

**galéjer** *v. (F)*. To tell tall stories, to exaggerate, to pitch it strong.

**galéjeur** *sm. (F)*. Tall story teller.

**galerie** *sf. (P)*. Grandstand play, grandstanding. Ex. : *Parler pour la galerie, amuser la galerie, étonner la galerie,* to grandstand.

**Galeries - Farfouillette** *(P)*. Nickname for the *Galeries Lafayette* (department store) in Paris. (See : *farfouillette*).

**galetouse** *sf. (Sl)*. Money, "gravy", "moolah", "wampum".

**galettard** *adj. (Sl)*. Same as : *galetteux*.

**galette** *sf. (Sl)*. Money, "dough", "jack", "moolah", "kale seed", "mazuma", "shekels", "dust", "tin", "cabbages". (Other French words for money : *fric, blé, pèze, braise, grisbi, beurre, pognon, oseille, des sous, des pesètes, des kopeks,* etc.). *Grosse galette,* heavy dough, heavy sugar, "pie", "big bankroll".

**galetteux** *adj. (Sl)*. Rich, wealthy, flush of money, full of beans, doughy, "well-heeled".

**galon** *sm. (F)*. *Gagner ses galons,* to earn promotion or distinction. *Rendre ses galons,* to resign one's rank.

**galonnard** *sm. (Sl)*. Pej. term for an army officer.

**galoper** *v. (Sl)*. To annoy, to weary, to plague. (Syn. : *courir*).

**galopin** *sm. (F)*. Little brat, whippersnapper, snippet.

**galure** *sm. (Sl)*. Hat, "skimmer", "lid".

**galurin** *sm. (Sl)*. Same as : *galure*.

**galvauder** *v. (Sl)*. To laze.

**gamin** *sm. (F)*. Boy, little boy.

**gamine** *sf. (F)*. Girl(ie).

**ganache** *sf. (Sl)*. *Vieille ganache,* old chowderhead, thickhead.

**garce** *sf. (Sl)*. Spiteful term for a woman. Drab, bitch, wench, beast.

**garder à carreau (se)** *(P)*. To stand on one's guard, to take every precaution.

**garder un chien de sa chienne à q.** *(P)*. To have a rod in pickle for one.

**garder une dent à q.** *(P)*. To owe a grudge.

**gare ! (à la)** *(Sl)*. Scram !

**garer** *v. (P)*. To salt away, to put in lavander, to stash away (for future use).

**gargariser (se)** *(P)*. To delight, to take delight in.

**gargote** *sf. (F)*. Cheap eating joint, eatery, beanery, hashjoint.

**gargotier** *sm. (P)*. Keeper of a law class restaurant, Ptomaine, Tommy.

**gargoulette** *sf. (Sl)*. Mouth, "grub", "trap" ; throat, "gargler".

**garno** *sm. (Sl)*. Furnished room.

**gars** *sm. (P)*. Boy, bud.

**gars "bien" (un)** *(P)*. Nice guy.

**gars de la marine (les)** *(P)*. Sailors, "gobs", "tars".

**gasconner** *v. (F)*. To boast, to draw the long bow. (The Gascon is famous for his bragging just as the Ozark story-teller in U.S. is noted for his "tall stories").

**gâte-sauce** *sm. (F)*. Cook's boy assistant, bad cook.

**gâteux** *sm. (F)*. Same as : *gaga*.

**Gaudissart** *(F)*. Nickname for a bragging commercial traveler. (The title character of Balzac's novel : *L'Illustre Gaudissart*).

**gaudriole** *sf. (P)*. Broad joking, spicy stories.

**gauler** *v. (Sl)*. To arrest, to capture, to "nab".

**gavroche** *sm. (F)*. Paris street child.

**gazer** *v. (P)*. *Ça gaze*, it works all right, everything is working smoothly.

**gazouiller** *v. (Sl)*. To work all right, smoothly. Ex. : *Ça gazouille*, it's O.K., it's going all right, it is working smoothly. To stink, to smell strongly.

**G.D.B. (avoir la)** *(Sl)*. Same as : *gueule de bois (avoir la)*.

**geler à pierre fendre** *(F)*. It is so cold you could spit ice cubes.

**gêné aux entournures (être)** *(P)*. To feel ill at ease, to be hampered (in one's work, plans, projects, etc.).

**genou** *sm. (P)*. Bald head.

**gens " bien " (des)** *(F)*. Nice people.

**(gens) de même farine** *(Sl)*. Tarred with the same brush, of the same stripe.

**gens du voyage (les)** *sm. pl. (P)*. Carnival people, " carnies ".

**gentil tout plein** *adj. (F)*. Very nice, cute.

**gerce** *sf. (Sl)*. Prostitute, whore, law class woman.

**gibier de potence** *sm. (F)*. Ruffian, gallows bird.

**gibus** *sm. (F)*. Top hat, collapsible silk hat, Opera hat. (From the name of the inventor of the crush hat).

**gigolette** *sf. (Sl)*. Girl of easy morals.

**gigolo** *sm. (Sl)*. Fancy man.

GIGOLO.

**gigoter** *v. (P)*. To kick (about), to fidget.

**gigots** *sm. pl. (Sl)*. Legs, "sticks".

**giroflée à cinq feuilles** *(P)*. Slap in the face.

GIROFLÉE A CINQ FEUILLES.

**girouette** *sf.* *(F)*. Turncoat, "weathercock".

**giton** *sm.* *(Sl)*. Catamite, "angelina".

**glaiseux** *sm.* *(Sl)*. Peasant, "rube", "hick", "hayseed".

**glass(e)** *sm.* *(Sl)*. Glass.

**glaviot** *sm.* *(Sl)*. Spittle.

**glavioter** *v.* *(Sl)*. To spit.

**glisser en douce** *(P)*. To tell confidentially.

**glissez, mortels, n'appuyez pas !** *(F)*. Fling at one who is trying to dwell on an unpleasant subject.

**gnaf** *sm.* *(Sl)*. Shoe repairer, cobbler.

**gnangnan** *sm. adj.* *(P)*. Milksop, mollycoddle, "zombie".

**gniaf** *sm.* *(Sl)*. Same as : *gnaf*.

**gniole** *sf.* *(Sl)*. Hard liquor, "panther sweat", booze.

**gnognotte** *sf.* *(P)*. Trifle, thing regarded as trivial, insignificant, paltry, etc., peanut(s), hogwash, doesn't amount to a row of pins, a "small order".

**gnon** *sm.* *(P)*. Blow, hit, "biff", "sock".

**gnouf** *sm.* *(Sl)*. Jail, booby(hatch), "college".

**gobe-mouches** *sm.* *(F)*. Gullible person, individual who'll swallow anything, gull, simpleton. Idler.

**gober** *v.* *(P)*. To swallow, to believe. Ex. : *il gobe tout ce qu'on lui dit.*

**gober (se)** *v.* *(P)*. To be chesty, conceited, to set full value on oneself, to think a lot of oneself, to get a swelled head.

**goberger (se)** *(P)*. To feast, to enjoy oneself, to live well.

**gobeur** *sm.* *(P)*. Sucker, "saperoo" (that'll "swallow" anything).

**godaille** *sf.* *(Sl)*. Feast, eatfest.

**godailler** *v.* *(Sl)*. To feast, to eat and drink lavishly.

**godasse** *sf.* *(Sl)*. Shoe. *Grosses godasses,* "clodhoppers", "violin case".

GODASSES.

**godelureau** *sm.* *(P)*. Fop, affected young man, "cookie-pusher", "jelly bean", "drugstore cowboy".

**godichard** *adj.* *(Sl)*. Silly, stupid, dimwit, "dopey", "simp", a "noodle".

**godiche** *adj.* *(P)*. Same as : *godichard*.

**godillots** *sm. pl.* *(Sl)*. Shoes, military shoes.

**gogo** *sm.* *(F)*. An easily fooled or misled person, sucker, "easy mark".

**\* goguenots** *sm. pl. (Sl).* Toilet, W.C., " Johnny ", " can ".

**goguette (être en)** *(P).* To be on a spree, on a binge, on the merry-go-round.

**goinfrer** *v. (P).* To eat greedily (and too much).

**gommeux** *sm. (P).* Snob, pretentious individual, fop, dandy.

**gonce** *sm. (Sl).* Another spelling for *gonze*.

**gondolant** *adj. (P).* Very amusing, too funny for words, side-splitting.

**gondoler (se)** *v. (P).* To laugh oneself silly, to laugh one's head off.

**gonflé à bloc** *adj. (Sl).* Full of pep and enthusiasm, full of beans.

**gonze** *sm. (Sl).* Individual, guy.

**gonzesse** *sf. (Sl).* Derogatory term for a woman, a girl, " broad ", biddy, floozey.

**gosier blindé (avoir le)** *(Sl).* To be able to drink the strongest liquors without inconvenience.

**gosier sec (avoir le)** *(F).* To be thirsty, to thirst for a drink.

**gosse** *sm. sf. (P).* Child, little boy or girl(ie).

**goualante** *sf. (Sl).* Popular hit-song.

**gouale** *sf. (Sl).* Swindle, racket.

**goualer** *v. (Sl).* To sing (a song), to confess, to " sing ", to come clean (at a police examination).

**gouape** *sf. (Sl).* Ruffian, hooligan, scissor(s)bill.

**goufre** *sm. (F).* Spendthrift. Long drawn-out and costly litigation, legal suit etc., bad business that continually eats up money.

**gougnotte** *sf. (Sl).* Lesbian, " dyke ".

**goujat** *sm. (P).* Skunk, cad.

**goulot** *sm. (Sl).* Throat, " gully ".

**goupiller** *v. (P).* To do, to maneuver, to handle.

**gourance** *sf. (Sl).* Mistake, bull, blunder, goofing.

**gourbi** *sm. (P).* House, cabin, case, shack, " shebang " funk-hole.

**gourde** *sf. (P).* Stupid person, silly person, dumbbell, chump, dope. *(Sl).* Head, " nut ", " pate ".

**gourdichon** *sm. (Sl).* Same as : *gourde*.

**gourer (se)** *v. (Sl).* To make a mistake. Ex. : *Tu t'es gouré jusqu'au trognon,* you made a bad mistake, you've goofed.

**gourgandine** *sf. (P).* Prostitute, street walker, " hooker ".

**gousse** *sf. (Sl).* Lesbian, " dyke ".

**gousset bien garni (avoir le)** *(P).* To be well-heeled.

**goût de revenez-y (avoir un)** *(P).* To taste like more.

**goutte** *sf. (F).* Small cup of liquor, a bit of the bottle, pick-me-up, bracer, " shot in the arm ".

**goutte dans la mer (une)** *(F).* A drop in the bucket.

**gouvernement** *sm. (P).* Humorous for one's wife. *Mon gouvernement,* my wife.

**grabuge** *sm. (P).* Quarrel, scramble, set-to, row, fracas. Ex. : *Il y aura du grabuge,* there will be a session, a bit of a scramble.

**grain (avoir son)** *(Sl).* To be slightly drunk, to be " lit " (a bit), to be " tuned up ".

**grain (avoir un)** *(P).* To be half crazy, not quite normal.

**graisser la patte à q.** *(P).* To bribe s.o., to offer a bribe, to grease the palm, to oil the palm, to " fix ", to " square ".

**grand carreau (le)** *(Sl).* Assize Court.

**grands couturiers** *sm. pl. (F).* Fashion designers (f.i. *Dior, Jacques Fath, etc.*). Their business, however, is not exclusively " *haute-couture* " ; most of them actually make the major part of their profit from accessories, stockings, perfumes, men's ties, etc., bearing their label.

**grande bringue** *sf. (P).* Same as : *grande perche.*

**grande muette** *sf. (F).* The Army.

**grande perche** *sf. (P).* A tall lanky woman.

**grand escogriffe** *sm. (P).* Disparaging term for a tall lout of a fellow.

**grande tasse (la)** *sf. (Sl).* Ocean, sea, " big drink ", " big ditch ".

**grande taule (la)** *sf. (Sl).* Police Prefecture : (Centrale Police H.Q. in Paris).

**grand format (un)** *sm. (Sl).* A 1.000-franc bill.

**grand manitou** *sm. (F).* Boss, poohbah.

**grand saut (faire le)** *(P).* To die, to " kick the bucket ".

**grand tra la la (en)** *(P).* In full feather, war-paint, dressed to kill.

**grasse matinée (faire la)** *(F).* To laze in bed till late hours in the morning.

**gratin** *sm. (P).* The *élite,* the upper ten thousand, the upper crust, the smart set, the four hundred, the " whipped cream " of society.

**gratouille** *sf. (Sl).* Itch, " scotch fiddle ".

**gratte** *sf. (P).* Small profits, rake-off. *(Sl).* Itch scabies, " scotch fiddle ".

**gratte-papier** *sm. (P).* An obvious nickname for an office worker, " ink slinger ", " scratcher ".

GRATTE-PAPIER.

**gratter (se)** *v. (Sl).* Same as . *fouiller (se), taper (se).*

**gratter du papier** *(P).* To work in an office (in a subordinate job), to " splash ink ".

**Grec (un)** *sm. (P).* Professional swindler at cards, cardsharp(er), " cold-decker ".

**greffier** *sm. (Sl).* Cat.

**grelots (avoir les)** *(Sl).* An occasional slang variant of *avoir les jetons.*

**greluchon** *sm. (P).* Fancy-man.

**grenouille** *sf. (Sl).* Cash box. Prostitute. (See also : *manger la grenouille*).

**grenouillère** *sf. (Sl).* Water-hole.

**grève perlée** *sf. (P).* Slowdown strike.

**grève sur le tas** *(P).* Sit-down strike.

**Gribouille** *(P).* Symbol of a boob(y).

**griffe** *sf. (Sl).* Army.

**griffeton** *sm. (Sl).* Same as : *griveton.*

**grigou** *sm. (P).* Pinchpenny, skin-flint, miser.

**grillé** *adj. (Sl).* Gone chicken. *Etre grillé,* to lose one's credit, reputation, etc. (not to be able to operate any more in a given place, town, etc.) ; *il est grillé,* his little game is up, his goose is cooked.

**griller** *v. (Sl).* To unmask. (See : *grillé*).

**grimpant** *sm. (Sl).* Trousers, pants.

**grincheux** *sm. (F).* Sorehead.

**gringaglet** *sm. (F).* Lean, skinny individual.

**grippe-sou** *sm. (P).* Same as : *grigou.*

**gris (être)** *(P).* To be slightly drunk, to be a bit " lit ", three sheets in the wind.

**grisbi** *sm. (Sl).* Money, " dough ", " moolah ".

GRISBI.

**grisbinette** *sf. (Sl).* A 100-franc coin.

**grise mine** *(F).* See : *faire grise mine à q.*

**grive** *sf. (Sl).* Army.

**griveton** *sm. (Sl).* French army private, buck private, serviceman. In U.S. : Joe, GI.

**groggy** *adj. (P).* Dazed by blows, dizzy, " cutting paper dolls ".

**grolles** *sf. pl. (Sl).* Shoes, " kick-ers ".

**grolles (avoir les)** *(Sl).* A variant of *jetons (avoir les).*

**gros bonnet** *(F).* A person of high position, a big shot, big noise, big wheel, big gun, big bug, VIP.

**gros bon sens (le)** *(P).* Horse sense, plain common sense.

**gros comme deux liards de beurre** *(P).* Quite small, tiny, dimin-utive.

**gros cul (du)** *(Sl).* Sort of ordinary rough-cut tobacco.

**gros Jean comme devant (être)** *(P).* To be no better off than before.

**gros lard** *sm. (Sl).* Same as : *gros tas.*

**gros lolos** *sm. pl. (Sl).* Woman's plump breasts.

**gros malin** *sm. (Pl).* Smart guy, smart aleck.

**gros numéro** *sm. (Sl).* Brothel, cat-house, red-light house.

**gros papa (un)** *sm. (Sl).* A 1.000-franc bill. Also a 5.000-franc bill.

**gros qui tache (du)** *(Sl).* Ordinary red wine, dago red. (Same as : *du gros rouge*).

**gros rouge (du)** *(Sl)*. Ordinary low-grade red wine.

**grosses légumes** *sf. pl. (P)*. Big shots, big wheels.

**gros sur la patate** *(Sl)*. See : *en avoir gros sur la patate*.

**gros tas** *sm. (Sl)*. Fatty, big slob.

**grouiller (se)** *v. (Sl)*. To hurry, to step lively, to make it snappy.

**grouillot** *sm. (Sl)*. Errand boy, pad boy, apprentice.

**grouper** *v. (Sl)*. To arrest, to capture, to " nab ".

**grue** *sf. (P)*. Prostitute, " chippy ", " floozey ".

**guelte** *sf. (F)*. Commission, premium, bonus paid to salesmen in a store, " push money ", " spiff ".

**gueulard** *sm. adj. (Sl)*. Big mouth, noisy, big-mouthed guy, a give-'em-hell sort of guy. Glutton.

✓ **gueule** *sf. (Sl)*. Mouth, " mug ". Face, " clock ", " pan ".

**gueule à caler les roues de corbillard** *(Sl)*. Very ugly face, a face that'll stop a clock.

**gueule à coucher dehors avec un billet de logement** *(Sl)*. A variant of preceding entry.

**gueule de bois** *sf. (Sl)*. A bibulous " hangover ", " hangover " after a debauch, stale mouth after a spree, " the morning after the night before ", the " moaning " after the night before.

**gueule de bois (avoir la)** *(Sl)*. To have a " hangover ", parched mouth after a drinking spree.

**gueule d'empeigne** *sf. (Sl)*. Very ugly face, a face that will stop a clock, " clock stopper ".

**gueule de raie** *sf. (Sl)*. Same as preceding entry.

**gueule en coin de rue** *(Sl)*. A colorful variant of two preceding entries.

**gueuler** *v. (Sl)*. To holler, to protest, to " kick ".

**gueuler comme un putois** *(Sl)*. To shout like madman.

**Gueules cassées (les)** *(P)*. Ex-servicemen whose wounded faces were disfigured (during World War I. 1914-1918).

**gueuleton** *sm. (P)*. A lavish meal, " blow-out ", eatfest, beano.

GUEULETON A DEUX.

**gueuletonner** *v. (P)*. To eat a lavish meal, to feast.

**Gugusse** *(P)*. Petname for Augustus. Gus, circus clown.

**guibolles** *sf. pl. (Sl)*. Legs, " drumsticks ", " shanks ".

**guiche** *sf. (F)*. Kiss-curl.

**guignard** *sm. adj. (P)*. Unlucky (individual).

**guigne** *sf. (P).* Bad luck, tough break.

**guigner** *v. (P).* To watch, to look.

**guignols** *sm. pl. (Sl). Gendarmes.*

**guimauve** *sf. (P).* Goo, insipid.

**guimbarde** *sf. (P).* Old ramshackle vehicle, " rattle-box ".

**guinche** *sm. (Sl).* Dance hall, " drag ".

**guincher** *v. (Sl).* To dance, to " shake a leg ", to " hoof it ".

**guitoune** *sf. (Sl).* House, shack, tepee, wigwam.

**gy** *(Sl).* Yes.

# H

**habiller de quatre planches (s')** *(Sl)*. To die, to "put on a wooden kimono".

**hâbleur** *sm. (F)*. Braggart, "fire-eater".

**hareng** *sm. (Sl)*. Man supported by a prostitute, pimp.

**haridelle** *sf. (P)*. Skinny and decrepit horse.

**harponner** *v. (Sl)*. To arrest, to capture, to put the collar on.

**hausser du col (se)** *(F)*. Same as : *pousser du col (se)*.

**haut comme trois pommes** *(F)*. Fling at a small kid, a snippet, a little mite, knee-high to a grasshopper.

**haut comme une botte** *(F)*. Same as : *haut comme trois pommes*.

**haute** *sf. (P)*. The upper classes, upper crust, the "whipped-cream" of society. Ex. : *Etre de la haute,* to be in the upper ten.

**haute main (avoir la)** *(F)*. To rule the roost.

**haute pègre (la)** *(P)*. The swell mob.

**hauteur (être à la)** *(F)*. To be equal to one's task, equal to the occasion.

**heure du berger (l')** *(F)*. The best, most favorable, hour of meeting for lovers.

**hic** *sm. (P)*. Difficulty, hitch, "bug". Ex. : *Voilà le hic ; c'est le hic.*

**hirondelle** *sf. (Sl)*. See : *vache à roulettes.*

**hirondelle d'hiver** *(P)*. Hot chestnut merchant in the streets in Paris.

**histoire à dormir debout** *(F)*. Incredible story, "bull", yarn, galley-yarn.

**histoire de** *(F)*. Merely for, just for, just to, etc. Ex. : *histoire de* *mentir,* just to tell a lie ; *histoire de respirer un peu,* just to take a bit of fresh air.

**histoire de rire** *(F).* Just for a joke, just to have a laugh.

**histoires de bonnes femmes** *(P).* Old wives tales.

**histoires marseillaises** *(F).* Tall stories, tall tales.

**hold-up** *sm. (P).* Stick-up, hold-up, heist (job).

**homme à passions** *(Sl).* Sexual pervert.

**homme à pogne** *(Sl).* Strong-man, dictator.

**homme de paille** *(F).* Dummy, " front ", a mere figurehead.

**homme fini** *(P).* See : *fini.*

**Honni soit qui mal y pense !** *(F).* Shamed be he who thinks evil of it !

**hôpital qui se moque de la charité (c'est l')** *(F).* The pot calling the kettle black. Satan rebuking sin. The sieve says to the needle : you have a hole in the tail.

**horizontale** *sf. (Sl).* Streetwalker, prostitute.

**hosto** *sm. (Sl).* Hospital.

**hôtel borgne** *sm. (F).* Cheap and disreputable hotel, flop-house.

**hôtel de passe** *sm. (Sl).* Assignation joint.

. **huile de bras** *(P).* Energy at work, physical effort, " elbow grease ".

**huile de coude** *(P).* Same as : *huile de bras.*

**huiles (les)** *(P).* Important persons, big shots, " big guns ", " big potatoes ", " bigwigs ". " Brass hats ", the big brass, top brass, (in the army).

**huître** *sf. (P).* Silly person, dope, chump, dumbbell. (See also : *andouille, cornichon, fourneau, gourde, moule, souche, tourte, ballot*).

**huit-reflets** *(P).* Top hat.

**humecter les amygdales (s')** *(Sl).* To have a drink, to " wet one's whistle ".

**huppé** *adj. (P).* Smart, ritzy, swell, la-de-da, posh, tip-top.

**hure** *sf. (Sl).* Face, " mug ".

**hurleur** *sm. (P).* Super-loud loudspeaker.

**hurluberlu** *sm. (P).* A thoughtless, harum-scarum, cockle-brained, scatter-brained individual.

# I

**il fera chaud !** *interj.* *(P)*. Nonsense ! Baloney ! Never !

**illico (presto)** *(P)*. Right away, at once, " tootey-sweetey ", p. d. q., pretty damn quick, right off the bat.

**il ne manquerait plus que ça !** *(P)*. That would be the limit !

**il n'en reste pas la queue d'un** *(P)*. Not one is left, absolutely nothing is left.

**il ne vaut pas la corde pour le pendre** *(P)*. He is not worth the hangman's rope.

**il n'y a pas âme qui vive** *(F)*. There is not a living soul.

**Il n'y a pas à tortiller** *(P)*. There is no getting away from it, there is no arguing about it.

**il n'y a pas de quoi fouetter un chat** *(P)*. Said of a mere trifle.

**il n'y a pas mèche** *(P)*. No soap ! No sale !

**il n'y a pas un chat** *(F)*. A coll. variant of *il n'y a pas âme qui vive*.

**il pleut comme vache qui pisse** *(Sl)*. A frequently heard but a rather vulgar expression meaning : it's raining cats and dogs (or pitchforks).

**il pleut des hallebarbes** *(P)*. A pop. variant of preceding slang phrase.

**il y a anguille sous roche** *(P)*. A nigger in the woodpile.

**il y a belle lurette** *(P)*. Long (time) ago.

**il y a du travail sur la planche** *(P)*. Popular phrase meaning that there is plenty of work to be done, a lot to do.

**il y a fagot et fagot** *(P)*. Popular saying meaning that there is a great difference between things that are seemingly alike.

**il y a plus d'un âne à la foire qui s'appelle Martin** *(F)*. There are more Johnnies than one at the fair.

**il y aura du sport !** *(P)*. Ironical fling meaning : you are going to see some row, some rookus, somebody will kick up hell !

**ils auront la graisse mais ils n'auront pas la peau !** They may make us suffer but they won't get us !

**imbuvable** *adj. (P)*. Unsociable, hard (if not impossible) to get along with, because of his (her) impossible character. Socially unacceptable.

**impair** *sm. (F)*. Blunder, mistake, error, " boo-boo ". *Faire un impair,* to make a " boo-boo ", a blunder.

**impasse** *sf. (P)*. Dead-end.

**imper** *sm. (Sl)*. Rain-coat.

**incendier** *v. (Sl)*. To abuse s.o. right and left, give s.o. a lick with the rough side of the tongue.

**incroyable, mais vrai** *(F)*. You won't believe it, yet it's true ; believe it or not !

**indécrottable** *adj. (P)*. Hopelessly incorrigible.

**indic** *sm. (Sl)*. Informer, police-spy, stool pigeon. (Same as : *indicateur*).

**indicateur** *sm. (P)*. Police informer, stool pigeon, " rat ", " finger ", " shamus ".

**infirme des méninges** *(Sl)*. Said of a very stupid person : dead from the neck up.

**inter** *sm. (Sl)*. Procurer, " hustler ", " steerer ".

**invitation à la valse** *(P)*. Ironic invitation for a person to do something he dislikes.

**itou** *adv. (P)*. Also, too. Ex. : *Moi itou !* me too ! me the same !

**Ivans (les)** *(P)*. An obvious nickname for Russians, " Russkies ".

# J

**jabot** *sm.* *(Sl)*. Stomach, " gizzard ", " breadbasket ".

**jaboter** *v.* *(P)*. To talk, to patter, to speechify.

**jacasser** *v.* *(P)*. To talk profusely and idly, to yackety-yack, to " gass ".

**jack** *sm.* *(Sl)*. Meter (of a cab), taxi meter.

**Jacques** *sm.* *(Sl)*. Safe, " crib ", " peter ". Burglar's jimmy, " buster ".

**Jacques (faire le)** *(P)*. To try to be funny, to try to pull funny stuff.

**Jacquot** *(Sl)*. Same as : *Jacques*.

**jacquots** *sm. pl.* *(Sl)*. Calves (of the leg).

**jactage** *sm.* *(Sl)*. Talk, gab, " chin music ", patter, yackety-yack.

**jactance** *sf.* *(P)*. Gift of the gab, gabbiness.

**jacter** *v.* *(Sl)*. To talk, to " spiel ", to palaver, to hold a conversation, to chew the fat, to chew the rag, to chin.

**jamais cœur faible n'a conquis une belle** *(F)*. Faint heart never won fair lady.

**jamais de la vie !** *(P)*. Never in all my born days !

**jambonner** *v.* *(Sl)*. To pester, to sicken, to importune, to tire, to plague s.o.

**janot** *sm.* *(P)*. Personification of a saphead, sap, " silly Willie ".

**jardin des refroidis** *sm.* *(Sl)*. Cemetery.

**jars** *sm.* *(Sl)*. Lingo, jive, cant.

**jaspiner** *v.* *(Sl)*. To talk, to palaver, to patter.

**jaunet** *sm.* *(Sl)*. 20-franc gold coin. (Also : *napoléon*).

**j'comprends !** *(P)*. You bet ! Sure !

**jean-foutre** *sm.* *(Sl)*. Imbecile, dumbbell, punk.

— 105 —

**jeannette** *sf. (P).* Small ironing board (especially for ironing delicate parts of linen, sleeves, collars, etc.), sleeve-board.

JEANNETTE.

**je suis comme Thomas, je suis incrédule !** *(P).* I don't believe your story ! I am skeptical until actual proof is demonstrated !

**Jésus** *sm. (Sl).* Fancy-man.

**jeter dedans** *v. (Sl).* To put s.o. in prison, to " run in ".

**jeter de la poudre aux yeux de q.** *(P).* To throw dust in the eyes, to pull wool over one's eyes. (See also : *poudre aux yeux*).

**jeter de l'huile sur le feu** *(F).* To add fuel to the fire, to add oil to the flames.

**jeter la pierre à q.** *(P).* To accuse, to blame one.

**jeter le manche après la cognée** *(F).* To throw the helve after the hatchet. *Il ne faut pas jeter le manche après la cognée*, never say die.

**jeter q. ch. à la figure de q.** *(P).* To reproach violently.

**jeter sa gourme** *(P).* To sow one's wild oats.

**jeter son bonnet par-dessus les moulins** *(P).* Said of a girl who commits herself to a love affair without regard to social conventions, who throws her decency to the winds, who flings aside all restraint. Ex. : *Elle a jeté son bonnet par-dessus les moulins*, she " threw her cap over the windmill ".

**je te vois venir !** *(P).* I guess what you want ! I see your little game !

**jetons (avoir les)** *(Sl).* To be frightened, to have " the shakes ".

**jettard** *sm. (Sl).* Jail, cooler.

**jeune** *adj. (Sl).* See : *trop jeune, un peu jeune*.

**jeunot** *adj. (Sl).* Young, not dry behind the ears, inexperienced, greenhorn.

**j' m'en-fichisme** *sm. (P).* Indifferentism. (See also : *j' m'en-fichiste*).

**j' m'en-fichiste** *sm. (P).* "Don't-care-a-damn " guy, an indifferentist, one who doesn't care a fig, one who is indifferent.

**j' m'en-foutisme** *sm. (Sl).* Same as : *j' m'en-fichisme*.

**j' m'en-foutiste** *sm. (Sl).* Same as : *j' m'en-fichiste*.

**job** *sm. (Sl).* Stupid person, dope, dumbbell.

**jobard** *sm. adj. (P).* A variation of *job* : a stupid person, chump, dumbbell.

**jockey** *sm. (Sl).* " Shill ", procurer in a gambling joint.

**joindre les deux bouts** *(P).* To make (both) ends meet.

**Jojo** *(P)*. Diminutive of *Joseph*.

**jouer au plus fin** *(F)*. To use finesse.

**jouer avec le feu** *(F)*. To court danger.

**jouer cartes sur table** *(F)*. To act loyally, openly and frankly.

**jouer de malheur (ou de malchance)** *(F)*. To have tough luck.

**jouer des compas** *(Sl)*. To flee, to scram, to "beat it".

**jouer des coudes** *(P)*. To elbow one's way through a heavy crowd.

**jouer des flûtes** *(Sl)*. Same as : *jouer des compas*.

**jouer des gambettes** *(Sl)*. Same as : *jouer des compas*.

**jouer des guibolles** *(Sl)*. Same as : *jouer des compas*.

**jouer des pattes** *(Sl)*. Same as : *jouer des compas*.

**jouer des quilles** *(Sl)*. Same as : *jouer des compas*.

**jouer la fille de l'air** *(Sl)*. Same as : *jouer des compas*.

**jouer rip** *(Sl)*. Same as : *jouer des compas*.

**jouer sur le velours** *(P)*. To gamble " on velvet ", without any risk.

**jouer un tour à q.** *(P)*. To play a trick on one.

**jouer un tour de cochon** *(Sl)*. To play a dirty trick on, to play hob with.

**joyeux** *sm. (Sl)*. Soldier of a disciplinary battalion in Africa.

**joyeux drille** *(P)*. Merry guy, jolly fellow, good-time Charlie.

**j' te crois !** You bet ! (for) sure !

**J 3** *sm. sf. (P)*. 15 to 20 year-old adolescent (boy or girl), teen-ager, teener.

LES J 3.

**jugeotte** *sf. (P)*. Brains, judgment.

**Jules** *sm. (Sl)*. Fancy man, souteneur. Nickname of the Germans during the occupation (1940-1944). Chamberpot.

**Julot** *sm. (Sl)*. Diminutive for *Jules*.

**jurer ses grands dieux** *(P)*. To swear by all that is sacred.

**jus** *sm. (Sl)*. Coffee, " mud ", " murk ". Electric current, " juice ".

**jusqu'à la gauche** *(Sl)*. Up to the last, up to the end, to the bitter end.

**jusqu'à plus soif** *(Sl)*. To repletion.

**jusqu'au bout des ongles** *(F)*. To one's finger-tips, through and through, every inch of it.

**jusqu'auboutiste** *(F)*. Bitterender.

**jusqu'au trognon** *(Sl)* To the very heart, into the very core, completely, thoroughly.

**juteux** *sm. (Sl)*. A variation of *adjupète.* (See this word).

# K

**kasbah** *sf. (Sl).* House, shanty, "shebang".

**kif (du)** *(Sl).* Abbr. variant of *kif-kif (bourricot).*

**kif-kif (bourricot)** *(Sl).* Same : similar, identical. Ex. : *C'est kif-kif bourricot,* it's the same ; *c'est du kif,* it's just the same, identical, no difference.

**kiki** *sm. (P).* Throat.

# L

**la barbe !** *interj.* *(Sl)*. Excl. of anger : You make me sick ! That makes me sick ! Botheration !

**labo** *sm. (P)*. Labo(ratory).

**la boucler** *v. (Sl)*. To shut up, to " clam up ".

**l'accrocher (se)** *v. (Sl)*. To go without food. (Also same as : *l'aligner (se)*.

**lâcher** *v. (Sl)*. To drop, to jilt, to throw over ; to throw up. To pay.

**lâcher la rampe (la perle)** *(Sl)*. To die, to give up the ghost, to " kick off ".

**lâcher le paquet** *(Sl)*. To confess, to " spill ", to " squeak ", to " squeal ", to " stool " on, to put the finger on, to " sing ".

**lâcher les dés** *(Sl)*. To give in, to yield, to throw up the sponge.

**lâcher q. d'un cran** *(Sl)*. To let one down, to throw one over.

**lâcher une perle** *(Sl)*. To let a fart.

**lâcheur** *sm. (P)*. Deserter, " flopper ", unreliable person.

**la connaître** *v. (Sl)*. To know the ropes, to know the " score " (Same as : *connaître la musique*).

**la connaître dans les coins** *(Sl)*. To know s. th. in every nook and corner. (Same as : *à la page (être)*.

**la crever** *v. (Sl)*. To be very hungry, to be starving.

**la danser** *v. (P)*. Ex. : *Gare à toi, mon gars, tu la danseras !* Watch out, my boy, you will get it in the neck.

**la faire à l'oseille** *(Sl)*. To gyp, to " hornswoggle ", to make a sucker.

**la faire à q.** *(P)*. To " hornswoggle ", to bamboozle, to fool one.

✓ **la ferme !** *(Sl)*. Shut up ! Dry up !

**laidasse** *sf. (Sl)*. Ugly woman, ugly jane, "lemon".

**laisser aller (se)** *v. (Sl)*. To become disheartened, discouraged.

**laisser choir** *v. (Sl)*. To drop s.o., to jilt.

**laisser courir** *v. (Sl)*. To give up, to drop.

**laisser des plumes** *(P)*. See : *y laisser des plumes*.

**laisser en carafe** *(Sl)*. To leave in the lurch.

**laisser en plan** *(P)*. A variant of *laisser en carafe*.

**laisser en rade** *(P)*. Another variation of *laisser en carafe*.

**laisser mijoter dans son jus** *(P)*. To let one stew in his own juice.

**\* laisser pisser** *(Sl)*. To let them talk away, to let them do as they like, "let George do it !".

**\* laisser pisser le mérinos** *(Sl)*. Not to act rashly, to wait till time is ripe.

**laisser q. le bec dans l'eau** *(P)*. To let one down, to leave one in trouble and needing help.

**laisser q. se débarbouiller** *(Sl)*. To let a person shift for himself, to let someone get out of a fix the best he can.

✓**laisser tomber q.** *(P)*. To let one down, to drop one.

**laisser tondre la laine sur le dos (se)** *(Sl)*. To allow oneself to be "sucked in", cheated, tricked, fleeced.

**laisser une queue** *(Sl)*. To depart without paying bills in full, to leave a debt after departure.

**laïus** *sm. (F)*. Chatter, babble, blah-blah, palaver.

**laïusser** *v. (P)*. To patter, to jabber, to shoot off one's mouth, to shoot off one's bazoo.

**la jambe !** *interj. (Sl)*. You make me sick ! that makes me sick !

**l'aligner (se)** *v. (Sl)*. *Tu peux te l'aligner, vous pouvez vous l'aligner*, you can whistle for it.

**lambin** *sm. adj. (P)*. Slow poke, slow coach.

**lambiner** *v. (P)*. To putter ; to loiter, to dawdle, to toy, to dally.

**lampe** *sf. (Sl)*. Throat, "gin lane", "whistle".

**lampe à souder** *sf. (Sl)*. Machine gun, tommy-gun, "violin".

**lampée** *sf. (P)*. Swill.

**lamper** *v. (P)*. To swig, to swill.

**lampiste** *sm. (P)*. Scapegoat, goat, fall guy, the least responsible member of an organisation who, should trouble arise, takes the blame for the really responsible higher-ups.

**lance** *sf. (Sl)*. Rain, water, urine.

**lance-parfum** *sm. (Sl)*. Machine gun, tommy-gun, "violin".

**lancequine** *sf. (Sl)*. Water, rain.

**lancequiner** *v. (Sl)*. To rain. To urinate, to make water.

**langue au chat** *(F)*. See : *donner sa langue au chat*.

**langue bien pendue (avoir la)** *(F)*. To have the gift of the gab.

**langue de vipère** *(P)*. Viperish tongue.

**langue trop longue (avoir la)** *(P)*. To be unable to hold one's tongue, unable to keep a secret.

**langue verte** *(P)*. Slang, cant.

**lanterner** *v.* *(P)*. To string one along.

**lapalissade** *sf.* *(P)*. Self-evident truth, truism, platitude. (See also : *vérité de La Palice*).

**lapin** *sm.* *(P)*. Date one failed to keep, " stand-up ".

**lapine** *sf.* *(P)*. Ex. : *Une mère lapine*, woman who has many children.

PAS D'ERREUR ! UNE VRAIE LAPINE.

**larbin** *sm.* *(P)*. Disparaging term for a male servant, flunkey.

LE LARBIN RESPECTUEUX.

**lard (se faire du)** *(P)*. To grow fat in a life of ease and indolence.

**lardon** *sm.* *(Sl)*. Child, baby, brat.

**larme (une)** *sf.* *(P)*. Very little, just a drop.

**lascar** *sm.* *(P)*. Guy, " ghee ", fellow, individual.

**la trouver mauvaise** *(P)*. To be very much dissatisfied. Ex. : *Vous la trouverez mauvaise,* you sure won't relish it, you will be dissatisfied.

**lavabo** *sm.* *(P)*. Toilet, W. C., rest-room.

**lavage** *sm.* *(Sl)*. Sale, selling. (See : *laver*).

**lavasse** *sf.* *(P)*. Hogwash.

**laver** *v.* *(Sl)*. To sell something quickly and usually in an underhand way and at any price, in order to turn it into money. (Syn. : *lessiver*).

**laver la tête à q.** *(P)*. To bawl out, to " dress down " a person.

**laver la tête d'un nègre, on perd sa lessive (à)** *(P)*. You can never make a purse out of a sow's ear.

**laver son linge sale en famille (il faut)** *(P)*. Don't wash your dirty linen in public.

**lavette** *sf.* *(Sl)*. Weakling, softie, " push-over ", washout, " fraidy-cat ".

**l'avoir échappé belle** *(F)*. Narrow escape, close shave ; escaped by the skin of one's teeth.

**lèche (faire de la)** *(Sl)*. To curry favor, to bootlick, to lick s.o.'s boots.

**lèche-bottes** *sm.* *(Sl)*. Apple polisher, bootlicker, toady.

**lèche-carreaux** *sm.* *(P)*. Window-shopping.

**lèche-cul** *sm. (Sl).* Same as : *lèche-bottes* (but stronger).

**lèche-motte** *sm. (Sl).* Same as : *lèche-bottes.*

**lèche-vitrines** *sm. (P).* Same as : *lèche-carreaux.*

**lécher les babines (se)** *(P).* See : *babouines.*

**lécher les bottes à q.** *(Sl).* To lick one's boots.

**lécheur de bottes** *(Sl).* Bootlicker.

**le donner en mille** *(F).* Ex. : *Je vous le donne en mille !* I bet you will never guess it !

**légitime** *sf. (Sl).* Wife, one's better half, "ball and chain". Ex. : *Ma légitime,* the missis, my better half.

LUI ET SA LÉGITIME.

**légume** *sm. (P).* " *Grosse* " *légume :* V.I.P., big shot, big wheel, bigwig.

**le prendre de (très) haut** *(P).* To show arrogance.

**les aligner** *(Sl).* To pay, to fork out, to shell out, to come across with the dough.

**les allonger** *(Sl).* Same as : *les aligner.*

**les avoir à l'envers (à la retourne)** *(Sl).* Said of an exceedingly lazy person.

**les avoir dans le dos** *(Sl).* To have police heat on one, to be chased, pursued or wanted by police.

**les avoir dans les reins** *(Sl).* Same as : *les avoir dans le dos.*

**les avoir longues** *(Sl).* To be very hungry.

**les avoir palmées** *(Sl).* To be extremely lazy.

**les doigts dans le nez** *(Sl).* Easily, with no great effort.

**les envoyer** *(Sl).* Same as : *les aligner.*

**les lâcher** *(Sl).* Same as : *les aligner.*

**les lâcher avec un élastique** *(Sl).* To give money parsimoniously, little by little. (Said of a miser, of a skinflint).

**les mettre** *(Sl).* To go away, to leave, to scram.

**lessive** *sf. (Sl).* Sale, selling. (See : *lessiver*).

**lessivé** *adj. (Sl).* Dog-tired, deadbeat, pooped (out), tuckered out, fagged out, ready to drop. To be financially broke (same as : *rincé*).

**lessiver** *v. (Sl).* To sell something quickly, usually in an underhand manner and at any price in order to turn it into money. (Syn. : *laver*).

**lessiver la tête à q.** *(Sl)*. Same as : *laver la tête à q.*

**lettre à cheval (une)** *(F)*. Letter written in stiff terms.

**lever** *v. (Sl)*. To arrest, to capture, to put the collar on. To make a " pick-up ".

**lever du pied gauche (se)** *(P)*. To get out of bed on the wrong leg.

**lever l'ancre** *(Sl)*. To go away, to depart, to lift anchor, to pull anchor.

**lever le coude** *(P)*. To lift an elbow, to " exercise the elbow ", to wet the whistle, to swizzle, to tipple.

ENCORE UN QUI AIME
A LEVER LE COUDE.

**lever le pied** *(P)*. To do a fade-out with the cash-box, to run away with the money.

**lever un lièvre** *(P)*. To raise a delicate and embarrassing question.

**lézard (faire le)** *(P)*. To take a sun-bath, to bake up in the sun.

**lézarder** *v. (P)*. Same as : *lézard (faire le).*

**licher** *v. (Sl)*. To drink (wine, beer, etc.).

**ligne (avoir la)** *(P)*. To be slender.

**limace** *sf. (Sl)*. Disparaging term for a woman, " tomato ".

**limogeage** *sm. (P)*. Removal, dismissal from office, shelving (of a high-ranking army officer or official).

**limoger** *v. (P)*. To shelve, to dismiss, to remove from office, to supersede a high-ranking army officer or official.

**lippe (faire sa (ou) faire la)** *(P)*. To pout.

**liquette** *sf. (Sl)*. Shirt, shimmy.

ÉLÉGANT MÊME EN LIQUETTE.

**liquider** v. (Sl). To kill, to murder, to "blot out", to bump off, to "erase".

**lit en portefeuille** (P). Short-sheet, apple-pie bed (practical joke : one of the sheets is removed and the other is doubled in the middle ; the unhappy person who goes into the bed is prevented getting more than half-way down as he can't stretch out his legs).

**livre (une)** sf. (Sl). Hundred francs.

**loche** sf. (Sl). Same as : chiffe.

**logé à la même enseigne** (P). In the same box, in the same boat.

**lolo** sm. (P). Milk.

**lolos** sm. pl. (Sl). Breasts, "milk bottles".

**long** sm. (Sl). Cigar, weed.

**lope** sf. (Sl). Male homosexual, pederast. Also : lopette.

**louche** sf. (Sl). Hand, "fin". Serrer la louche, to shake hands, to "flip a fin".

**louchébem** sm. (Sl). Butcher.

**louf** adj. (Sl). Same as : loufoque.

**loufiat** sm. (Sl). Waiter (in a café).

**loufoque** sm. adj. (Sl). Crazy, crackpot, screwy, zany. Ex. : Histoire loufoque, shaggy-dog story, hairy-dog story.

**louftingue** sm. adj. (Sl). Same as : loufoque.

**louis** sm. (F). Abbr. of louis d'or, French 20-franc gold coin.

**loulou** sm. (P). Term of endearment : darling.

**lou(lou)te** sf. (P). Term of endearment : sweetie-pie.

**louper** v. (P). To miss, to muff, to bungle, to make a mess of. Ex. : J'ai loupé mon tour, I muffed my turn.

**loupiot** sm. (P). Little child, brat, baby, bunny, kiddie.

**lourd** adj. (P). Stupid, silly, dopey, lunkheaded.

**lourde** sf. (Sl). Door. Ex. : Boucler la lourde, to close the door.

**loustic** sm. (P). Fellow, guy, wag, mick(ey). Un drôle de loustic, a funny duck, a strange duck, a peculiar duck.

**lumignon** sm. (P). Very dim light.

**lune** sf. (Sl). Posteriors, fanny.

**lupanar** sm. (Sl). Brothel, cat-house.

# M

**maboul** *sm. adj. (Sl)*. Crackpot(ty), cuckoo, loony, dingdong daffy, one who has a loose screw, off one's bean, off one's trolley.

**mac** *sm. (Sl)*. Procurer, "cadet", pimp, mac.

**macadam (faire le)** *(Sl)*. A variant of *faire le tapin*.

**macaroni** *sm. (P)*. Nickname for an Italian, dago, "spaghetti".

**mac(c)habée** *sm. (P)*. Corpse, "stiff".

**machin** *sm. (P)*. Anything whose name has slipped the memory. Same as : *truc*.

**machin-chose** *sm. (P)*. A variation of *machin*. (Frequently also : *machin-chouette*).

**madré** *adj. (F)*. Foxy, sly.

**maffia** *sf. (P)*. Ring, crime syndicate.

**magner (se)** *(Sl)*. To hurry up, to make it snappy. A pop. adjuration that one should hurry : *Magne-toi !* Make it snappy ! Get a move on !

**magner le popotin (se)** *(Sl)*. A variant of preceding entry : to hurry up. *Magne-toi le popotin !* Rustle your bustle ! Get a move on !

**maigre comme un cent de clous** *(P)*. Said of an exceedingly skinny person.

**maigre comme une lame de rasoir** *(P)*. Variant of *maigre comme un cent de clous*.

**maigrichon** *adj. (P)*. Lean, skinny.

**maille à partir avec (avoir)** *(F)*. To have a crow to pluck with s.o., to be in Dutch with s.o., to have a brush with s.o.

**main de fer dans un gant de velours (une)** *(F)*. An iron hand in velvet gloves. *Ayez une main de fer dans un gant de velours*, "tread softly but carry a big stick".

— 116 —

**main malheureuse (avoir la)**
*(F).* To be unlucky in doing s.th., in dealing with one.

**mains dans les poches (les)**
*(P).* Easily, with no efforts at all, hands down.

**mains liées (avoir les)** *(F).*
To be hog-tied.

**maintes et maintes fois** *(F).*
Time after time, over and over.

**maison** *sf. (Sl).* Brothel.

**maison d'abattage** *(Sl).* Cheap brothel.

**maison de tolérance** *(P).* Brothel, red light house.

**maison de verre** *(P).* The " glass house " where there is no secret.

**maison tire-bouchon** *(Sl).*
*Liaison* between two lesbians.

MAL FICELÉ.

**malagauche** *adj. (P).* Clumsy, " butterfingers ".

**mal aux cheveux** *sm. (F).*
Hang-over, stale mouth after a binge, katzen-jammer. (See also : *gueule de bois*).

**mal blanchi** *(Sl).* Nigger, ebony.

**mal embouché** *(F).* Rough, coarse of speech, rude, vulgar.

**mal ficelé** *(F).* Badly dressed.

**mal fichu** *(P).* Slovenly. Slightly ill. Ex. : *Je suis mal fichu,* I don't feel quite well, I feel out of sorts.

**mal foutu** *(Sl).* Same as : *mal fichu* (but more vulgar).

**malheureux comme les pierres** *(P).* Very unhappy, extremely miserable.

**malheureuse** *sf. (Sl).* Prostitute.

**malin, malin et demi (à)**
*(F).* Diamond cut diamond, outwitting.

**malle (faire la)** *(Sl).* To walk out ; to jilt.

**mallette et paquette** *(Sl).*
Desertion, jilting (of a lover), bust-up.

**mal loti** *adj. (P).* Poor, hard up, behind the eight ball.

**mal vissé** *adj. (Sl).* In an ugly mood, out of temper.

**mamie** *sf. (F).* Same as : *mémé.*

**mamours** *sm. pl. (F).* Used mostly in the phrase : *Faire des mamours,* caressing, courting, billing and cooing.

**manche à balai** *(P).* Very skinny person. " Joy stick " (aviation).

**manche à gigot** *sf. (P).* Leg-o'-mutton sleeve.

**mandarin** *sm. (P).* Intellectual.

**mandarines** *sf. pl. (Sl)*. Derisive for a girl's small, tiny breasts, "tea-cups".

**mangeaille** *sf. (P)*. Food, "grub", "chaw".

**manger à plusieurs rateliers** *(P)*. To derive income from several sources, to serve several bosses.

**manger avec les chevaux de bois** *(P)*. To go without food, to skip lunch or dinner.

**manger de la vache enragée** *(F)*. To rough it.

**manger la consigne** *(P)*. Same as : *avaler la consigne*.

**manger la grenouille** *(Sl)*. To steal and make off with the cash-box. (Said generally of a dishonest cashier who steals money and makes off with it).

**manger le morceau** *(Sl)*. To confess, to blow the gaff, to "sing". (See also : *mettre à table (se)*.

**manger le nez (se)** *(P)*. To quarrel.

**manger le pif (se)** *(Sl)*. Same as preceding entry.

**manger les pissenlits par la racine** *(P)*. To be dead and buried, to push up daisies.

**manger son blé en herbe** *(F)*. To spend one's earnings or income in advance.

**manger son pain blanc le premier** *(F)*. To start first in a happy situation which can't or won't last ; to begin with the cake, with one's finest hour ; to eat the best part first.

**manger sur le pouce** *(P)*. To eat a small and hurried meal, to eat a snack, to snatch a bite.

**manier le derrière (se)** *(Sl)*. To hurry up, to make it snappy.

**manier le popotin (se)** *(Sl)*. Same as : *magner le popotin (se)*.

**manigancer** *v. (P)*. To contrive, to concoct, to plot.

**manigances** *sf. pl. (P)*. Maneuvers, intrigue, wirepulling.

**manque de bol** *(Sl)*. A variant of *manque de pot*.

**manque de pot** *(Sl)*. Bad luck, tough luck.

**manquer le coche** *(P)*. To miss the bus.

**manouche** *sm. (Sl)*. Gipsy.

**maousse** *adj. (Sl)*. Large, strong, beefy, hefty.

**ma pomme** *(Sl)*. Oneself, the speaker, uncle Dudley.

\* **maquereau** *sm. (Sl)*. Fancy man, pimp, cadet, man supported by a woman, souteneur who lives on the earnings of a prostitute.

\* **maquerelle** *sf. (Sl)*. Brothel hostess, Madame, procuress, white-slaver.

**maquille (faire de la)** *(Sl)*. To hustle "hot" cars.

**marchand de sable est passé (le)** *(F)*. The sand-man has come, children must go to bed.

**marchand de soupe** *(P)*. Inferior restaurant, keeper of an eating house.

**marchand de tuyaux** *(P)*. Dopester, one with inside information on races.

**marché aux puces** *(P)*. Flea market, second-hand goods market in Paris.

**marcher** *v. (P)*. To accept or to refuse a bid. Ex. : *Je marche*, count me in. *Je ne marche pas*, count me out.

**marcher sur les empeignes** *(P)*. To be on one's uppers.

**marcher sur les traces de q.** *(P)*. To follow in one's footsteps.

**mare aux harengs** *(F)*. Sea, Atlantic Ocean.

**margoulette** *sf. (Sl)*. Mouth, "smacker".

**margoulin** *sm. (P)*. Said of one who botches up work, a bungler, blunderer, tinker. A dishonest small shopkeeper. Fig. : a third-rater.

**mariage à la colle** *(Sl)*. Cohabitation of an unmarried couple.

**mariage de la main gauche** *(P)*. Left-handed marriage. (Same as : *mariage à la colle*).

**Marianne** *(F)*. Affectionate nickname for the French Republic.

**Marie-Chantal** *(F)*. Fashionable name for a girl, personification of bourgeois cynism.

**mariée est trop belle (la)** *(F)*. Sarcastic fling at one who complains about something nice in which he ought rather to rejoice.

**Marie-graillon** *(P)*. Said of an untidy kitchen wench, dishwasher girl, slut.

**Marie-salope** *(P)*. A variant of preceding entry : an untidy woman, slut, slattern.

**marier à la mairie du 21ᵉ (se)** *(P)*. Said humorously of a man and a woman who live together, as man and wife, without being married ; to marry over the broomstick, to "shack up".

**marin d'eau douce** *(P)*. Landsman, landlubber.

**marlou** *sm. (Sl)*. Pimp, "cadet".

**marmaille** *sf. (P)*. Small fry, small children.

**marmite** *sf. (Sl)*. Prostitute who supports a fancy man, "meal ticket". (Syn. : *boulangère*).

**marmite norvégienne** *(P)*. Pressure cooker.

**marmiter** *v. (Sl)*. To shell, to bombard.

**maroquin** *sm. (P)*. Ministry, portfolio.

**marotte** *sf. (F)*. Fad, fancy.

**marquise (la)** *sf. (Sl)*. Hostess of a brothel, madame.

**marrant** *adj. (Sl)*. Funny, amusing, comical.

**marre (en avoir)** *(Sl)*. To be fed up.

**marrer (se)** *(Sl)*. A very frequent variant of : *gondoler (se)*, *bidonner (se)*.

**marron** *sm. (Sl)*. Blow, hit (to the body, on the nose, etc.), crack, sock in the face, on the nose, punch on the snoot.

MARRON SUR LA FIGURE.

**marron** *adj. (P)*. Unqualified. See : *courtier marron, médecin marron*. *(Sl)*. Taken, caught red-handed. See also ; *faire marron*. *Etre marron*, to be a victim, dupe, bag holder.

**marronnant** *adj. (Sl)*. Annoying.

**marronner** *v. (Sl)*. To grumble, to grouch.

**marron sur la figure (un)** *(Sl)*. A slap, a blow in the face, a punch on the nose.

**marsouin** *sm. (Sl)*. Marine, gyrene, leatherneck.

**marteau** *adj. (Sl)*. Mentally deranged, crazy as a betsey bug, cracked-up, loony, " off ", pixilated.

**martel en tête** *(P)*. Ever-recurring worry, headache (used chiefly in the phrase : *se mettre martel en tête*).

**massacrer** *v. (P)*. To mess up, to louse up, to " murder ". (Same as : *bousiller*).

**mastic** *sm. (Sl)*. Disorder, mess, mix-up, damage.

**mastoc** *adj. (P)*. Heavy, lubberly.

**mastroquet** *sm. (P)*. Barkeeper, wine seller.

CHEZ LE MASTROQUET.

**m'as-tu-vu** *sm. (P)*. Ham actor.

**ma tante** *(P)*. Pawnshop, hock-shop, Uncle Benny, Uncle's.

**matelas** *sm. (Sl)*. Billfold, wallet, pocket-bock (especially well filled).

**matérielle** *sf. (P)*. Money needed for daily existence.

**maternelle** *sf. (P)*. Nursery school. Kindergarten.
*(Sl)*. Mother, mom(my), ma.

**math** *sm. pl. (P)*. Mathematics.

**matheux** *sm. (P)*. Student expert in mathematics.

**matraque** *sf. (F)*. Bludgeon, blackjack.

**Maub' (la)** *(Sl)*. *Place Maubert*, hobos' meeting place in Paris (left bank).

**mauvais comme la gale** *(P)*. Pop. variant of *méchant comme la gale*.

**mauvais comme une teigne** *(P)*. Another variant of *méchant comme la gale*.

**mauvais coucheur** *sm. (F)*. Quarrelsome, troublesome individual, hard to get along with ; cantankerous, rantankerous fellow, a sorehead, cross-patch.

**mauvais crin (être de)** *(P)*. A variation of *mauvais poil (être de)*.

**mauvais pas** *(F)*. Difficult situation, predicament, fix. Ex. : *Tirer q. d'un mauvais pas*, to help one out of a fix.

**mauvaise passe** *(F)*. *Etre dans une mauvaise passe*, to be in a tight spot, behind the eightball.

**mauvais poil (être de)** *(P)*. To be ill-tempered, in an ugly mood.

**mauvais sang (se faire du)** *(F)*. To worry oneself.

**mauviette** *sf. (P)*. Said of a delicate, weak person, feeble creature ; weakling, " sissy ".

**ma vieille branche** *(P)*. My old pal, my buddy.

**mazette !** *(P)*. Exclamation meaning admiration, surprise, etc.

**mec** *sm. (Sl)*. Individual, guy, gazabo, ghee.

**mec à la redresse** *(Sl)*. A hep guy.

**mécano** *sm. (P)*. Mechanic, "grease monkey".

**mec de la rousse** *(Sl)*. Policeman, cop.

**méchant comme la gale** *(P)*. Extremely nasty.

**méchant comme un âne rouge** *(P)*. Said of a very mean person or child.

**méchant comme une teigne** *(P)*. Same as : *méchant comme la gale.*

**mèche avec (de)** *(P)*. To be in cahoots with, to be hand in glove with s.o.

**mecton** *sm. (Sl)*. Small, insignificant individual, snippet.

**médecin marron** *sm. (P)*. Unqualified doctor.

**mégère** *sf. (F)*. A scolding, nagging woman, a woman of violent temper, a shrew.

**mégot** *sm. (P)*. Cigar or cigarette butt, "snipe", "dead soldier".

**mélasse** *sf. (Sl)*. Predicament, fix. *Dans la mélasse,* in a jam, in a fix, in the "barrel", in "hot water".

**méli-mélo** *sm. (P)*. Hotch-potch, mess-up, "screw-up", mish-mash.

**mélo** *sm. (P)*. Abbr. of *mélodrame,* melodrama.

**mémé** *sf. (F)*. Grand-mother, granny, gammy.

**mémère** *sf. (P)*. Same as : *mémé.* Also : any aged woman (pej.).

**même trempe (être de la)** *(P)*. To be of the same kidney, tarred with the same brush.

**mémoire de lièvre (avoir une)** *(F)*. To have a very poor memory.

**ménage** *sm. (Sl)*. Cohabitation of an unmarried couple. Homosexual liaison between two males or two females.

**ménage à la colle** *(Sl)*. Concubinage, unlawful marriage. (See also : *collage*).

**ménage à trois** *(P)*. The triangle of husband, wife and the latter's lover.

**ménager la chèvre et le chou** *(F)*. To manage so as to keep on good terms with both parties (both sides), to run with the hare and hold with the hounds.

MÉGÈRE.

**mendès (un)** *sm. (Sl).* A cup of milk (named after *Mendès-France* who recommended drinking milk instead of wine).

**mendiants** *sm. pl. (F).* Almonds, raisins, nuts and figs (eaten as dessert).

**mendigot** *sm. (P).* Beggar, bum, panhandler.

**mendigoter** *v. (P).* To beg, to panhandle, to bum.

**mener en barque** *(P).* To bamboozle, to make a fool of, to string along.

**mener en bateau** *(P).* Same as : *mener en barque.*

**mener la vie à grandes guides** *(F).* To kick over the traces, to kick up one's heels, to dissipate.

**mener par le bout du nez** *(P).* To lead one by the nose.

**ménesse** *sf. (Sl).* Pej. for a woman, floosey, broad, " tomato ".

CHEZ LE MERLAN.

**mentir comme un arracheur de dents** *(P).* To be an egregious liar.

**menton en galoche** *(P).* Slipper-chin.

\* **merdaillon** *sm. (Sl).* Sloppy child, dirty and pretentious child.

☞ **merde** *sf. (Sl).* Very vulgar " four-letter word ". *Merde !* Nuts !

\* **merdeux** *sm. (Sl).* Any contemptible guy, dirty skunk.

**merlan** *sm. (Sl).* Nickname for a barber, hairdresser.

**merle blanc** *sm. (F).* Rarity, an unusual or extraordinary individual.

**mes oignons (c'est)** *(Sl).* That's my business, that's my funeral.

**messe basse** *(P).* Secret conversation or talk in an undertone.

**mesurer les autres à son aune** *(P).* To judge others by one's own standards.

**métallo** *sm. (P).* Metal-worker.

**métèque** *sm. (P).* Pej. term for a certain category of foreigners living in France, particularly from South and Central America and South-Eastern Europe.

**mets cela dans ta poche et ton mouchoir par-dessus** *(P).* Put that in your pipe and smoke it.

**mettre à gauche** *(Sl).* To salt away money, to stash away (often ill-gotten money).

**mettre à la boîte** *(Sl).* To jail one, to put one in jail.

**mettre à la page** *(P).* To post(up), to smarten up, to wise(n) up, to put in the know.

**mettre à la page (se)** *(P).* To get wise to, to get hep to.

**mettre à l'ombre** *(P)*. To put s.o. in prison, to " run in ".

**mettre à poil** *(Sl)*. To strip to the buff.

**mettre à table (se)** *(Sl)*. To confess, to " sing ".

**mettre au bloc** *(Sl)*. To put in prison, in jail.

**mettre au clou** *(P)*. To hock, to put " in soak ".

**mettre au pas** *(P)*. To enforce obedience.

**mettre au rancart** *(P)*. To junk, to " deadline ".

**mettre à zéro** *(P)*. To cancel, to wipe out.

**mettre dans le ballon** (Sl). To put in prison, in jail.

**mettre dans le même sac** *(P)*. To put in the same basket, in the same category.

**mettre dans le mille** *(P)*. To be successful, to succeed, to hit the right spot.

**mettre de côté pour un coup dur** *(P)*. To save for a rainy day.

**mettre dedans** *(Sl)*. To put in prison, to slap in the can. To best one, to swindle, to " suck in ", to gyp, to hornswoggle, to make a sucker out of, to " sell a goldbrick ".

**mettre de l'eau dans son vin** *(F)*. To grow softer, less exacting ; to soften down, to come down a peg or two.

**mettre des bâtons dans les roues** *(F)*. To throw a monkey wrench into the transmission, to throw a spanner in the works.

✓**mettre des gants** *(F)*. To do something tactfully (in order not to hurt a person's feelings).

**mettre du beurre dans les épinards** *(F)*. To make things easier, to bring grist to the mill. (See also : *beurre dans les épinards*).

**mettre du foin dans ses bottes** *(P)*. Same as : *faire sa pelote*.

**mettre en boîte** *(P)*. To guy, to rib, to needle, to " spoof ", to poke fun at, to " razz ", to " give the razz (berry) ".

**mettre en boule** *(P)*. To get one's monkey up.

**mettre en caisse** *(Sl)*. Same as : *mettre en boîte*.

**mettre en quatre (se)** *(P)*. To make a whole-hearted, sustained effort, to exert oneself to the utmost limit of one's strength, to bust a gut, to lay (put) oneself out for.

**mettre en veilleuse** *(P)*. To slow up the pace, the tempo, the rhythm. *Mettre une usine en veilleuse*, to reduce output to a minimum.

✓**mettre la bride (se)** *(Sl)*. To go without food, to tighten one's beet.

✓ **mettre la ceinture (se)** *(Sl)*. Same as : *mettre la bride (se)*.

**mettre la charrue devant les bœufs** *(F)*. To put the cart before the horse.

**mettre la corde au cou (se)** *(P)*. To get married, to get spliced, to " put a halter round one's own neck " (joc. term).

**mettre la dernière main à q. ch.** *(P)*. To put the finishing touch.

**mettre la main à la pâte** *(P)*. To take an active part in the work, to put one's shoulder to the wheel.

**mettre la puce à l'oreille** *(P)*. To awaken one's suspicions.

**mettre la tringle (se)** *(Sl)*. Same as : *mettre la bride (se)*.

**mettre le couteau sur la gorge** *(P)*. To employ coercion, to threaten with violence, to "strong-arm".

**mettre le doigt dans l'œil (se)** *(P)*. To be in the wrong box, to be mistaken, to bark up the wrong tree.

**mettre le doigt dessus** *(P)*. To hit the nail on the head.

**mettre le doigt sur la plaie** *(P)*. Same as : *mettre le doigt dessus.*

**mettre le feu aux poudres** *(P)*. To stir up a hornets' nest, to cause an explosion (of anger, indignation, etc.).

**mettre le grappin dessus** *(P)*. To get hold of.
*(Sl)*. To arrest, to capture, to run in.

**mettre le paquet** *(Sl)*. To open (up) the gun, to go it at full speed (in cycle racing).

**mettre le pied à l'étrier à q.** *(F)*. To give one a leg up, to help one into a position, into a job.

**mettre les bâtons** *(Sl)*. See : *mettre les bouts.*

**mettre les bouts** *(Sl)*. To go away, to depart hurriedly, to flee, to duck out, to scram, to take a powder. (Syn. : *mettre les bâtons*).

**mettre les bouts de bois** *(Sl)*. A variant of *mettre les bouts.*

**mettre les petits plats dans les grands** *(P)*. To entertain lavishly, to spare no expense.

**mettre les pieds dans le plat** *(P)*. To give one a piece of one's mind, to put one's foot down. Ex. : *J'en ai plein le dos ! je finirai par mettre les pieds dans le plat.*

**mettre les points sur les " i "** *(F)*. To spell out, to speak plainly to s.o., to make the meaning plain, perfectly clear. To dot the i's and cross the t's.

**mettre les pouces** *(Sl)*. To yield, to knuckle down, to knuckle under, to submit.

**mettre les voiles** *(Sl)*. To go away, to depart, to clear out, to check out, to scram, to do a bunk.

**mettre martel en tête (se)** *(P)*. To worry about s. th., to make oneself very uneasy.

**mettre q. à toutes les sauces** *(P)*. To put one to all kind of jobs, hence : to compel one to shoulder all sorts of undesired responsibilities.

**mettre q. au pied du mur** *(P)*. To corner one.

**mettre q. en capilotade** *(P)*. To knock the stuffing out of one, to knock into a cocked hat.

**mettre son grain de sel** *(P)*. See : *y mettre son grain de sel.*

**mettre sous les verrous** *(P)*. To put in jail, to "run in", to lock up.

**mettre sur la paille** *(P)*. To ruin utterly.

**mettre sur le tapis** *(P)*. To bring up for discussion.

**mettre sur son trente-et-un (se)** *(P)*. To put on one's best clothes, to don one's best bib and tucker.

**me voilà frais !** *(P)*. Same as : *me voilà propre !*

**me voilà propre !** *(P)*. I am in a nice fix !

**mézigue** *(Sl)*. Oneself, the speaker, uncle Dudley.

**miché** *sm.* *(Sl)*. A prostitute's paying guest.

**micheton** *sm. Sl).* A variation of *miché.*

**micmac** *sm. (P).* Jumble, medley, mess-up, mess, muddle.

MIDINETTE.

**midinette** *sf. (P).* Young work-girl in Paris in the fashion, millinery or dressmaking business.

**mignon** *sm. (Sl).* Catamite, " angelina ".

**mignon comme tout** *(F).* Cute as a bug's ear.

**mijoter** *v. (P). Qu'est-ce qui se mijote ?* What's cooking ? What's up ?

**milieu (le)** *sm. (Sl).* World of *souteneurs* and prostitutes in large cities and ports in France.

**mince !** *interj. (Sl).* Excl. of surprise : Gosh !

**minet** *sm. (F).* Puss, pussy.

**minute, papillon !** *(P).* Pop. catch phrase : Wait a minute !

**mioche** *sm. sf. (P).* Affectionately coll. for a child, baby, kid, brat.

MIOCHE.

**mirer** *v. (Sl).* To look at.

**mirettes** *sf. pl. (Sl).* Eyes, " peepers ".

**mirobolant** *adj. (P).* Prodigious, stunning, out of this world.

**mironton** *sm. (Sl).* Guy, ghee. *Un drôle de mironton,* a queer customer.

**mise en boîte** *(P).* Poking fun at s.o., guying s.o., spoof.

**mise en caisse** *(Sl).* Same as : *mise en boîte.*

**miser** *v. (P).* To bet, to stake.

**misérable** *sm. (Sl).* Nickname of a 500-franc bill (a " bill that won't buy much ") bearing Victor Hugo's effigy (obviously in reference to Victor Hugo's famed novel : " *Les Misérables* ").

**miser sur les deux tableaux** *(P)*. To stake on two (opposite) issues, to " hedge ".

**mistoufle** *sf. (P)*. Extreme poverty. *Faire des mistoufles à q.*, to be nasty with s.o.

**mitard** *sm. (Sl)*. Cooler, disciplinary cell in a jail.

**miteux** *adj. (P)*. Out at the elbows, shabby, down at (the) heels, bum, worthless, lousy.

**mitraille** *sf. (Sl)*. Small coins, " chicken feed ".

**mobilard** *sm. (Sl)*. Policeman, cop (of a special mobile squad).

**moche** *adj. (P)*. Ugly, lousy, rotten, dime-a-dozen ; no bloody good.

**mochetée** *sf. (Sl)*. Plain woman, ugly face.

**mocheton** *sm. (Sl)*. Bum looker, a very ugly female.

**moco** *sm. (Sl)*. Derisive nickname for a man from Marseille.

**mœurs (les)** *sm. pl. (Sl)*. Policemen of the Paris vice-squad.

**moineau** *sm. (P)*. *Drôle de moineau*, funny guy, strange individual.

**moins une (il était)** *(P)*. It was a narrow escape, a close shave, a close call, escape from a disaster by an infinitely small margin.

**moïse** *sm. (F)*. Coll. term for a small cot for a baby, " Moses basket ".

**moisir** *v. (Sl)*. To wait, to cool one's heels. *Moisir en prison*, to rot in stir.

**moitié** *sf. (P)*. Joc. for wife, one's better half, " sparring partner ". *Ma moitié*, my better half.

**molard** *sm. (Sl)*. Spittle, spit.

**molarder** *v. (Sl)*. To spit, to expectorate.

**mollasse** *adj. (P)*. Soft, lifeless, gutless.

**mollo** *adv. (Sl)*. Gently. *Vas-y mollo !* Go it easy !

**môme** *sm. sf. (Sl)*. Young boy, girl, young woman.

**mômerie** *sf. (Sl)*. Kid stuff.

**momie** *sf. (P)*. Zombie.

**momignard** *sm. (Sl)*. Same as : *môme*.

**mominette** *sf. (P)*. Small glass of *absinthe*.

**mon chou** *(P)*. My little lovebird, pussy cat. (Term of endearment). Sometimes : *mon petit chou en sucre* or : *mon petit chou en susucre*.

**mon coco** *(P)*. Another coll. term of endearment : darling, my little chipmunk, my little honey-bee.

**(ben) mon colon !** *(Sl)*. Excl. conveying surprise or admiration.

**monde au balcon (il y a du)** *(Sl)*. Said of a woman's well-developed breasts.

IL Y A DU MONDE
AU BALCON.

**monde fou (un)** *(F)*. Large crowd, large gathering.

**monnaie de singe** *(P)*. See : *payer en monnaie de singe*.

**mon nœud !** *interj. (Sl)*. A vulgar variant of *mon œil !*

**mon œil !** *interj. (Sl)*. Excl. of disbelief : Nothing doing ! Baloney ! Apple sauce ! My eye ! You can't fool me ! (Excl. generally accompanied by a gesture of pulling down the lower lid of the right eye with the right index finger).

**mon (petit) rat** *(P)*. Pop. petting term : my little chipmunk, my pussy-cat.

**Monsieur de Paris** *(P)*. The hangman (who operates the guillotine).

**Monsieur Tout-le-Monde** *(P)*. The man-in-the-street, the average citizen.

**montagne qui accouche d'une souris (la)** *(P)*. Mountains labor and bring forth a mouse.

**monté (être)** *(Sl)*. To be slightly drunk.

**monte-en-l'air** *sm. (P)*. Burglar, porch-climber, yeggman, " second-story man ".

**monter à l'échelle** *(Sl)*. To get angry, to get one's monkey up.

**monter en épingle** *(P)*. To make a show of, to exaggerate the importance of.

**monter en graine** *(F)*. To be getting on in years, to be getting an old maid.

**monter la tête (se)** *(P)*. To get excited, to get enthusiastic about.

**monter la tête à q.** *(P)*. To work one up, to excite one.

**monter le bobéchon (se)** *(Sl)*. A variation of *monter la tête (se)*.

**monter le bourichon (se)** *(Sl)*. Another variation of *monter la tête (se)*.

**monter le coup à q.** *(P)*. To take s.o. in, to " let in ", to " suck in ", to put up a job on.

**monter sur le billard** *(P)*. To undergo a surgical operation.

**monter sur ses ergots** *(P)*. Same as : *dresser sur ses ergots (se)*.

**monter sur ses grands chevaux** *(P)*. To ride the high horse, to be on one's high horse.

**monter un bateau à** *(P)*. To hoax, to spoof, to hand a line of baloney.

**Montparno** *(Sl)*. Slang name of *Montparnasse*, artists' district in Paris (left bank).

**montrer patte blanche** *(P)*. To show a distinctive mark, to make oneself recognizable, to identify oneself.

**mon trognon** *(P)*. Sweetie-pie (term of endearment).

**monts et merveilles** *(F)*. *Promettre monts et merveilles*, to promise the moon.

**mon vieux !** *(P)*. Pop. vocative : old cock! my old friend !

**moquer du tiers comme du quart (se)** *(P)*. Not to care a damn.

**morceau sur le pouce** *(P)*. Snack, a bite of food.

**mordre (c'est à se les)** *(Sl)*. Exceedingly funny, very amusing.

**mordre dans le truc** *(Sl)*. To fall into the trap, to drop in for it.

**mordre la poussière** *(P)*. To bite the dust.

**mordu** *adj. (Sl)*. In love with. Ex. : *Il est bien mordu*, he's nuts over the girl.

**mornifle** *sf. (P)*. Slap in the face.

**mort aux vaches !** *(P)*. Insult for policemen.

**mort et enterré** *adj. (P)*. Dead and gone.

**morue** *(Sl)*. Term of contempt for a dirty, dissipated woman. Slut, bitch, prostitute, " blimp ", " floozey ".

**motard** *sm. (P)*. Speed cop, motor cop.

MOTARD.

**mot de Cambronne** *sm. (P)*. Four-letter word, in French euphemism for : *merde*.

**mots avec q. (avoir des)** *(P)*. To quarrel with s.o.

**mot sur le bout de la langue (avoir le)** *(P)*. To have the word on the tip of one's tongue.

**motus !** *interj. (P)*. Keep it secret ! don't say a word !

**mouchard** *sm. (P)*. Police inform-er, police-spy, stool pigeon.

**moucharder** *v. (P)*. To inform on, to act as a police-spy, to rat on.

**mouche du coche (faire la)** *(F)*. To play the fly on the coach-wheel. Said of one who imagines himself to be a person of importance, who plays the busybody and thinks that his influence is very important ; one who plays the " fly on the wheel ".

**moucher** *v. (Sl)*. To beat up badly, to bawl out severely.

**mouiller (se)** *v. (Sl)*. To expose oneself to a great danger or a heavy punishment.

**mouillette** *sf. (P)*. Same as : *trempette*.

**mouise** *sf. (Sl)*. Great poverty, tough sledding. *Etre dans la mouise*, to be on the rocks, " on the hog ".

**moukère** *sf. (Sl)*. Derogatory for : woman, wife ; " broad ".

**moule** *sf. (P)*. Dull and stupid person, dumbbell, dope.

**moulin** *sm. (Sl)*. Automobile or airplane motor, " mill ".

MOUMOUTE.

**moulin à paroles** *(P)*. A very talkative person, a chatterbox.

**moulinette** *sf. (Sl)*. Tommy gun, submachine gun.

**moulu** *adj. (P)*. Exhausted, dead tired, pooped (out).

**moumoute** *sf. (Sl)*. Wig.

**mourant** *adj. (P)*. Awfully funny, killing.

**mourir de rire** *(P)*. To laugh oneself sick.

**mouscaille** *sf. (Sl)*. Euphemistic variation of *merde*.

**moussante** *sf. (Sl)*. Beer.

**moutard** *sm. (P)*. Child.

**moutarde après dîner (c'est de la)** *(P)*. Day after the fair, anything coming too late when it's no longer needed.

**moutarde lui monte au nez (la)** *(P)*. He gets angry, he gets his monkey up.

**mouton** *sm. (Sl)*. Police informer, stool pigeon, steerman.

**mouvement (être dans le)** *(P)*. To be in the swim, to be hep to, to be " in ".

**M.R.P.** *Abbr.* of *Mouvement Républicain Populaire,* important French political party, left center.

**muet comme une carpe** *(P)*. Silent as the grave.

**mufle** *sm. (F)*. Skunk, cad, an ill-bred, ill-mannered fellow.

**muflerie** *sf. (F)*. Caddishness.

**mûr** *adj. (Sl)*. Drunk, " ripe ", " plastered ".

**museau** *sm. (Sl)*. Mouth, " mug ", " muzzle ".

**musette** *sm. (Sl)*. Same as : *bal-musette*.

**musicien** *sm. (Sl)*. Flatterer, " soft-soap artist ". Crook.

**mystère et boule de gomme !** *(Sl)*. Excl. meaning : Mystery inside an enigma, any enigmatical or inexplicable thing.

# N

**nager dans l'encre** *(Sl)*. To be in the dark.

**nana** *sf. (Sl)*. Girl, young girl, "broad".

**nanan** *sm. (P)*. Tasty stuff, yummy.

**nap** *sm. (Sl)*. Short for a *napoléon*.

**naphtaline** *sf. (Sl)*. Cocaine, "coke", "gold dust".

**napoléon** *sm. (F)*. 20-franc gold coin.

**nature** *adj. (F)*. Neat, straight (without any addition). Ex. : *café nature,* black coffee ; *une personne nature,* blunt, plain speaking person.

**navarin** *sm. (F)*. Mutton stew with turnips, carrots and potatoes.

**nave** *sf. (Sl)*. An exceedingly silly person, dumbbell.

**navet** *sm. (P)*. Unsuccessful and bad show, bad film, "turkey".

**navette (faire la)** *(P)*. To go back and forth, to ply.

**n'avoir ni rime ni raison** *(F)*. To have neither rhyme nor reason, neither head nor tail, senseless.

**n'avoir ni queue ni tête** *(P)*. Pop. saying meaning a nonsense.

**n'avoir ni sou ni maille** *(P)*. Not to have a red cent, a copper, not even a plugged nickel.

**n'avoir que la peau sur les os** *(F)*. Same as : *maigre comme un cent de clous.* Said of an extremely skinny person : bag of bones, rattle-bones, nothing but skin and bones.

**n'avoir rien à se mettre sous la dent** *(P)*. Popular way of saying that one has nothing to eat.

**ne casse pas les vitres (ça)** *(P)*. Cuts no ice.

**ne casse rien (ça)** *(P)*. Same meaning as preceding entry.

**né coiffé (être)** *(P)*. Born under a lucky star.

**ne connaitre ni d'Eve ni d'Adam** *(P)*. Not to know one from Adam, not to know one at all.

**ne faire ni chaud, ni froid** *(P)*. To have no influence on, not to change matters in the least.

**ne faire ni une ni deux** *(P)*. Without hesitating.

**nèfles (des)** *sf. pl. (Sl)*. Nothing! nothing at all ! (Syn. : *des clous, des dattes, des radis, du vent*).

**nègre** *sm. (P)*. Ghost writer.

**neige** *sf. (Sl)*. Cocaine.

**n'en avoir pas dans le ventre** *(Sl)*. To be a coward, chicken, a scaredy-cat, not to have any guts.

**nénés** *sm. pl. (Sl)*. Humorous slang for breasts, "bubbies".

**nénette** *sf. (Sl)*. Girl, "tomato".

**ne nous emballons pas !** *(P)*. Let us be calm ! Keep your shirt on !

**n'en pas...** See : *ne pas en...*

**n'en pouvoir mais** *(P)*. *Je n'en peux mais*, I can't help it !

**ne pas avoir de plomb dans la cervelle** *(P)*. To be scatterbrained, foolish, flighty.

**ne pas avoir froid aux yeux** *(P)*. To have guts, to have plenty of cheek, not to be afraid.

**ne pas avoir inventé la poudre** *(P)*. Pop. variant of *ne pas avoir inventé le fil à couper le beurre*.

**ne pas avoir inventé le fil à couper le beurre** *(P)*. Said of a person who is not intelligent, who has not much brains.

**ne pas avoir la langue dans sa poche** *(P)*. Said of a person who has the gift of the gab, who has a ready retort to anything.

**ne pas avoir le rond** *(Sl)*. To be broke, penniless.

**ne pas avoir q. en odeur de sainteté** *(P)*. To have s.o. in one's black books.

**ne pas avoir un fifrelin** *(F)*. Not to have a red cent.

**ne pas avoir un pelot** *(Sl)*. Frequent variant of *ne pas avoir un fifrelin*.

**ne pas blairer** *(Sl)*. To hate, to detest. Ex. : *Je ne peux pas le blairer*, I detest him.

**ne pas en avoir pour sa dent creuse** *(P)*. Not enough to fill a bad tooth. (Said of a very tiny portion).

**ne pas encaisser** *(P)*. To hate, to detest. (Same as : *ne pas blairer*). *Je ne peux pas encaisser ce type-là*, I can't bear that guy.

**ne pas en ficher un coup** *(Sl)*. Not to do a stroke of work, to loaf, to idle, to bum around.

**ne pas en ficher une datte** *(Sl)*. Same as : *ne pas en ficher un coup*.

**ne pas en ficher une rame** *(Sl)*. Same as : *ne pas en ficher un coup*.

**ne pas en ficher une secousse** *(Sl)*. Same as : *ne pas en ficher un coup*.

**\* ne pas en foutre un coup (une datte, une rame, une secousse)** *(Sl)*. Same as : *ne pas en ficher un coup* (but more vulgar).

**ne pas en mener large** *(P)*. To be in a tight spot.

**ne pas être à la noce** *(P)*. To be in an uncomfortable position, in serious trouble, in a pretty to-do, in a sorry fix.

**ne pas être à prendre avec des pincettes** *(P)*. To be irritable, in an ugly mood. *Il n'est pas à prendre avec des pincettes*, he's not fit to be touched with a barge-pole, (or with a ten foot pole).

**ne pas être bon** *(Sl)*. To refuse. Ex. : *Je ne suis pas bon*, I refuse, I don't agree. (Syn. : *Je ne marche pas*).

**ne pas être dans son assiette** *(F)*. To feel all-overish, not to feel up to the mark, up to par, not to be up to dick.

**ne pas être si bête qu'on en a l'air** *(P)*. Not to be such a fool as one looks.

**ne pas faire long feu** *(P)*. Flash in the pan.

**ne pas ficher un coup de rame** *(Sl)*. Same as : *ne pas en ficher un coup*.

**ne pas l'avoir volé** *(P)*. To well deserve it (sarcastically). Ex. : *Tu ne l'as pas volé !* It serves you right ! you deserve it and how !

**ne pas l'emporter au Paradis** *(P)*. *Tu ne l'emporteras pas au Paradis !* You won't get away with that ! (Fling carrying disapproval, blame, for a discreditable action).

**ne pas mâcher ses mots** *(P)*. Not to mince words, matters.

**ne pas manquer de toupet** *(P)*. To be cheeky, to be a sauce-box, a smarty.

**ne pas marcher** *(P)*. To refuse. (Same as : *ne pas être bon*).

**ne pas mettre le pied dehors** *(P)*. Not to go out, to stay at home.

**ne pas pouvoir blairer q.** *(Sl)*. Slang variant for *ne pas pouvoir sentir*.

**ne pas pouvoir encaisser q.** *(P)*. Pop. variant for *ne pas pouvoir sentir*.

**ne pas pouvoir gober** *(Sl)*. Same as : *ne pas pouvoir sentir*.

**ne pas pouvoir sentir** *(P)*. Not to bear, not to stand, a person.

**ne pas pouvoir tenir sa langue** *(P)*. Not to be able to hold one's tongue.

**ne pas pouvoir voir q. en peinture** *(P)*. *Je ne peux pas la voir en peinture*, I can't bear the mere sight of her.

**ne pas quitter q. d'une semelle** *(P)*. Not to let one get an inch out of one's sight.

**ne pas rigoler** *(Sl)*. To be in a fix, to be annoyed. Ex. : *Je ne rigolais pas*, I was in an awful fix, I was very much annoyed.

**ne pas se donner de coups de pied** *(P)*. To brag, to boast, to pat oneself on the back, to "spread oneself ".

**ne pas se fouler le poignet** *(Sl)*. Not to break one's back working. (Said of a lazy person).

**ne pas se fouler le pouce (la rate)** *(Sl)*. Same as : *ne pas se fouler le poignet*.

**ne pas se moucher du pied** *(P)*. Said of a pretentious individual who denies himself nothing, who does things in an elegant style.

**ne pas s'en faire** *(P)*. Not to worry. Ex. : *Ne t'en fais pas !* Don't worry !

**ne pas sourciller** *(F)*. Not to bat an eye, without batting an eyelash.

**ne pas tourner rond** *(P)*. *Ça ne tourne pas rond*, something is wrong somewhere, it just doesn't "add up ".

**ne pas valoir chipette** *(P)*. Worthless, not worth a whoop, not worth shucks, not worth a continental,

**ne pas valoir pipette** *(P)*. Same as : *ne pas valoir chipette*.

**ne pas valoir tripette** *(P)*. Another variant of *ne pas valoir chipette*.

**ne pas valoir un clou** *(P)*. Still another variant of *ne pas valoir chipette*.

**ne pas valoir un pet de lapin** *(P)*. Frequent pop. variant of *ne pas valoir chipette*.

**ne pas venir à la cheville de q.** *(P)*. Not to be a patch upon, not fit to hold a candle to.

**ne pas voir plus loin que le bout de son nez** *(P)*. Not to see an inch beyond one's nose, to be real shortsighted.

**ne pas y aller avec le dos de la cuiller** *(P)*. Same as : *ne pas y aller par quatre chemins*.

**ne pas y aller de main morte** *(P)*. To go it hammer and tongs, to put plenty of vim into it.

**ne pas y aller par quatre chemins** *(P)*. Not to mince words, to tell straight from the shoulder.

**ne pas y couper** *(P)*. Not to be able to avoid something.

**ne pas y regarder de si près** *(P)*. Not to be overdainty, overcritical.

**ne rêver que plaies et bosses** *(P)*. Said of a "scrappy" individual (always ready to fight or quarrel).

**nerfs en pelote (avoir les)** *(P)*. To be very nervous, jittery, very irritated.

**ne rien casser** *(P)*. See : *ça ne casse rien !*

**ne rien dire** *(F)*. *Cela ne me dit rien*, il doesn't appeal to me.

**ne rien se casser** *(P)*. Said of a lazy person.

**ne rimer à rien** *(P)*. *Cela (ça) ne rime à rien*, it's senseless.

**nervi** *sm. (Sl)*. Marseille gunman, gangster.

**ne savoir où donner de la tête** *(P)*. (So busy as) not to know which way to turn.

**ne savoir sur quel pied danser** *(P)*. Not to know what to do, how to behave, which way to turn, etc.

**nespasien** *sm. (P)*. Joc. term for a person who, in speaking, uses excessively often : *n'est-ce pas ?*

**(ne) t'occupe pas du chapeau de la gamine !** *(P)*. See : *t'occupe pas du chapeau de la gamine !*

**nettoyé** *adj. (Sl)*. Ruined, kicked out, "liquidated".

**ne valoir que dalle** *(Sl)*. To be worth nothing, worthless.

**ne vouloir rien savoir** *(P)*. To refuse, not to agree. Ex. : *Il ne veut rien savoir*, he refuses, he won't agree.

**ne vous emballez pas !** *(P)*. Keep your shirt on ! don't lose your temper ! don't get excited ! (See : *emballer (s')*.

**nez (avoir dans le)** *(Sl)*. To hate, to detest.

**nez (avoir du)** *(Sl)*. To have a good nose.

**nez creux (avoir le)** *(Sl)*. Same as : *nez (avoir du)*.

**nez de poivrot** *sm. (P)*. Bibulous nose.

**nez en pied de marmite** *(P)*. Flat nose.

**nez long (avoir le)** *(P)*. To cut a long face.

**nez piqué (avoir le)** *(Sl)*. To be drunk, to be "cooked", "plastered".

**nez sale (avoir le)** *(Sl)*. Same as : *nez piqué (avoir le)*.

**nib** *(Sl)*. Nothing. *Nib de nib*, nothing at all, nix.

**ni chair ni poisson (n'être)** *(P)*. Neither fish, flesh nor good red herring.

**nichons** *sm. pl. (Sl)*. A woman's breasts, " ninnies ".

**Nicodème** *sm. (P)*. Simpleton, chump.

**nigaudinos** *sm. (P)*. Same as : *niguedouille, nicodème*.

**niguedouille** *sm. (Sl)*. Stupid person, fool, simpleton, sap, saperoo.

**nipper** *v. (P)*. To fit out. *Bien nippé*, well supplied with clothes, well dressed.

**nippes** *sf. pl. (P)*. Clothes, dresses.

**ni rime ni raison** *(F)*. See : *n'avoir ni rime ni raison*.

**ni sou ni maille** *(P)*. See : *n'avoir ni sou ni maille*.

**ni vu, ni connu, j't'embrouille !** *(P)*. Popular joc. phrase to refer to a cheap trickery, hocus-pocus, switcheroo, a clever trick of substitution : " And here is a muddle, now try and sort it out ! ".

**noce** *sf. (P)*. Binge, high jinks. *Faire la noce*, to go on a spree, on a bust, on a binge, to paint the town red. (See also : *ne pas être à la noce*).

**noceur** *sm. (P)*. Reveller, hellraiser, " cutup ", hellbender.

**noir (le)** *sm. (Sl)*. Opium. Black market. *Au noir*, on the black market. *adj. (Sl)*. Drunk, boozy, " plastered ", " blotto ". Illicite, as in : *marché noir, travail noir*, etc.

**noircir (se)** *v. (Sl)*. To get drunk, to get tight.

**noir comme dans un four (il fait)** *(F)*. It's pitchdark.

**noix** *sf. (Sl)*. Silly person, muff, goof, dumbbell.

**noix (à la)** *(Sl)*. See : *à la noix*.

**nom de baptême** *(F)*. First name, given name.

**nom de D... !** *(Sl)*. Chrissake !

**nom de deux !** *(Sl)*. Euphemism for : *nom de D... !*

**nom de nom !** *(Sl)*. Expletive.

**nom d'un chien !** *(P)*. Mild oath.

**nom d'une pipe !** *(P)*. Another mild oath.

**nom d'un petit bonhomme !** *(P)*. Still another mild oath.

**nom d'un tonnerre** *(P)*. Expletive, stronger than preceding entries.

**nom qui se dévisse** *(P)*. Humorous pop. term for a high-sounding aristocratic name carrying the nobiliary particle(s). Ex. : *Monsieur du Fond du Jardin*.

**non, mais des fois !** *(P)*. Spiteful excl. meaning : don't be ridiculous ! don't make me laugh ! don't try to fool me !

**note (être dans la)** *(P)*. To be hep to, to be in the swim.

**nouba** *sf. (P)*. Binge, bender, hellraising. *Faire la nouba*, to go on a bust, on a binge.

**nougat (du)** *(Sl)*. Easy job, " velvet ", " pushover ", " duck soup ", " pie ", " snap ".

**nougats** *sm. pl. (Sl)*. Feet, " dogs ".

**nouille** *sf. (P)*. Silly person, sap, dumbbell, dope, chump, lunkhead, chowderhead, noodlehead, doughhead, beanhead.

NOUNOU.

NUE COMME UN VER.

**nounou** *sf. (F)*. Wet nurse, nursie.

**nous voilà frais !** *(P)*. Same as : *nous voilà propres !*

**nous voilà propres !** *(P)*. We are in a nice fix !

**nu comme un ver** *(P)*. Entirely naked, without a stitch on.

**numéro** *sm. (P)*. Odd fellow, screwball, a "case".

**numéro cent** *(Sl)*. W.C., "hoosegow".

**n'y aller que d'une fesse** *(Sl)*. To do a thing only half-heartedly.

**n'y entraver que dalle** *(Sl)*. Not to understand a damn thing.

**n'y plus être du tout** *(P)*. Ex. : *Il n'y est plus du tout,* he's not in the picture at all, he didn't get it.

**n'y voir goutte** *(P)*. To see nothing.

**n'y voir que du bleu** *(P)*. Not to realize, unable to see through it.

# O

**obéir au doigt et à l'œil** *(F)*. To be at one's beck and call.

**occase** *sf. (Sl)*. Bargain, real bargain.

**occasion fait le larron (l')** *(P)*. Opportunity makes the thief.

**occupe-toi de tes oignons** *(Sl)*. Mind your own business ! Tend your own potatoes ! Stick to your own potatoes !

**œil (avoir l')** *(P)*. To watch out, to keep one's eyes peeled.

**œil (avoir q. à l')** *(P)*. To watch one, to keep an eye on a person.

**œil américain** *sm. (P)*. Watchfulness, weather eye, peeled eye, the cautious eye.

**œil américain (avoir l')** *(P)*. To have very sharp eyes, to have one's eyes open.

**œil au beurre noir** *(P)*. Eye heavily bruised by a blow, black eye, "mouse", "shiner".

**œil en boule de loto** *(P)*. Goggle-eye.

**œil en coulisse** *(P)*. *Faire les yeux en coulisse à q.,* to ogle one.

**œil pour œil, dent pour dent** *(F)*. Tit for tat.

**œil qui dit zut à l'autre** *(P)*. Cross-eye, squinting eye, swivel eye.

**œufs à la neige** *(F)*. "Floating island" (boiled custard with meringue).

OIGNON.

**œufs sur le plat** *(Sl)*. Humorous slang for a woman's flat and tiny breasts.

**oignon** *sm. (Sl)*. An old fashioned large watch, "turnip".

**oiseau** *sm. (P)*. Pej. term for a strange individual. *Drôle d'oiseau*, a funny guy.

**olive** *sf. (Sl)*. Bullet, "slug", "Chicago pill", "lead".

**ombre (être à l')** *(Sl)*. To do time (in jail), to be in stir.

**onduler de la toiture** *(Sl)*. Humorous for : to be crazy, loony, to have a screw loose.

**on en mangerait** *(P)*. Said of anything very appetizing.

**ongles en deuil** *(P)*. Dirty nails.

**on lui donnerait le bon Dieu sans confession** *(P)*. He (she) looks innocent, looks as if butter would not melt in his (her) mouth.

**on mangerait par terre** *(P)*. Popular saying conveying the notion of : very clean, well kept. (Said principally of a tidy, well kept room, kitchen, house, etc.).

**on ne sait jamais** *(P)*. You never can tell.

**orgueilleux comme un paon (pou)** *(P)*. As proud (as vain) as a peacock.

**orphelin** *sm. (Sl)*. Cigarette butt, "snipe".

**oseille** *sf. (Sl)*. See : *galette*.

**ostrogoth** *sm. (P)*. Man who does not know how to behave, coarse-mannered individual.

**oublier les mois de nourrice** *(P)*. To pretend to be younger than one really is. (See : *... plus les mois de nourrice*).

**ours mal léché** *(P)*. Unlicked cub, unsociable person.

**ouste !** *(P)*. Interj. Ex. : *Et ouste, il détale en vitesse*, so he up and scurries off.

**outil** *sm. (Sl)*. Clumsy, awkward person. Ex. : *Va donc, eh ! outil !*

**outsider** *sm. (P)*. Dark horse.

**ouvrir à q. (s')** *v. (P)*. To open one's heart to s.o., to unbosom oneself to s.o.

**ouvrir les écluses** *(Sl)*. To burst into tears, to weep bitterly.

**ouvrir l'œil et le bon** *(P)*. To watch out, to keep one's eye skinned.

# P

**pacquelin** *sm. (Sl)*. Same as : *patelin*.

**pacqueson** *sm. (Sl)*. Same as : *pacson*.

**pacson** *sm. (Sl)*. Parcel, small package.

**paf** *adj. (Sl)*. Tight, boozed up, boozy, " plastered ".

**pagaie** *sf. (P)*. Same as : *pagaille*.

**pagaille** *sf. (P)*. Mess, mess-up, holy mess, hell of a mess.

**pageot** *sm. (Sl)*. Bed.

**pagnot** *sm. (Sl)*. Bed.

**pagnoter (se)** *v. (Sl)*. To hit the hay (the bed), to turn in.

**paillasse** *sf. (Sl)*. Woman of loose morals, " push-over ", " free-for-all ".

**paillasson** *sm. (Sl)*. Woman of easy morals, floozy, tomato, a zipper-moraled girl, an easy Jane.

**paille (mettre sur la)** *(P)*. To ruin. Ex. *Ça ne nous mettra pas sur la paille*, it won't land us in the poorhouse.

**paille ! (une)** *sf. (P)*. A flea-bite ! a mere trifle !

**paille et la poutre (la)** *(F)*. One is always apt to criticize merciless-ly other people's little failings while one winks light-heartedly at one's own more serious faults or defects.

**paillons (des)** *sm .pl. (Sl)*. *Faire des paillons*, said of an unfaithful lover. (Syn. : *faire des queues*).

**pain** *sm. (Sl)*. *Recevoir un pain*, to get a punch on the nose ; *flanquer un pain à q.*, to deal a blow.

**pain bénit ! (c'est)** *(P)*. It serves him (her) right.

**pain sur la planche (avoir du)** *(P)*. To have money in reserve, to have a nest-egg. To have a lot of work in view, plenty to do.

**pajot** *sm. (Sl)*. Bed.

**palabrer** *v. (P)*. To talk idly, to chitter and chatter, to yackety-yack.

**palabres** *sf. (P)*. Idle talk, "gassy" talk.

**palasser** *v. (Sl)*. To talk, to palaver, to "gass".

**paletot de sapin** *(Sl)*. Coffin, casket, "wooden overcoat".

**"Palm Beach"** *(F)*. Marina.

**palper** *v. (P)*. To draw money, to cash one's salary. *C'est moi qui travaille et c'est lui qui palpe,* I am doing the job and he is getting the money.

**palpitant** *sm. (Sl)*. Heart, "ticker".

**paltoquet** *sm. (P)*. Palooka, "kike", "jake".

**panade** *sf. (P)*. Great financial straits, predicament. *Etre dans la panade,* to be on the rocks, "on the hog", "broke".

**Panam(e)** *(Sl)*. A slang nickname for Paris, capital of France.

**panards** *sm. pl. (Sl)*. Feet, "dogs", "purps".

**pandore** *sm. (P)*. Gendarme.

**panier à deux anses (faire le)** *(P)*. Gentleman with a lady on each arm. (This is called sometimes a "sandwich" in England).

**panier à salade** *(P)*. Patrol wagon, paddy wagon. Black Maria, police car with windows latticed with iron for transportation of prisoners.

PANIER A SALADE.

**panier percé** *(P)*. Spendthrift, highroller who spends money recklessly, prodigally.

**paniquard** *sm. (P)*. "Jitterbug".

**panne** *sf. (Sl)*. Utter poverty, hardship, pinches (as in : to be in the pinches).

**panné** *adj. (Sl)*. Broke, clean broke, on the hog, ruined, busted (in the pocketbook).

**panouillard** *sm. (Sl)*. Stupid guy, blockhead, "chump", "goof".

**panouille** *sm. (Sl)*. Same as : *panouillard.*

PANIER A DEUX ANSES.

**panse** *sf. (P). Grosse panse,* big, prominent abdomen, "corporation".

**pante** *sm. (Sl).* Dull-witted guy, stupid person, dummy.

**Pantin** *(Sl).* A slang nickname of Paris, capital city of France.

**pantouflard** *sm. (P).* Home-bird, man who loves his comfort at home.

**Pantruchard** *sm. (Sl).* Parisian, inhabitant or native of Paris.

**Pantruche** *(Sl).* A slang nickname for Paris, capital of France. (See also : *Panam(e).*

**papa (à la)** *(Sl).* In a simple, homely and unhurried manner. Ex. : *Faire les choses à la papa,* to do things normally and in an unhurried fashion.

**papa gâteau** *(P).* Sugar daddy.

PAPA GATEAU.

**papaout** *sm. (Sl).* Male homosexual, pansy.

**Pape (le)** *(Sl).* Director of Naval Academy at Lanvéoc-Poulmic (school slang).

**papeau** *sm. (Sl).* Humorous slang for : hat.

**papelard** *sm. (P).* Paper, piece of paper, letter, small printed notice.

**papelards** *sm. pl. (Sl).* Identity papers. Newspapers.

**paperasserie** *sf. (F).* Red-tapery.

**paperasses** *sf. pl. (F).* Paper work, red-tape, long-winded and mostly useless papers, files, documents, etc.

**paperassier** *sm. (F).* One who likes red-tape(ry).

**papier à douleur** *(Sl).* Protested unpaid note (commerce). Rent bill presented by the landlord.

**papotages** *sm. pl. (F).* Chitterchatter, chit-chat, small talk.

**papoter** *v. (F).* To chitter-chatter, to talk idly, to chew the rag.

**papouille** *sf. (Sl).* Hug, caress, embrace.

**paqueson** *sm. (Sl).* Same as : *pacson.*

**Pâques ou à la Trinité (à)** *(F).* Said of an undefined later date, practically never. When pigs fly, when hell freezes over.

**paquet (avoir son)** *(Sl).* To have what one deserves, a good thrashing. *Il a eu son paquet,* he got his comeuppance.

**paradis** *sm. (P).* Top gallery in a theater, "paradise", "peanut gallery", "chicken roost".

**parages** *sm. pl. (P).* Diggin's. Ex. : *Venez nous voir quand vous passerez dans nos parages.*

**parallèle (le)** *sm. (P).* Euphemism fort the currency black market.

**parbleu !** *(P).* Sure ! You bet !

**par-dessus la tête** *(P).* See : *en avoir par-dessus la tête.*

**pardi !** *(P).* Sure ! You bet !

**paré** *adj.* *(Sl)*. Flush of money, well-heeled.

**pareil au même (c'est du)** *(P)*. It's six of the one and half a dozen of the other, it's practically the same.

**paresseux comme une couleuvre** *(P)*. Pop. saying of a particularly lazy individual.

**Parigot** *sm.* *(Sl)*. Native Parisian.

**Paris ne s'est pas fait en un jour** *(F)*. Rome was not built in a day.

**parler affaires** *(P)*. To talk turkey, to talk business.

**parler à tort et à travers** *(P)*. To talk irrevelantly or without knowlegde, to talk through one's hat, to talk tripe.

**parler chiffon** *(P)*. To talk fashion, to talk dress.

**parler dans le vide** *(P)*. To talk without being listened to.

**parler de la pluie et du beau temps** *(P)*. To chitter-chatter, any small talk.

**parler en l'air** *(P)*. To talk idly.

**parler français comme une vache espagnole** *(F)*. To speak French very badly, to murder the language.

**parler petit nègre** *(P)*. To talk "pidgin French", to speak incorrect French (as little negro boys do) especially in using infinitive instead of *verbum finitum*, such as : *moi pas connaître*, instead of : *je ne le connais pas*.

**parlotte** *sf.* *(P)*. Idle talk, yacketyyack, yattity-yattity.

**paroissien** *sm.* *(Sl)*. Sarcastic euphemism for : guy, individual, fellow. (See : *drôle de paroissien*).

**parole d'évangile (c'est)** *(F)*. You may take it for gospel truth.

**parti (être)** *(Sl)*. To be drunk, to be boozy, to be "boiled", to be "cooked".

**particulière** *sf.* *(Sl)*. Sa *particulière* : one's sweetheart, "steady".

**partie carrée** *(P)*. Party of two couples, double date.

**partir en bombe** *(Sl)*. To go on a bust, to raise hell, to make hoopla.

**partir en virée** *(Sl)*. To go the dizzy rounds, to make hell pop loose.

**partir pour le grand voyage** *(P)*. Same as : *grand saut (faire le)*.

**parvenu** *sm.* *(P)*. Social climber.

**pas bésef** *(Sl)*. Not much. Ex. : *Y en a pas bésef,* there isn't very much, it doesn't amount to much.

**pas ça !** *(P)*. Nothing at all ! (usually said with a gesture that consists in clicking the thumbnail against the inside of the front teeth to stress absolute nothingness).

**pas chic** *(P)*. Paltry, mean.

**pas commode** *(F)*. Not easy to get along with.

**pas croyable** *(P)*. Pop. for *incroyable ;* unbelievable, incredible.

**pas de ça, Lisette !** *(P)*. No soap ! No sale !

**pas de clerc (faire un)** *(P)*. To make a slip-up, to make a blunder.

**pas de danger que** *(P)*. No fear of. Ex. : *Pas de danger qu'elle le fasse,* no fear of her doing so.

**pas épatant** *(P)*. Nothing to write home about.

**pas facile** *(P)*. Not easy, "no picnic".

**pas folichon** *(P)*. Sad, annoying, uncomfortable (affair).

**pas foutu de** *(Sl)*. Not fit to, not able to.

**pas grand'chose** *sm. (P)*. Bad lot, good-for-nothing, worthless person, cheapie.

**pas la queue d'un (e)** *(P)*. Not (a blessed) one.

**pas lourd** *(Sl)*. Very little.

**pas mal** *(P)*. Tolerable, not so bad.

**pas marrant** *(Sl)*. Very annoying.

**pas méchant** *(P)*. Harmless.

**pas mèche** *(Sl)*. Nothing doing, impossible, no soap ! no sale !

**pas piqué des vers** *(P)*. Anything nice and good, bang-up, first-rate.

**pas plus compliqué que ça** *(P)*. It's as simple as that, easy like taking candy from a baby.

**passade** *sf. (P)*. Short love affair, passing fancy.

**passage à tabac** *(P)*. Severe thrashing (generally by police).

**passe** *sf. (Sl)*. Quick amorous session with a prostitute, " quickie ".

**passer à gauche** *(Sl)*. To be deprived of one's fair share.

**passer à la casserole** *(Sl)*. Said of a woman upon whom rape is being committed.

**passer à l'as** *(P)*. To disappear without any visible trace.

**passer à tabac** *(P)*. To beat severely, to give the works, to give one a working-over, to let one have it.

**passer à travers** *(P)*. To escape danger or punishment, to beat the rap.

**passer au bleu** *(P)*. To spirit away, to hush up.

**passer au traviol (l) e** *(Sl)*. A slang variant of *passer à travers*.

**passer comme une lettre à la poste** *(P)*. Said of anything that can be done immediately and effortlessly, with no difficulty involved. Ex. : *Ça passe comme une lettre à la poste,* easy like pie, like taking candy from a baby.

**passer (de) la pommade** *(Sl)*. To flatter fulsomely, to hand out (the) soft soap, to butter up.

**passer la main** *(Sl)*. To give in, to yield, to toss up the sponge. To let someone else have a try.

**passer la main dans le dos** *(P)*. To flatter, to butter up.

**passer la main dans les cheveux** *(P)*. A variant of *passer la main dans le dos*.

**passer la pogne** *(Sl)*. To make peace. Ex. : *Passe la pogne !* Let's shake hands and make peace !

**passer l'arme à gauche** *(Sl)*. To die, to " go west ".

**passer l'éponge** *(P)*. *Passons l'éponge là-dessus !* Let's forget it once for all ! Let bygones be bygones !

**passez-moi la rhubarbe, je vous passerai le séné** *(F)*. Tradelast.

**passer sur le billard** *(P)*. To undergo an operation, to be operated on.

**passer un savon** *(P)*. To bawl out, to dress down.

**passer un suif** *(Sl)*. Same as : *passer un savon* (but more vulgar).

**pas si bête** *(P)*. Nobody's fool.

**pas si bête qu'il en a l'air**

*(P)*. Not so fool(ish) as might be assumed, not such a fool as he looks.

**pas sorcier** *(P)*. Easy like taking candy from a baby, a " pushover ", " duck soup ".

**pastis(se)** *sm. (Sl)*. Ersatz for *absinthe*. Predicament, fix, annoyance, trouble, mess, mix-up, " razzle-dazzle ". *Etre dans le pastis(se)*, to be in a fix, in trouble. *Quel pastis(se) !* What a hell of a mess !

**pas très catholique** *(P)*. Not very honest, dubious, of doutful honesty. Ex. : *Ça ne m'a pas l'air très catholique.*

**pas très chaud** *(P)*. Not very keen on, not very enthusiastic about.

**pas un chat** *(P)*. No one, nobody, not a soul.

**pas un radis** *(Sl)*. Not a red cent, not a plugged nickel, totally broke.

**pas un rotin** *(Sl)*. A variation of *pas un radis.*

**pas verni** *adj. (P)*. Not lucky, unlucky.

**patache** *sf. (P)*. Old ramshackle carriage.

**patapouf** *sm. (P)*. Heavy, bloated guy, fat kid, greaseball, a fat podge.

**pataquès** *sm. (P)*. Slip, mistake made in the *liaison* (for instance, *vingt hommes* pronounced : *vingt-s-hommes*). Malapropism, " double-dutch ".

**patate** *sf. (Sl)*. A large nose, schnozzle, " schnozzola ". Spud (potato). " Hayseed ", " rube ".

**patati et patata (et)** *(P)*. Onomatopoeia to ridicule an endless confab, chit-chats or people who are real chatterboxes. " Talkathon ".

**patatras** *interj. (F)*. Crash !

**patatrot** *sm. (Sl)*. Hasty flight, quick escape. Horse races.

**pâtée** *sf. (Sl)*. Beating, licking, hiding.

**patelin** *sm. (P)*. Country, one's native land (or village).

**paternel** *sm. (P)*. Father, dad(dy), pa, pop, the old man.

**patin** *sm. (Sl)*. Tongue, " clacker ", " lapper ".

**patoches** *sf. pl. (Sl)*. Hands, " fins ", " dukes ".

**patouille** *sf. (Sl)*. Delicate caress. Mud.

**patouiller** *v. (Sl)*. To splash in the mud.

**patraque** *adj. (P)*. Out of order, sick, on the blink, on the terrific Fritz.

**patte d'oie** *sf. pl. (P)*. Small wrinkles near (or round) the eyes, " crow's feet ".

**pattes** *sf. pl. (Sl)*. Hands, " fins ". Human feet.

**pattes d'araignée** *sf. pl. (Sl)*. Delicate caresses with the fingers, " goose ".

**pattes de lapin** *sf. pl. (Sl)*. Short side whiskers, burnsides.

**pattes de mouche** *sf. pl. (P)*. Sprawling (and often) illegible handwriting, scrawl.

**paumer** *v. (Sl)*. To arrest, to " nab ", to " run in ".

**pauvre diable** *sm. (P)*. Poor devil.

**pavoiser** *v. (Sl)*. To go about with a blackened eye, with a " shiner ".

**paxon** *sm. (Sl)*. Parcel, small package.

**payer (le)** *(P)*. *Tu vas me le*

*payer !* You will pay for that ! (threat implying punishment in store).

**payer (se)** *v. (P).* To treat one-self to. (See : *s'envoyer*).

**payer cash** *(Sl).* To pay cash (derived from American and " natural-ized " in French slang).

**payer de sa personne** *(P).* To do one's bit, to take a hand in the work oneself.

**payer de toupet (se)** *(P).* To call one's bluff ; to " braze it out ".

**payer en monnaie de singe** *(F).* Smiles, fine promises and blarney instead of money. To flatter, to soft-soap, to humbug (a creditor). *Il m'a payé en monnaie de singe,* I got fine promises, but no money.

**payer la figure de q. (se)** *(P).* Same as : *payer la tête de q. (se).*

**payer la tête de q. (se)** *(P).* To ridicule, to guy one, to give the razz, to make fun of, to get a rise out of. (Other sl. synonyms : *se payer la fiole, la poire, la gueule de q.*).

**payer les pots cassés** *(P).* To face the music, to pay the piper.

**payer les violons** *(P).* To pay the piper, to assume financial respon-sibility.

**payer recta** *(P).* Same as : *payer rubis sur l'ongle.*

**payer rubis sur l'ongle** *(P).* To pay on the nail, to pay punctually, cash on the barrel-head, cash on the nail.

**payer une tournée** *(P).* To buy a drink for several persons in a bar, to pay for a round of drinks.

**pays** *sm. (P).* Fellow-countryman, man of one's own country.

**payse** *sf. (P).* Fellow-countrywom-an, woman compatriot.

**P.D.** *sm. (Sl).* Pederast. (Same as : *pédé*).

**peau** *sf. (Sl). Une vieille peau,* an old prostitute, an old zook, old and ugly wench.

**peau (la) !** *(Sl).* Nothing ! nothing doing !

**peau (en)** *adv. (Sl).* With a very low *décolleté.*

**peau (faire la)** *(Sl).* To mur-der, to kill, to " erase ", to " blot out ", to bump off.

**peau de balle !** *(Sl).* Nothing (at all), not a thing !

**peau de balle et balai de crin !** *(Sl).* A variant of *peau de balle.*

**peau de balle et variété !** *(Sl).* Another variant of *peau de balle.*

**peau de nœud !** *(Sl).* Same as : *peau de balle.* Also interj. to express displeasure.

**peau de q. (avoir la)** *(Sl).* To kill s.o., to " rub out " s.o.

**peau de saucisson** *(Sl).* Very low grade ware, junk, inferior goods.

**peau de vache** *(Sl).* Lousy bum, insult for a despicable individual, contemptible person.

**peau de zébi** *(Sl).* Nothing at all, rubbish, swosh, junk, worthless good, any vague, fictitious thing.

**peau d'hareng** *(Sl).* Junk, no good.

**peau neuve (faire)** *(P).* To straighten up, to square oneself.

**pébroque** *sm. (Sl).* Umbrella, bumbershoot, brolly.

**pêcher en eau trouble** *(P).* To fish in troubled water.

**pédale (la)** *sf. (Sl).* Pansyland, the world of male homosexuals.

**pédé** *sm. (Sl).* Pederast, pansy, fairy, faggot.

**pédéro** *sm. (Sl).* Same as : *pédé.*

**pédoque** *sm. (Sl).* Same as : *pédé.*

**pedzouille** *sm. sf. (P).* Peasant, " hayseed ", rube, " apple knocker ", yokel.

PEDZOUILLE.

**pègre** *sf. (P).* Underworld gangdom, world of *souteneurs* and their prostitutes. *Basse pègre,* the lowest class of the underworld.

**pégriot** *sm. (Sl).* Small thief.

**peigne-cul** *sm. (Sl).* Contemptuous term for a miser, pinchpenny.

**peignée** *sf. (Sl).* Beating, rubdown, licking, thrashing.

**peigner (se)** *v. (Sl).* To have a fight.

**peigner la girafe** *(P).* To be idle, to laze, to do nothing.

**peinard (être)** *(Sl).* See : *pénard.*

**pékin** *sm. (Sl).* Civilian, non-military.

**pelot** *sm. (Sl).* Five-centime coin, nickel. (See : *n'avoir pas un pelot*).

**pelotage** *sm. (Sl).* Petting (of a woman), cuddle-bugging, fondling, " courting with the hands ".

**pelote** *sf. (P).* Money, piled up money, savings. (See also : *faire sa pelote*).

**peloter** *v. (Sl).* To pet, to caress a woman.

**peloteur** *sm. (Sl).* Petter, cuddle-bug, a " sexplorer ".

**pelousard** *sm. (P).* Turfman, horse-racing fan, racing bug.

**pelure** *sf. (Sl).* Top-coat, overcoat.

**pénard (être)** *(Sl).* To have it soft, to take things easy, to take it easy. (Also spelt : *peinard*).

**pendre au nez** *(P).* Bound to happen. (Said of some impending unpleasantness bound to happen to somebody). Ex. : *Méfie-toi, ça te pend au nez !*

**pendre la crémaillère** *(F).* To give a house-warming party (to inaugurate a new home). *Pendaison de la crémaillère :* house-warming party.

**pendu au téléphone (être toujours)** *(P).* To be always hanging on the 'phone.

**pendu aux basques de q. (être)** *(P).* To be always hanging on one's coat-tails.

**penses-tu ! (pensez-vous !)** *(P).* Excl. conveying refusal or negation : Oh, come off !

**pépée** *sf. (Sl).* Any girl, cutie. Also applied to a prostitute : " tomato ", " hustler " " broad ".

**pépère** *sm. (P)*. Friendly coll. for a quiet, good old man.
*adj.* Comfortable, cozy, pleasant, dandy, first rate.

**pépète** *sf. (Sl)*. Money, " dough ", " moolah ".

**pépie (avoir la)** *(Sl)*. To be thirsty.

**pépin** *sm. (P)*. Umbrella. An unexpected difficulty, " bug ", hitch, snag. *(Sl)*. Love, fancy. *Avoir le pépin pour q.,* to have a crush on s.o.

JE NE SORS JAMAIS
SANS MON PÉPIN.

**péquenot** *sm. (P)*. Peasant, countryman or provincial clown, " hayseed ", " apple knocker ", " palooka from the sticks ", yokel.

**percer** *v. (P)*. To succeed, to get there.

**perche** *sf. (P)*. See : *grande perche.*

**percher** *v. (Sl)*. To live, to hang out. *Où perches-tu ?* Where do you hang out ?

**perdreau** *sm. (Sl)*. Cop, plainclothes man.

**perdreaux (les)** *sm. pl. (Sl)*. Cops of the *Paris Sûreté* (Criminal Investigation Dept.).

**perdre la boule** *(Sl)*. To go off one's rocker.

**perdre la boussole** *(P)*. Same as : *perdre le nord.*

**perdre la face** *(P)*. To lose face.

**perdre le goût du pain** *(Sl)*. To die, to " go over to the great majority ".

**perdre le nord** *(P)*. To get mixed up, to lose one's head.

**perdre les pédales** *(P)*. To lose control of.

**perdre sa salive** *(P)*. To talk idly, to no purpose, in vain.

**perdre son latin** *(F)*. See : *y perdre son latin.*

**péril en la demeure (il n'y a pas)** *(F)*. No need for worrying, there is no immediate danger.

**perle** *(sf). (P)*. A gem of a, a pearl of a, a jewel of a. *Notre bonne est une perle,* our maid is a treasure (=hard-working and in every way satisfactory).
*(Sl)*. Fart.

**perlot** *sm. (Sl)*. Tobacco.

**perlouse** *sm. (Sl)*. Pearl.

**perme** *sf. (Sl)*. Furlough, leave of absence.

**péronnelle** *sf. (P)*. Silly talkative girl (or woman), saucy girl, hussy.

**Pérou (le)** *(P)*. *Ce n'est pas le Pérou,* not so well paid as one would think ; not, in any way, a fortune.

**perpète (à)** *adv. (P).* For ever.

**perruque** *sf. (Sl).* Hair.

**peser le pour et le contre** *(F).* To weigh the pros and cons, to look at both sides of a question.

**peser ses paroles** *(F).* To weigh one's words.

**pesètes** *sf. pl. (Sl).* Money, dough, " shekels ".

**peste !** *interj. (P).* Bless me ! Hang it !

**pester** *v. (P).* To swear at, to fret and fume.

**pétarader** *v. (Sl).* To be angry, mad, to make the fur fly.

**pétard** *sm. (P).* See : *faire du pétard.*
*(Sl).* Posteriors, rear-end, fanny. Revolver, oscar, roscoe, " smoke ".

**pétarder** *v. (Sl).* To raise hell.

**pétasse** *sf. (Sl).* Fright, funk (-iness), fear, " creeps ". Abusive term for a woman, " broad ".

**pétasse (avoir la)** *(Sl).* To be frightened, to have the " shakes ".

**pétaudière** *sf. (P).* A noisy assemblage where all are talkers with no hearers, a house mismanaged where every one is master. Any disorderly and misruled place.

**pet de lapin** *(P). Ne pas valoir un pet de lapin,* not worth shucks, not worth a continental. Ex. : *Ça ne vaut pas un pet de lapin.*

**pet de nonne** *(P).* Sinker(s), dumpling(s).

**pet-en-l'air** *(P).* Man's short house jacket, " bum-freezer ".

**péter** *v. (Sl).* To burst, to bust. *Ça pète,* hellzapoppin'.

**péter le feu** *(Sl).* To be very lively, peppy, to be full of beans, to be on one's toes, to be a hustler.

**pète-sec** *sm. (P).* Unpleasant man with gruff manners. Martinet.

**péteuse** *sf. (Sl).* Feminine form of *péteux,* snob. Motorbike.

**péteux** *sm. (P).* Coward, fraidy-cat, chicken-hearted individual. *Foutre le camp comme un péteux,* to flee through fear, to " punk out ".
*(Sl).* Snob.

**petiot** *adj. (P).* Tiny, little.

**petit ami (son)** *(P).* Her boy friend.

**petit blanco (un)** *(Sl).* A little glass of white wine.

**petit bonheur la chance (au)** *(P).* Excl. meaning that one is relying on one's good luck.

**petit bout d'homme** *(P).* Snippet, a tiny little chap.

**petit cadeau** *(Sl).* Prostitute's word for the money she receives from a man.

**petit Caporal (le)** *(F).* Nickname for Napoleon I.

**petit carreau (le)** *(Sl).* Police court.

**petite** *sf. (P).* Little girl, very young girl.

**petite bière** *(P).* See : *ce n'est pas de la petite bière !*

**petite bouche (faire la)** *(P).* To pick at one's meal, to nibble, to be overdainty.

**petit endroit (le)** *(P).* W.C., toilet, " johnny ". *Aller au petit endroit,* to go " see a man about a dog ".

**petite reine** *(F).* Bicycle. (Term much in vogue 50 years ago. Now rare).

**petit fripon** *(P)*. Little skeesicks, little scamp.

**petit juif** *(P)*. Funny bone.

**petit-lait** *sm. (P)*. See : *boire comme du petit-lait (se)*.

**petit nègre** *(P)*. "Pidgin French", bastard French, broken French. (See : *parler petit nègre*).

**petit noir** *(P)*. Cup of black coffee.

**petit salé** *(Sl)*. New-born baby.

**petit somme** *(P)*. Forty winks, a short sleep.

**pétochard** *sm. (Sl)*. Coward, "chicken".

**pétoche** *sf. (Sl)*. Fear, funk. Ex. : *Avoir la pétoche,* to be afraid, to be jittery.

**peton** *sm. (P)*. Small, tiny foot. (Said generally of a child's tiny feet, tootsies).

**pétrin** *sm. (P)*. Predicament, fix. Ex. : *Etre dans le pétrin,* to be in a fix, in a jam, in a spot, behind the eight ball.

**pétrole** *sm. (Sl)*. Liquor, booze, "vitriol", "hardware".

**pétrolette** *sf. (P)*. Small motor-bike.

PÉTROLETTE.

**pétrousquin** *sm. (P)*. A variant of *pedzouille*.

**pétrus** *sm. (Sl)*. Posterior, rear-end, fanny.

**pétzouille** *sm. (P)*. Another spelling for *pedzouille*.

**pèze** *sm. (Sl)*. Same as : *galette*.

**P.G.** *(P)*. Abbr. of *prisonnier de guerre*, prisoner of war, P.O.W.

**pharamineux** *adj. (P)*. Astonishing, stunning, big-time.

**phénix** *sm. (P)*. Remarkable person, top-notcher, lollapaloosa, "wizard".

**phénomène** *sm. (P)*. Strange person, queer fish, a "card", a "screw-ball". Looloo, lulu.

**philistin** *sm. (P)*. Lowbrow *bourgeois*, term applied by artists to those of the *bourgeois* class who do not appreciate literature and art.

**piailler** *v. (P)*. To blubber.

**piano-piano** *adv. (P)*. Quietly.

**piaule** *sf. (Sl)*. House, dump, "shebang", room, "pokey hole", "coop".

**piauler (se)** *v. (Sl)*. To go home.

**picaillons** *sm. pl. (Sl)*. Money, dough, "moolah".

**pichenette** *sf. (P)*. Flip (with the fingers), fillip.

**picoler** *v. (Sl)*. To drink frequently, to tipple, to souse. Generally used in reference to devotees of wine.

**picoleur** *sm. (Sl)*. Elbow bender, tippler, wine-guzzler.

**pictance** *sf. (Sl)*. Drink, alcoholic beverage.

PICOLEUR EN FORME.

PIED DE NEZ.

**pied de nez (faire un)** *(P).* To thumb one's nose, to give a "finger-wave" (to put one's thumb to one's nose and extend one's fingers at s.o., a gesture meaning contempt).

**pied levé (au)** *(P).* See : *au pied levé.*

**pied marin (avoir le)** *(F).* To be a good sailor.

**pieds (faire les)** *(Sl). Ça lui fera les pieds,* that will teach him a good lesson.

**pieds dans les reins (avoir les)** *(Sl).* To be wanted (chased) by police, to have the police heat on.

**pieds devant (s'en aller les)** *(Sl).* To die, to "kick the bucket", to "go home feet first".

**pieds et des mains (faire des)** *(P).* To move heaven and earth.

**pieds humides** *sm. pl. (P).* Pej. for outside brokers (Stock Exchange), dealing in "cats and dogs". Also : low-grade or dubious securities.

**pieds nickelés (avoir les)** *(Sl).* To refuse to move, to budge or to work.

**picter** *v. (Sl).* Same as : *picoler.*

**pictonner** *v. (Sl).* Another variant of *picoler.*

**pièce de résistance** *(P).* High spot. Main course.

**pied** *sm. (P).* Silly person, dumbbell, sap, fathead.

**pied à l'étrier (avoir le)** *(P).* To be lifted into a comfortable position.

**pied dans la tombe (avoir un)** *(P).* To be half-dead, very old, with one foot in the grave.

**pied de cochon** *(Sl).* Nasty trick, nastiness, dirty trick.

**pied de grue (faire le)** *(P).* To wait for a long time, to be kept waiting, to kick (cool) one's heels waiting for s.o., to dance attendance.

**pie-grièche** *sf. (P)*. Shrew, vixen.

**pierreuse** *sf. (Sl)*. Low-class prostitute, " zook ".

**pierrot** *sm. (Sl)*. Odd guy. Ex. : *Un drôle de pierrot.*

**pieu** *sm. (Sl)*. Bed.

**pieuter (se)** *v. (Sl)*. To go to bed, to turn in, to hit the sack, to hit the hay.

**pif** *sm. (Sl)*. Nose, " bugle ", " conk ", " schnozzo ".

DIEU ! QUEL PIF !

**piffard** *sm. (Sl)*. Same as : *pif.*

**piffer** *v. (Sl)*. Same as : *blairer.* Ex. : *J'peux pas le piffer,* I can't stand him.

**piffomètre** *sm. (Sl)* Rough estimate, guesswork. Ex. : *Mesurer, calculer au piffomètre,* to " guesstimate ".

**pige** *sf. (P)*. See : *faire la pige à.* *(Sl)*. One year (to designate age or term in jail).

**pigeon** *sm. (Sl)*. Victim, sucker, dupe, " gull ", cheatee.

**pigeonné (être)** *(Sl)*. To be victimized, taken in, " sucked in ".

**pigeonner** *v. (Sl)*. To deceive, to take in, to swindle.

**piger** *v. (P)*. To understand it, to grasp the significance of it, to get it. Ex. : *Il pige vite,* he's quickwitted, he understands things very quickly.

**pignon sur rue (avoir)** *(F)*. To own a home, a house of one's own, hence : to be well-off, well-to-do.

**pignouf** *sm. (P)*. Cad, an unmannerly fellow.

**pile** *sf. (Sl)*. Beating, licking, shellacking.

**pile (une)** *sf. (Sl)*. 100 francs.

**pile !** *adv. (P)*. To a nicety, with utmost precision, in the very nick of time. Ex. : *Tu arrives pile !* You are coming in the very nick of time !

**pilier de cabaret** *(P)*. Habitual drinker, bar fly.

**pilonner** *v. (P)*. To shell, to bombard, to prang.

**pilule** *sf. (P)*. See : *avaler la pilule.*

**pinard** *sm. (P)*. Wine, ordinary wine.

**pince** *sf. (Sl)*. Hand, " fin ". Ex. : *Serrer la pince à q.,* to shake hands with s.o. (See also : *cuiller, louche*).

**pinceaux** *sm. pl. (Sl)*. Feet, " dogs ".

**pince-cul** *sm. (Sl)*. Low-class dance hall, low-class juke joint.

**pince-fesses** *sm. (Sl)*. A variation of *pince-cul.*

**pince-monseigneur** *sf. (P)*. Jimmy(-bar), jemmy (a burglar's tool).

**pincer** *v. (P)*. To arrest, to capture, to pinch, to catch, to " nab ".

**pince-sans-rire** *sm. (P)*. Dry joker.

**pincettes** *sf. pl. (P)*. Thin shanks.

**pingler** *v. (Sl)*. Same as : *pincer*.

**pingre** *sm. (P)*. A variant of *radin* : a pinchpenny, cheap screw.

**pinter** *v. (Sl)*. To drink habitually (wine, beer, etc.), to tipple.

**piocher** *v. (P)*. To work, to study hard, to grind.

**pioncer** *v. (Sl)*. To snooze, to snoozle, to sleep, to do a doss.

**pioupiou** *sm. (P)*. Affectionate nickname for the French soldier around the turn of the century.

LE PETIT PIOU-PIOU.

**pipard** *sm. (Sl)*. Pipe smoker.

**pipe** *sf. (Sl)*. Cigarette, " gasper ".

**pipelet** *sm. (P)*. Housekeeper, *concierge*, janitor.

**pipelette** *sf. (P)*. Housekeeper (woman), *concierge* (feminine of *pipelet*).

**piper** *v. (Sl)*. To arrest, to " nab ", to " nail ".

**pipé sur le tas** *(Sl)*. To be caught red-handed.

**pipette** *sf. (Sl)*. Cigarette "gasper".

**pipo** *sm. (Sl)*. Student of *Ecole Polytechnique* in Paris.

**piqué** *adj. (P)*. Crazy, cracked.

**pique-assiette** *sm. (P)*. Parasite, sponger, bum.

**piquer** *v. (Sl)*. To steal, to pinch, to swipe. To arrest, to capture, to " nail ", to " nab ".

**piquer au truc** *(Sl)*. To try, to attempt.

**piquer dans le tas** *(P)*. To pick up at random.

**piquer le nez (se)** *(Sl)*. To booze, to tipple, to get drunk.

**piquer une crise** *(P)*. To fly into a passion, to make the fur fly, to hit the ceiling.

**piquer une sèche** *(Sl)*. To bum a cigarette.

**piquer un fard** *(P)*. To blush, to turn poppy-red.

**piquer un laïus** *(Sl)*. To make a speech.

**piquer un soleil** *(P)*. Same as : *piquer un fard*.

**piqueur** *sm. (Sl)*. Pickpocket, " picker ", " dipper ", " whiz ".

**piqueur de clopes** *(Sl)*. One who picks up discarded cigarette butts, " snipe shooter ".

**piquouse** *sf. (Sl)*. Narcotic injection, hypo, shot (in the arm).

**pisseuse** *sf. (Sl)*. Derisive term for a little girl, or a baby girl.

**piston** *sm. (P)*. Patronage, backing, backstairs influence. Student at the *Ecole Centrale*.

**pistonner** *v. (P)*. To use one's influence in s.o.'s favor, to recommend s.o. for a post, a job, etc., to "push" s.o.

**pitaine** *sm. (P)*. Same as : *capiston*.

**P.J.** *sf. (P)*. Abbr. of *Police Judiciaire* : Criminal Investigation Dept.

**placard** *sm. (Sl)*. Jail, box, "cooler", "college".

**placeur** *sm. (Sl)*. Procurer, individual who procures women for brothels.

**plafond** *sm. (Sl)*. Head, "bun", "pate".

**plaindre que la mariée est trop belle (se)** *(F)*. See : *mariée est trop belle (la)*.

UNE VRAIE PLANCHE A PAIN.

**planche à pain** *(P)*. Skinny woman (with very small and flat breast).

**planche à repasser** *(P)*. A variant of *planche à pain*.

**plancher des vaches** *sm. (P)*. *Terra firma*, land (as compared with sea ; term originally used by seamen).

**planque** *sf. (Sl)*. Hide-out, hiding place, "stash", "plant", funk-hole.

**planquer** *v. (Sl)*. To hide, to stash away.

**planquer (se)** *(Sl)*. To go into hiding, to hide.

**planter un drapeau** *(Sl)*. To go away, to decamp, without paying a debt, a bill, etc.

**plaquage** *sm. (Sl)*. Desertion, "chucking", jilting, bust-up.

**plaquer** *v. (P)*. To leave s.o. in the lurch, to throw over, to jilt, to walk out on, to abandon suddenly.

**plastronner** *v. (P)*. To be conceited, chesty, to swank it, to put on the dog, to brag, to blow one's bazoo.

**plat** *sm. (Sl)*. See : *faire du plat, en faire tout un plat*.

**plate(s) couture(s) (à)** *(P)*. See : *battre à plate(s) couture(s)*.

**plat garni** *(F)*. Plate lunch.

**plein (être)** *(Sl)*. To be drunk, tight, to be full as a fiddle, to be "plastered".

**plein aux as** *(Sl)*. To have a lot of money, to be rich, well-heeled, to be flush (of money).

**plein comme un boudin** *(Sl)*. Dead-drunk, "blotto", "cooked", "full to the brim".

**plein comme une bourrique** *(Sl)*. A variation of *plein comme un boudin*.

**plein comme un œuf** *(P)*. Full to the brim, chuck-full, jam-up. *(Sl)*. Dead-drunk, boozed up.

**plein gaz** *(P)*. See : *donner plein gaz*.

**plein le dos** *(P)*. See : *en avoir plein le dos*.

**plein ses bottes** *(Sl)*. See : *en avoir plein ses bottes*.

**pleurer comme une Madeleine** *(P)*. To shed bitter tears, to weep bitterly.

ELLE PLEURE COMME
UNE MADELEINE.

**pleurer comme un veau** *(P)*. A pop. variant of *pleurer comme une Madeleine*.

**pleurer dans le gilet de q.** *(P)*. To cry poor mouth.

**pleutre** *sm. (P)*. Contemptible individual, cad, yellow dog.

**pleuvoir comme vache qui pisse** *(Sl)*. See : *il pleut comme vache qui pisse*.

**plier bagage** *(P)*. To decamp, to dust off, to clear out.
*(Sl)*. To die, to "kick the bucket".

**plomb dans l'aile (avoir du)** *(P)*. To be severely hit, to carry the germs of a deadly disease.

**plomb dans la tête (avoir du)** *(P)*. To be staid, sedate. *Mettre du plomb dans la tête à q.*, to knock some sense into one's head.

**plombe** *sf. (Sl)*. Hour.

**pluie et le beau temps (la)** *(F)*. See : *faire la pluie et le beau temps*.

**plumard** *sm. (Sl)*. Bed, "feather(s)".

**plumer** *v. (P)*. To gyp, to skin, to fleece.

**plumes** *sf. pl. (Sl)*. Hair, "wool".

**plumet (avoir son)** *(Sl)*. Same as : *nez piqué (avoir le)*.

**plus belle fille du monde ne peut donner que ce qu'elle a (la)** *(P)*. Pop. phrase meaning that no one can be expected to do more than he possibly can.

**plus d'un tour dans son sac (avoir)** *(P)*. To have other shots in the locker, to have other tricks in one's locker.

**plus fort que de jouer au bouchon (c'est)** *(P)*. That beats the Dutch, it beats the band.

**plusieurs cordes à son arc (avoir)** *(F)*. To have several strings to one's bow, to be versatile, many-sided.

**... plus les mois de nourrice** *(P)*. Jocular catch phrase meaning that a person is older than he (or she) pretends to be. Ex. : How old is she ? - She says she is thirty. - Yeah, thirty...

*plus les mois de nourrice* (= yes, thirty... plus a bit).

**plus on est de fous, plus on rit** *(P)*. The more, the merrier ; the greater number of people, the better.

**pochard** *sm. (P)*. Drunkard, "stew", "soak", "lush", "booze-hound".

**pocher les yeux au beurre noir** *(P)*. To blacken one's eyes through hard blows, a nasty one in the eyes, to give one a "shiner", to "mouse" one's eyes.

**pochetée** *sf. (Sl)*. Silly guy, chump, dumbbell.

**pochette** *sf. (P)*. Hanky.

**pochette-surprise** *sf.* Pig in a poke.

**pogne** *sf. (Sl)*. Hand, grip, strength of hand, energy, vigor. (See : *passer la pogne*).

**pognon** *sm. (Sl)*. Same as : *galette*.

**poil (à)** *(Sl)*. Naked.

**poil (au)** *(Sl)*. Perfect, faultless, precise, accurate, on the nose. *C'est au poil,* 100 % perfect, accurate.

**poilant** *adj. (Sl)*. Exceedingly funny, very amusing, comical.

**poil dans la main (avoir un)** *(P)*. To be lazy, a lazy bum. (Often : *avoir un fameux poil dans la main*).

**poil de carotte** *(P)*. Red (carroty) hair, redhead. Nickname for a red-haired child.

**poiler (se)** *(Sl)*. A variant of *bidonner (se)*.

**poilu** *sm. (P)*. French soldier during World War I.

**point-de-côté** *(Sl)*. Creditor (particularly a hard-boiled or a troublesome one).

**pointe (avoir sa)** *(Sl)*. To be slightly drunk, to be "lit" a bit.

**pointeau** *sm. (P)*. Timekeeper in a factory.

**poire** *sf. (P)*. Victim, sugar sucker, gullible person, easy mark.
*(Sl)*. Face, "mug", "pan". Head, "bulb", "nob", "nut", "noodle".

**poireau (faire le)** *(Sl)*. A variation of *poireauter*.

**poireauter** *v. (Sl)*. To be kept waiting, to cool one's heels.

**poire est mûre (la)** *(P)*. The opportunity is ripe to be seized.

**poire pour la soif (garder une)** *(P)*. To keep something in reserve for future needs; savings, something put aside for a rainy day.

**poissard** *sm. adj. (Sl)*. Unlucky (person).

**poisse** *sf. (Sl)*. Hard luck, tough luck. (Stronger and more vulgar than *guigne*).

**poisse (avoir la)** *(Sl)*. To have tough luck, to be hoodooed. *C'est la poisse,* that's tough luck, that's a lousy break, T.S.

**poisser** *v. (Sl)*. To arrest, to capture, to "nab", to "run in".

**poisson** *sm. (Sl)*. A euphemistic variant of *maquereau : souteneur,* a prostitute's lover, man supported by a woman.

**poisson d'Avril** *(F)*. April fool ; practical or other joke on April 1.

**poivre (être)** *(Sl)*. To be drunk, to be boozy, "blotto".

**poivrer** *v. (Sl)*. To contaminate (V.D.). To intoxicate, to make one drunk.

**poivrot** *sm.* *(P)*. Drunkard, rumpot, "soak", "stew".

**polichinelle dans le tiroir (avoir un)** *(Sl)*. To be pregnant, big with child, "heir conditioned". Ex. : *Elle a un polichinelle de quatre mois (dans le tiroir)*.

**politicailleur** *sm.* *(P)*. A peanut politician.

**polka** *sf.* *(Sl)*. Woman.

**polochon** *sm.* *(P)*. Bolster.

**pommade** *sf.* *(Sl)*. Blarney, flattery, applesauce, "sugar", "oil", "banana oil", "butter", "eyewash". (See : *passer (de) la pommade*).

**pommadin** *sm.* *(Sl)*. Pej. for a hairdresser, barber.

**(pommes) frites** *sf. pl.* *(P)*. French fries.

**pompé (être)** *(Sl)*. To be completely run-down, pooped out, (after big physical strain).

**pompelard** *sm.* *(Sl)*. Fireman.

**pomper** *v.* *(Sl)*. To drink (wine, beer, liquor, etc.), to swizzle, to booze.

**pompes** *sf. pl.* *(Sl)*. Shoes, "kicks", "kickers", "dogs".

**pompette (être)** *(P)*. To be drunk, to be (half)shot, to be soused, to be tanglefooted (mainly of a woman).

**pompon** *sm.* *(P)*. *A lui le pompon !* He takes the cake !

**pompon (avoir son)** *(P)*. A variant for *pompette (être)*.

**pont (faire le)** *(F)*. To keep holiday on a working day between a legal holiday and a Sunday (or vice-versa).

**pont aux ânes** *(P)*. Problem that anybody but a fool can solve.

**ponte** *sm.* *(P)*. V.I.P., king-pin. *(Sl)*. Backer, gambler. Ex. : *Un gros ponte*, a heavy backer, gambler.

**pontifier** *v.* *(F)*. To use pompous language, to speak with pomposity.

**Popofs (les)** *sm. pl.* *(P)*. Obvious nickname for Russians, "Ruskies".

**popote** *sf.* *(P)*. "Chow", "grub". Army mess.

**popotin** *sm.* *(Sl)*. Posteriors, fanny, tail(end), pratt.

**populo** *sm.* *(Sl)*. Many people, the undistinguished crowd. Ex. : *Il y aura du populo*, there will be a crowd.

POPULO.

**porte-fafiots** *sm.* *(Sl)*. Pocketbook, wallet.

**porte-pipe** *sm.* *(Sl)*. Face, "mug".

**porter aux nues** *(F)*. To praise one excessively, to praise up to the skies.

**porter comme un charme (se)** *(F)*. To be fit as a fiddle, to be physically in perfect condition, in the pink of health, in fine fettle.

**porter la culotte** *(P)*. Said of a woman, "wearer of the pants", who is the dominant partner in a marriage, who bosses the household, who rules the home. Petticoat rule in a house.

**porter le grimpant** *(Sl)*. A pop. variant of *porter la culotte*.

**porté sur la bagatelle (être)** *(P)*. Said of a fast man or a sexually responsive woman. (See : *bagatelle*).

**porté sur le truc (être)** *(Sl)*. A variation of *porté sur la bagatelle (être)*.

**portion congrue** *(P)*. Scanty supply, hardly enough for existence. Ex. : *Etre réduit à la portion congrue*.

**portrait** *sm. (Sl)*. Face, "pan", "mug", "portrait".

**portrait tout craché (le)** *(P)*. Spitting image. Ex. : *C'est le portrait tout craché de sa mère*, she is the spit and image of her mother.

**poser** *v. (P)*. To wait, to kick one's heels. *Faire poser q.*, to keep one waiting.

**poser là cinq minutes (se)** *(Sl)*. To be strong, hefty, beefy.

**poser sa chique** *(Sl)*. To die, to "kick the bucket", to "cash in one's checks", to "lay down one's knife and fork".

**poser un lapin** *(P)*. To fail to keep a date, an appointment, to "stand up", to let one down.

**poseur de lapin** *(P)*. Person who fails to keep a date, "stander-upper".

**posséder q.** *v. (P)*. To deceive, to fool, to dupe, to double-cross one. Ex. : *On m'a possédé*, I've been had, I have been "sucked in".

**postérieur** *sm. (P)*. Fanny, seat of the pants.

**postiche** *sf. (Sl)*. Ballyhoo, outside talk (in a side show), sales talk.

**postiches** *sf. pl. (Sl)*. Street-vendor's spiel, persuasive sales talk. Ex. : *Faire des postiches aux clients*.

**posticheur** *sm. (Sl)*. Ballyhooer, "barker" in a side show (carnival) ; spieler.

**postillon** *sm. (P)*. See : *envoyer des postillons*.

**pot** *sm. (Sl)*. A drink, "shot", "snort".

**pot (avoir du)** *(Sl)*. To be lucky. *Manque de pot*, bad luck, tough luck, a lousy break.

**pot de terre contre le pot de fer (c'est le)** *(F)*. The weak against the strong.

**potache** *sm. (P)*. High school boy. In France : *collégien, lycéen*.

**potard** *sm. (P)*. Nickname for a chemist.

**potasser** *v. (P)*. To work (or study) hard, to bone up on. Ex. : *Potasser l'histoire*, to study hard history, to bone up on history.

**pot-à-tabac** *sm. (P)*. Short and stocky individual.

**pot-au-feu** *sm. adj. (P)*. Said of a stay-at-home sort of individual.

**pot-de-colle** *sm. (Sl)*. Derisive term for a person one can't get rid of.

**pote** *sm. (Sl)*. Chum, buddy.

**poteau** *sm. (Sl)*. *Mon poteau,* my dear pal.

**poteau (avoir son)** *(Sl)*. To be drunk, tight, boozy.

**poteaux** *sm. pl. (Sl)*. Thick feminine legs, unshapely legs.

**potée** *sf. (P)*. Great quantity of, oodles of.

**potin** *sm.* *(P)*. Noise, din.

**potins** *sm. pl.* *(P)*. Gossip, " scuttlebutt ", " grapevine telegraph ".

**potron-minet** *(F)*. See : *dès potron-minet*.

**poubelle** *sf.* *(P)*. Garbage can, G-can, trash can.

**poudre aux yeux (de la)** *(P)*. Bluff, " eyewash ".

**poudre de perlimpinpin** *sf.* *(P)*. Quack medicine (hence : baloney).

**poudre d'escampette** *sf.* *(F)*. Flight, escape, hasty or sudden departure, " run-out powder ".

**pou du ciel** *sm.* *(P)*. Small 'plane, sky-auto.

**pouffant** *adj.* Very amusing, funny.

**pouffer (se)** *v.* *(P)*. To laugh coarsely, to guffaw.

**pouffer de rire** *(P)*. Same as : *pouffer (se)*.

**pouffiasse** *sf.* *(Sl)*. Abusive term for a woman of loose morals, " blimp ", floozey.

**pouilleux** *sm. adj.* *(P)*. Crumby, crummy, bummy, lousy.

**poulailler** *sm.* *(P)*. Top gallery in a theater, " chicken roost ", " nigger heaven ". (Same as : *paradis*).

**poule** *sf.* *(Sl)*. Derisive term for a girl, a woman. A loose woman, " tomato ", " broad ".

**poule (la)** *sf.* *(Sl)*. Police.

**poule aux œufs d'or (la)** *(F)*. The goose that lays the golden eggs.

**poule à chanter devant le coq (ce n'est pas à la)** *(P)*. Pop. phrase meaning that a wife should not lay down the law for her husband.

**poule mouillée** *(P)*. Sissy, fraidy cat, scaredy-cat, milquetoast.

**poulet** *sm.* *(P)*. Jocularly or ironically : love letter, *billet-doux* (to a girl, a woman). Often, by antiphrasis : an unpleasant letter, a complaint, a request for payment from a creditor or a tax-collector.
*(Sl)*. Detective, plain-clothes man, cop, Dick, " slapman ".

**poulette** *sf.* *(Sl)*. Sarcastic term for a young woman, a girl, bunny, chick, baby. Also : pretty young thing.

**pouliche** *sf.* *(Sl)*. Filly. Humorously pej. term for a woman, a girl, " tomato ", " broad ", " bunny ", " flossy ".

**poupée** *sf.* *(Sl)*. Woman, prostitute, " tomato ". (Same as : *pépée*).

**poupoule** *sf.* *(P)*. Darling.

**pour des pruneaux** *(P)*. Same as : *pour des prunes*.

**pour des prunes** *(P)*. For mighty little (or practically for nothing).

**pour en finir** *(F)*. To get it over with.

**pour la bonne bouche** *(F)*. *Garder pour la bonne bouche,* to leave something nice for the last bite, to keep a tidbit for a finish.

**pour la gloire** *(F)*. For nothing (at all). Ex. : *Nous ne travaillons pas pour la gloire.*

**pour le roi de Prusse** *(F)*. For nothing (at all), for shucks. Ex. : *Je ne veux pas travailler pour le roi de Prusse,* I won't work for nothing.

**pour ses frais** *(F)*. See : *en être pour ses frais.*

**pour tout potage** *(P)*. All told, in all.

**pour une bouchée de pain** *(P)*. For a mere song. Ex. : *Il a eu*

*cette maison pour une bouchée de pain,*
he got this house for a song.

**pousse-au-crime** *sm. (Sl).* Strong
liquor, knock-out drop.

**pousse-café** *sm. (P).* Small cup
of brandy taken after coffee, a chaser,
a digester.

**pousse-cailloux** *sm. (P).* Infantryman.

**pousser à la roue** *(P).* To help
along, to work hard to achieve success
of an undertaking.

**pousser des cris de paon** *(P).*
To scream out, to raise an outcry.

**pousser du col (se)** *(P).* To
boast, to get a swelled head, to put on
side.

**poussières** *sf. pl. (P).* Said
mainly of a small supplementary
amount of francs that is added to a
basic (big) amount. Ex. : *Cent mille
francs et des poussières,* 100.000 and
a few francs.

**pouvoir se fouiller** *(P).* Same
as : *pouvoir toujours courir.*

**pouvoir toujours courir** *(P).*
*Tu peux toujours courir !* Fling at
one : Nothing doing ! You won't get
it ! You can whistle for it !

**prêcher à un sourd** *(P).* To
pour water over a duck's back. (Said
of an action that has no effect).

**prêcher dans le désert** *(P).*
Same as : *prêcher à un sourd.*

**préchi-précha** *sm. (P).* Extend-
ed or endless speech, talk, lecture,
debate, etc., talkathon, "blabfest".
Talkative speaker.

**première** *sf. (P).* First salesgirl in
a fashion or haute-couture shop.

**première (de)** *(Sl).* Excellent,
A N° 1, first-rate, classy.

**premier venu (le)** *sm. (P).*
Anybody, anyone. *Ce n'est pas le premier venu,* he isn't a mere nobody.

**prendre à la rigolade** *(P).* Not
to take seriously, to laugh it off.

**prendre de la bouteille** *(P).*
To become older, to age.

**prendre de la graine (en)**
*(F).* To take pattern by s.o., to follow
one's example.

**prendre des gants** *(F).* To
handle with much tact.

**prendre la balle au bond** *(F).*
Same as : *saisir la balle au bond.*

**prendre la clé des champs**
*(P).* Same as : *prendre la poudre
d'escampette.*

**prendre la goutte** *(P).* To drink
a small cup of liquor, to have a
"bracer".

**prendre la mouche** *(P).* To get
miffed, to get one's dander up.

**prendre la poudre d'escam-
pette** *(P).* To flee, to escape, to
scram, to decamp.

**prendre la tangente** *(Sl).* To
leave hurriedly, to scram, to "take it
on the lam", to "beat it".

**prendre le large** *(P).* To leave,
to decamp, to clear out, to duck out.

**prendre le taureau par les
cornes** *(P).* To take the bull by the
horns.

**prendre mesure d'un paletot
de sapin** *(Sl).* To die, to "put on a
wooden overcoat".

**prendre pour q. (se)** *(P).* To
think no small beer of oneself, to be
all swelled up with oneself, to be pretentious, haughty, a "stuffed shirt",
conceited, arrogant, setting full value
on oneself.

**prendre q. ch. pour argent comptant** *(P)*. To take a thing for sure(-fire stuff).

**prendre q. ch. pour son grade** *(P)*. A variant of *prendre q. ch. pour son rhume.*

**prendre q. ch. pour son rhume** *(P)*. To get a raking over the coals, to get a bawling-out, a severe panning.

**prendre q. ch. sous son bonnet** *(P)*. To take something into one's head, (imagine it).

**prendre q. en grippe** *(P)*. To take a dislike to one.

**prendre q. la main dans le sac** *(P)*. To catch one in the very act, to catch one red-handed.

**prendre ses cliques et ses claques** *(P)*. To take one's traps (one's personal belongings), to go away, to leave, to "take a powder", to "clear out".

**prendre ses jambes à son cou** *(P)*. To scram, to "take it on the lam".

**prendre son courage à deux mains** *(P)*. To pluck up courage.

**prendre un billet de parterre** *(P)*. To fall, to come a cropper, to take a spill.

BILLET DE PARTERRE.

**prendre une cuite** *(Sl)*. To get drunk, boozy.

**prendre une culotte** *(Sl)*. To lose big money (at gambling). To get drunk, tight.

**près de ses sous (être)** *(P)*. To be tight-fisted.

**presto** *adv. (P)*. Very quickly, as speedily as possible, like a streak of greased lightning.

**prétentiard** *adj. (Sl)*. Pompous (style or person).

**prêter à la petite semaine** *(F)*. Said of a loan shark who loans (lends) money at high weekly interest.

**primeur** *sf. (Sl)*. Virginity.

**prise (être)** *(Sl)*. To be pregnant, " knocked up ".

**prise de bec** *sf. (P)*. Spat, quarrel, violent argument.

**P.R.L.** Abbr. of *Parti Républicain de la Liberté,* French political party, right wing.

**pro** *sm. (P)*. Professional, pro.

**prof** *sm. (Sl)*. Professor, schoolmaster.

**profonde** *sf. (Sl)*. Pocket, "kick", " poke ".

**prolo** *sm. (Sl)*. Proletarian.

**promener (se)** *(P)*. To be lying around, to be kicking around. Ex. : *J'ai vu un livre qui se promenait par ici,* I saw a book kicking around here somewhere.

**prophète de malheur** *(P)*. Calamity Joe, Calamity Jane.

**propos de botte(s) (à)** *(P)*. Without rhyme or reason.

**proposer la botte** *(Sl)*. To proposition.

**proprio** *sm.* *(Sl)*. Owner, proprietor.

**propriote** *sf.* *(Sl)*. Owner (female), proprietress.

**prune** *sf.* *(Sl)*. Ticket given by a traffic policeman. *Coller une prune,* to give a ticket.

**pruneau** *sm.* *(Sl)*. Severe hit, hard hit, " Sunday punch ". Pistol bullet, " hot lead ", " Kentucky pill ". *Envoyer un pruneau dans la peau,* to send one a bullet, to " slip one the heat ".

**prunes (des)** *sf. pl.* *(Sl)*. Nothing (at all), " nix ".

**puce à l'oreille (mettre la)** *(P)*. To make one aware of, to awaken one's suspicions.

**puceau** *sm.* *(P)*. Virgin young man.

**pucelage** *sm.* *(Sl)*. Maidenhood, virginity.

**pucier** *sm.* *(Sl)*. A lousy or filthy bed, " fleabag ".

**puçot** *sm.* *(Sl)*. Another way of spelling *puceau.*

**puer** *v.* *(P)*. To stink strongly.

**punaise** *sf.* *(P)*. Term of contempt for a bad woman, a bad girl. Shrew.

**punaise de sacristie** *(P)*. Disparaging term for an exceedingly devout woman.

**purée** *sf.* *(Sl)*. Great poverty, " tight corner ", fix. *Etre dans la purée,* to be busted, broke.

**purge** *sf.* *(Sl)*. Beating, " shellacking ", a " dose of strap oil ".

**purotin** *sm.* *(Sl)*. Poor, hard-up fellow ; man always in the pinches, " broker ", bum.

**putain** *sf.* *(F)*. Prostitute, " hooker ", whore, bitch, harlot.

# Q

**qu'à cela ne tienne !** *(F)*. Never mind !

**quand le bâtiment va, tout va !** *(P)*. Semi-proverbial saying meaning that flourishing building trade entails prosperity in all other branches of the country's industries.

**quand les poules auront des dents** *(F)*. When the cows give beer, hence : never.

**quand on parle du loup on en voit la queue** *(F)*. Talk of the devil and he is sure to appear.

**quarante** *sf.* *(Sl)*. Street-vendor's table.

**quart** *sm.* *(Sl)*. Police station, commissariat

**quart de brie** *sm.* *(Sl)*. Derisive term for a big nose, "honker", big "schnozzle".

**quart d'heure (pour le)** *(P)*. For the moment, for the time being.

**quart d'heure de Rabelais** *(P)*. Great fix, predicament, difficult moment.

**quart (d'œil)** *(Sl)*. Police commissioner in Paris.

**quatre à quatre** *(F)*. Very quickly, p. d. q., pretty damn quick.

**quatre pattes (à)** *(F)*. On all fours.

**quatrième vitesse (en)** *(F)*. As fast as your legs can carry you, faster than greased lightning, lickety-split.

**quatt'crans** *(Sl)*. Very strict sergeant or any non-commissioned officer who often threatens "*quatre crans*". Ex. : *j'vais te foutre quatt'crans!* (See : *cran*).

**quel culot !** *(Sl)*. I like your nerve ! Some cheek ! Some gall !

**quelle mouche te pique ?** *(F)*. What's eating you ?

— 161 —

**quelque chose dans le ventre (avoir)** *(P)*. To have talent, to have the goods.

**quelque chose de soigné** *(P)*. Dandy, anything first class. (Used mainly sarcastically). Ex. : *Une rossée, quelque chose de soigné,* a first-class licking, a very thorough thrashing.

**quelqu'un** *(P)*. Capable man, hep guy, someone who excels, "big potato". Ex. : *Ce type est quelqu'un,* this guy is an ace.

**quelqu'un dans la peau (avoir)** *(Sl)*. To be madly in love with s.o., to love s.o. with passion, with violent love. Ex. : *Elle l'avait dans la peau.*

**quémander** *v. (F)*. To cadge.

**quenotte** *sf. (F)*. Dimin. for a tooth, a child's tooth.

**que pouic** *(Sl)*. Nothing (at all).

**qu'es-aco ?** Joc. for : *qu'est-ce que c'est que cela ?* What's that ? What's the idea ?

**que tu dis !** *(Sl)*. Sez you !

**queue** *sf*. See : *faire la queue, faire des queues, il n'en reste pas la queue d'un.*

**queue de cervelas** *(Sl)*. Daily walk of convicts in the prison yard.

**queue de pie** *(P)*. Dress coat, tails.

**queue de poisson** *(P)*. Among autoists : tail-wobble.

**quilles** *sf. pl.* Another variant of *guibolles.*

**quimper** *v. (Sl)*. To arrest, to "nab".

**quinquets** *sm. pl. (P)*. Eyes, "blinkers", "peekers".

**quiqui** *sm. (P)*. Throat, guzzle.

**qui se fait brebis le loup le mange** *(F)*. He who is too confiding is easily imposed upon.

**quitte pour la peur** *(F)*. See : *en être quitte pour la peur.*

# R

**rab** *sm. (Sl).* Short for *rabiot.*

**rabattre le caquet de q. q.**
*(F).* To take one down a notch or two,
(a peg or two), to check an arrogant
or conceited person.

**rabibochage** *sm. (P).* Reconcilia-
tion.

**rabibocher (se)** *v. (P).* To
make it up, to get reconciled, to become
friends again.

**rabiot** *sm. (Sl).* Surplus food,
surplus profit, etc. Overtime (in office,
factory) or extra period of military
service.

**rabioter** *v. (Sl).* To manage to
get surplus food, surplus profit (or any
special advantage on top of one's normal share).

**rabougri** *adj. (F).* Runty.

**racaille** *sf. (P).* The rabble, mob,
riffraff, the rough part of the popula-
tion.

**raccourcir** *v. (Sl).* To execute by
guillotine, to guillotine.

**raccrocher** *v. (Sl).* To " hook ",
to solicit men in the street (said of a
prostitute, a " hooker ").

**raclée** *sf. (Sl).* Beating, licking,
" shellacking ", a " dose of strap oil ".

**racler** *v. (Sl).* To shave.

**racloir** *sm. (Sl).* Razor.

**raclure** *sf. (Sl).* Strong abuse for
a lowclass woman.

**racoler** *v. (F).* To hustle (customers).

**racoleur** *sm. (P).* Steerer, hustler.

**racontars** *sm. pl. (F).* Old wives'
tales.

**radin** *adj. (Sl).* Cheap screw, pinchpenny, cheap skate.

**radiner** *v. (Sl).* To show up, to
turn up, to come back.

**radis (des)** *sm. pl. (Sl).* Nothing, nope, not a cent.

**radis (pas un)** *(Sl).* Not a cent, not a plugged nickel.

**radoter** *v. (P).* To drivel, to dote.

**raffoler de** *(F).* To be nuts over.

**raffut** *sm. (P).* Noise, row, rumpus, rookus, " hell ".

**raffut (faire du)** *(P).* To make the fur fly, to raise hell.

**rafistoler** *v. (P).* To patch up.

**rafle** *sf. (P).* Roundup, dragnet.

**rafler** *v. (Sl).* To arrest, to " nab ".

**ragots** *sm. pl. (P).* Old wives' tales.

**ragougnasse** *sf. (Sl).* Inferior food, slipslop.

**raidard** *adj. (Sl). Etre raidard,* to be stone-broke. (Same as : *être raide, fauché*).

**raide** *sm. (Sl).* 1.000-franc bill. Brandy, booze, very strong liquor. Ex. : *boire du raide,* to drink strong liquor.

**raide** *adj. (P).* Stiff. Ex. : *C'est un peu raide !* That's a bit steep ! a bit stiff !

**raide (être)** *(Sl).* To be drunk, to be boozy, tight. To be broke (stone-broke). See further : *raide comme un passe-lacet.*

**raide comme la justice** *(Sl).* A variant of *raide comme un passe-lacet.*

**raide comme un passe-lacet** *(Sl).* To be broke, clean broke, " cleaned up ".

**raisonner comme une pantoufle** *(P).* To argue, to reason, incorrectly, absurdly, to no purpose.

**raisonner comme un sabot** *(P).* A variant of *raisonner comme une pantoufle.*

**raisonner comme un tambour mouillé** *(P).* Another variant of *raisonner comme une pantoufle.*

**râler** *v. (Sl).* To bellyache, to gripe.

**râleur** *sm. (Sl).* Fault-finder, bellyacher, griper, sorehead.

**râleuse** *sf. (Sl).* Feminine form of *râleur.*

**rallonge** *sf. (P).* Complement, addition, supplement, " rider ", anything added to the main body.

**ramasser** *v. (Sl).* To arrest, to " nab ", to " haul in ", to " run in ". To reprimand, to scold, to blow up, to bawl out.

**ramasser (se)** *(P).* To stand up, to rise (after a fall).

**ramasser à la cuillère (à)** *(P).* Dead tired, dog-tired, dogged out.

**ramasser une bûche** *(P).* To fall, to come a cropper, to take a flop, to take a spill.

JEUNE HOMME
RAMASSANT UNE BUCHE.

**ramasser une pelle** *(P).* Same as : *ramasser une bûche.*

**ramasser une veste** *(P)*. To suffer a defeat, to be " sent Salt River ".

**ramasseur de clopes** *(Sl)*. Man who picks up cigarette butts in the street, " snipe shooter ".

**ramolli** *adj. (P)*. Pop. variant of the slangy *ramollo(t)*.

**ramollo(t)** *adj. (Sl)*. *Vieux ramollo(t)*, old dodo, old dodderer.

**ramoner** *v. (Sl)*. To scold, to reprimand, to bawl out.

**rampant** *sm. adj. (P)*. Military slang word for a man on ground duty, not qualified for flying service, " kiwi ".

**ramponneau** *sm. (Sl)*. Heavy blow, " Sunday punch ", lick, " sock ", " paste ", " biff ", " punch on the snoot ", a " sock " in the jaw, " haymaker ".

RAMPONNEAU.

**rapapilloter** *v. (P)*. To reconcile people (after disagreement, quarrel, etc.)

**râpé** *sm. (P)*. Grated cheese.

**rapiat** *sm. adj. (P)*. Miser, stingy individual, " lickpenny ", " cheap screw ", " cheap skate ".

**rapiate** *sf. adj. (P)*. Feminine form of *rapiat* : close-fisted, stingy woman.

**rapido** *adv. (P)*. Very quickly, lickety-quick, p. d. g.

**rapin** *sm. (P)*. Nickname for a young or mediocre painter, dauber.

RAPIN EN PLEIN BOULOT.

**raplapla** *adj. (P)*. Exhausted, tired(out), pooped(out), bushed, faded to a frazzle.

**rappliquer** *v. (Sl)*. To turn up, to come back.

**rapporter** *v. (P)*. To tell on s.o., to snitch.

**raquettes** *sf. pl. (Sl)*. Feet, " dogs ".

**raser** *v. (P)*. To bore s.o. stiff, to tire s.o. to death.

**rasoir** *sm. adj. (P)*. A person that is a bore (or a nuisance). *Il est rasoir, ce qu'il peut être rasoir !* he is an awful bore, what a bore ! Something extremely dull and boring.

**rat (petit)** *sm. (F)*. Very young ballet girl at the Opera.

**rat** *adj. (Sl)*. Same as : *radin*. Ex. : *Il est d'un rat !* What a miser he is !

**rata** *sm. (P)*. See : *rata(touille)*.

**rata(touille)** *sf. (P)*. Mulligan, slipslop, slumgullion.
*(Sl)*. Beating, licking, thrashing.

**rater** *v. (P)*. To miss (out), to muff, to get off to a bum start. Ex. : *Rater son coup,* to muff one's shot.

**rater le coche** *(P)*. See : *manquer le coche*.

**ratiboiser** *v. (P)*. To chisel out of, to gyp, to gyp out of.

**ratichon** *sm. (Sl)*. Catholic priest, " galaway ", holy Joe.

**ratisser** *v. (P)*. To gyp out of, to chisel, to flimflam out of.

**rayer de ses papiers** *(F)*. A coll. variant of *rayer de ses tablettes*.

**rayer de ses tablettes** *(F)*. To write off, to consider as lost, to give up. *Rayez-moi de vos tablettes !* count me out !

**raz-de-marée** *sm. (P)*. Landslide (in politics), a sudden and sensational triumph of a political party at an election.

**rebiffer au truc** *(Sl)*. Same as : *repiquer au truc*.

**recalé** *adj. (P)*. Flunked, "failed".

**recaler** *v. (P)*. To plough, to " fail out " one at an exam.

**réceptionniste** *sm. sf. (F)*. Room-clerk (hotel).

**recevoir des pommes cuites** *(P)*. Said of bad actors who are booed and hissed. U.S. equivalent : to get the bird (Bronx cheer). (Sound made with the lips to demonstrate disgust, displeasure or disapproval).

**recevoir q. comme un chien dans un jeu de quilles** *(F)*. To give a very cold or bad reception.

**recevoir son paquet** *(P)*. To get a bawling out, a thrashing. *Il a reçu son paquet,* he got his comeuppance.

**recevoir un coup de bambou** *(P)*. To become crazy, cracked.

**réchauffé (du)** *adj. (P)*. Something rehashed.

**recta** *adv. (P)*. Correctly, punctually.

**reculer pour mieux sauter** *(P)*. To step back in order to jump all the farther (meaning figuratively : to hesitate in making an unpleasant decision one will necessarily have to make sooner or later).

**redorer son blason** *(F)*. To restore one's former fortune. (Said mainly of a man of noble birth who marries a wealthy girl beneath his social standing).

**redresse (à la)** *(Sl)*. *Un type à la redresse,* a hep guy, hep ghee.

**refaire** *v. (P)*. To trick, to dupe, to " fool, to swindle, to do s.o., to " suck in ".

**refaire (se)** *v. (P)*. To regain one's strength (physically or financially).

**refiler** *v. (Sl)*. To palm off s. th. on s.o., to give, to hand over. Ex. : *On m'a refilé un faux billet,* I have been given a phoney bill.

**refroidi** *sm. (Sl)*. Corpse, " stiff ",

**refroidir** *v. (P).* To throw cold water on.
*(Sl).* To kill, to "erase", to "wipe out", to bump off.

**régaler** *v. (P).* To entertain, to feast s.o.

**regarder** *v. (P).* See : *Tu ne m'as pas regardé !*

**regarder en chiens de faïence (se)** *(P).* To stare at each other.

**réglé comme un papier de musique** *(P).* Very punctual, regular.

**règles (dans les)** *(P).* Fair and square.

**régulier** *adj. (P).* Correct.

**régulière** *sf. (Sl). Sa régulière,* one's lawful wife.

**reins solides (avoir les)** *(P).* To be financially strong.

CE GARS A LES REINS SOLIDES.

**relever le gant** *(P).* To accept a challenge.

**reluquer** *v. (P).* To keep looking at s.o. or s. th. To eye, to ogle s.o. or s. th. To observe.

**rembarrer q.** *v. (P).* To bawl out, to tell off.

**rembourré avec des noyaux de pêches** *(P).* Joc. phrase meaning anything very hard.

**remède de bonne-femme** *(P).* Old folk cure, old wives' cure.

**remède contre l'amour** *(P).* Ugly woman (girl), ugly face.

**remercier** *v. (P).* To dismiss, to sack, to fire one.

**remettre ça** *v. (P).* To start again, to repeat.

**remettre q. à sa place** *(P).* To put one in his (her) place, to put one back where he belongs.

**rempiler** *v. (P).* To re-enlist (army).

**remplir (se)** *v. (Sl).* To get rich, to amass a fortune.

**remplumer (se)** *v. (P).* To regain health.

**remporter une veste** *(P).* To fail, to be defeated at election, to be "sent Salt River".

**remuer ciel et terre** *(F).* To leave no stone unturned.

**remuer l'argent à la pelle** *(P).* To have money to burn.

**renâcler à la besogne** *(P).* To shirk one's work.

**rendez-vous** *sm. (P).* Hangout. Ex. : *Rendez-vous des clochards,* hangout of hobos, hobos' joint.

**rendre à q. la monnaie de sa pièce** *(P).* To give one his comeuppance, to pay out, to pay one back (in his own coin).

**rendre son tablier** *(P).* To resign from one's post, to give up (throw up) one's job, to walk out.

**rengaine** *sf. (P).* Tiresome repetition, old story. Ex. : *Toujours la même rengaine,* always the same old story.

**reniflette** *sf. (Sl).* Cocaine.

**rentrer bredouille** *(P).* To come home empty-handed (said of a sportsman, or of a hunter).

**rentrer dans la gueule** *(Sl).* To hit hard in the face, on the nose, to beat up, to administer rough treatment to.

**rentrer dans le chou à q.** *(Sl).* To attack s.o., to pitch into, to sock into one.

**rentrer dans le décor** *(Sl).* Said of a driver who collides with a lamp-post, a wall, a house, etc. causing material damage.

CIEL ! JE SUIS RENTRÉ
DANS LE DÉCOR !

**rentrer dans le lard** *(Sl).* To hit hard, to sail into.

**rentrer dans le portrait** *(Sl).* To hit hard in the face, " sock in the pan ".

**rentrer dans sa coquille** *(P).* To draw in one's horns, to withdraw into one's shell.

**renversant** *adj. (P).* Staggering, stunning.

**renverser la vapeur** *(P).* To stop and reverse steam, to change over.

**renvoyer la balle** *(P).* To retort promptly.

**repapilloter** *v. (P).* To reconcile people (after quarrel, disagreement, etc.).

**repapilloter (se)** *v. (P).* To get reconciled, to kiss and make up.

**repêchage** *sm. (F).* A second-chance exam. for those who failed previously.

**repêcher** *v. (F).* To give a second chance (at exam.).

**repiquer** *v. (Sl).* To retake, to recapture.

**repiquer au truc** *(Sl).* To start over again, to repeat, to re-enlist.

**replâtrage** *sm. (P).* Patched-up peace (which usually can't last).

**répondre du tac au tac** *(P).* To make a prompt (flashing) retort, to retaliate blow for blow, to give tit for tat.

**répondre en Normand** *(F).* To give a canny, shrewd, evasive answer (neither affirmative nor negative).

**réponse à tout (avoir)** *(P).* To have always a ready retort.

**réponse de Normand** *(F).* Canny, shrewd, equivocal or evasive answer. (See also : *répondre en Normand*).

**réponse du berger à la bergère (la)** *(P).* Decisive (or conclusive) point in an argument, a " clencher ", a " corker ".

**repousser** *v. (Sl).* To stink, to " hum ", to smell strongly.

**repousser du goulot** *(Sl).* To have strong halitosis.

**repoussoir** *sm. (P)*. Foil to one's beauty.

**reprendre du poil de la bête** *(P)*. To react, to regain advantage over.

**reprendre le collier (de misère)** *(P)*. To resume work, to get back to drudgery, after a period of rest, such as vacation, holiday, weekend, etc.

**requin** *sm. (P)*. Shark, swindler.

**requinquer** *v. (Sl)*. To buck up, to spruce up, to perk up.

**requinquer (se)** *(Sl)*. To pick up, to recover, to restore one's health, to perk up.

**respectueuse** *sf. (Sl)*. Prostitute.

**respirette** *sf. (Sl)*. Cocaine.

**resquille** *sf. (Sl)*. Gate-crashing, getting into a theater, movie, party, etc. without a ticket or an invitation, wangling.

**resquiller** *v. (Sl)*. To crash the gate, to chisel, to wangle.

**resquilleur** *sm. (Sl)*. Gate-crasher, person who gets into a theater, party, etc. without a ticket or invitation. Uninvited guest, chiseler, wangler.

**ressembler comme deux gouttes d'eau (se)** *(P)*. To be as much alike as two peas.

**rester court** *(P)*. To be nonplused, squelched.

**rester en carafe** *(Sl)*. To get stuck, to be left in the lurch.

**rester en plan** *(P)*. Same as : *rester en carafe.*

**rester sur le carreau** *(P)*. To be left high and dry, to be left dead on the field. (Used often fig.).

**rester (tout) pantois** *(P)*. To be astounded, astonished, flabbergasted.

**resucée** *sf. (Sl)*. Renewal, starting over again.

**rétamé** *adj. (Sl)*. Drunk, " plastered ".

**retaper** *v. (P)*. To renovate, to touch up, to buck up.

**retaper (se)** *v. (P)*. To recover, to pick up again.

**retire ton blair de là que je voie la Tour Eiffel** *(Sl)*. Fling at one with a prominent nose.

**retoquer** *v. (Sl)*. Same as : *recaler.*

**retourner le fer dans la plaie** *(P)*. To rub it in, to rake up unpleasant memories.

**retourner sa veste** *(P)*. To change one's opinion, to bolt one's party.

**revenir à la charge** *(P)*. To renew obstinately an effort, an attempt, a demand, etc.

**revenir à ses moutons** *(F)*. *Revenons à nos moutons,* let us go back to the subject. This semi-proverbial phrase is taken from the old French comedy, *la Farce de Maître Pathelin.*

**revenir bredouille** *(P)*. See : *rentrer bredouille.*

**revenir de loin** *(P)*. To have escaped a great danger, to recover from a severe illness.

**revenir de Pontoise (avoir l'air de)** *(P)*. Said of an absentminded or day-dreaming person.

**revoyure (à la)** *(P)*. Slang term of farewell : See you later ! see you later, alligator ! see you in church !

**revue (être de la)** *(P)*. To be done for, to be washed out, to be done up brown. Ex. : *Il est encore de la revue !* he has been " done " again !

**ribambelle** *sf. (P)*. Scads of, oodles of, large order, a heap of, slathers.

**ribote** *sf. (Sl)*. Drinking bout, booze-up, binge.

**ribouis** *sm. (Sl)*. Shoe (of inferior quality).

**ribouldingue** *sf. (Sl)*. Drunken spree, binge, big soak, hellraising, high-jinks, booze-fest.

**ribouldinguer** *v. (Sl)*. To go on a drunken spree, on a binge.

**Ricains (les)** *sm. pl. (Sl)*. Americans, Yankees.

**richard** *sm. (P)*. Wealthy man. *Un gros richard,* a zillionaire, " plute ".

**riche comme Crésus** *(F)*. Same as : *cousu d'or.*

**rideau !** *(P)*. Shut up ! button your face ! lay off !

**rien à chiquer !** *(Sl)*. Nothing doing ! No soap !

DEUX SOUS LE MÊME RIFLARD.

**rien à faire !** *(P)*. Nothing doing ! No soap !

**rififi** *sm. (Sl)*. Scuffle, free-for-all, fracas, " fireworks ".

**riflard** *sm. (P)*. Umbrella.

**riflette** *sf. (Sl)*. War, " fracas ".

**rigolade** *sf. (Sl)*. Amusement, fun, merry-making, hearty laugh, joke. (Said of anything that cannot be taken seriously). *C'est de la rigolade !* That's a joke ! *Ce n'est pas de la rigolade !* It's serious business, no laughing matter !

**rigolard** *adj. (Sl)*. Funny, comical.

**rigolboche** *adj. (Sl)*. An occasional variant of *rigolo.*

**rigoler** *v. (Sl)*. To laugh, to joke.

**rigolo** *sm. (Sl)*. Funny guy. Revolver, " oscar ", rod, " equalizer ".

**rigolo** *adj. (Sl)*. Funny, amusing.

**rigolote** *adj. (Sl)*. Feminine form of : *rigolo adj.* (see this word).

**rigouillard** *adj. (Sl)*. Very amusing, very funny.

**rincé** *adj.* Exhausted, dog-tired, frazzled, deadbeat, (syn. in French sl. : *flapi, sur les genoux, sur les rotules, lessivé*). Dead-broke.

**rince-cochon** *sm. (Sl)*. A glass of mineral water after a heavy drinking party.

**rincée** *sf. (Sl)*. Beating-up, licking, " shellacking ".

**rincer la dalle (se)** *(Sl)*. To drink (wine, beer, liquor, etc.).

**rincer l'œil (se)** *(P)*. To eye something with particular pleasure (especially a girl's or a woman's charms), to get an " eyeful ".

**rincette** *sf. (Sl)*. A variation of *pousse-café.*

**ripaille** *sf.* *(P)*. See : *faire ripaille.*

**ripailler** *v.* *(Sl)*. Same as : *faire ripaille.*

**ripatonner** *v.* *(Sl)*. To foot it, to hike, to walk.

**ripatons** *sm. pl.* *(Sl)*. Feet, "purps", "dogs".

**ripincelle** *sm.* *(Sl)*. Another spelling for *riz-pain-sel.*

**riquiqui** *sm.* *(Sl)*. Diminutive person. The little finger, "pinky". Low-grade brandy.

**rire à la barbe de q.** *(P)*. Same as : *rire au nez de q.*

**rire au nez de q.** *(P)*. To laugh in one's face.

**rire aux anges** *(F)*. Said of a baby who smiles sweetly in its sleep.

**rire (rigoler) comme un bossu** *(P)*. To have a belly-laugh, to laugh heartily.

**rire dans sa barbe** *(P)*. To laugh in one's sleeve.

**rire jaune** *(P)*. To laugh out on the wrong side of the mouth.

**rire sous cape** *(P)*. To snicker, to snigger, to chuckle.

**risquer le paquet** *(P)*. To chance it.

**risquer le tout pour le tout** *(P)*. Same as : *risquer le paquet.*

**risquer un œil** *(P)*. Jocular phrase meaning : to have a looksee (usually at some suggestive or *risqué* scene).

**risque-tout** *sm.* *(P)*. Daredevil, break-neck.

**Ritals (les)** *sm. pl.* *(Sl)*. Italians, "Eyeties".

**river son clou à q.** *(P)*. To silence one, to compel silence, to give one a decisive answer, a squelch. (Syn.: *clouer le bec à q.*).

**riz-pain-sel** *sm.* *(P)*. Nickname for a soldier employed in a Commissariat.

**rodomont** *sm.* *(P)*. See : *faire le rodomont.*

**roberts** *sm. pl.* *(Sl)*. A woman's breasts, "ninnies", "titties".

**rogaton** *sm.* *(Sl)*. Worthless thing, junk. In plural : leftovers (food).

**Roger-Bontemps** *sm.* *(P)*. Good-time Charley.

**rogne** *(P)*. Anger, rage, temper. Ex. : *Ça me met en rogne,* that's what makes me angry, that's what gives me a pain in the neck.

**rogne (être en)** *(P)*. To be angry, mad, in an ugly mood.

**roi de Prusse (travailler pour le)** *(P)*. See : *travailler pour le roi de Prusse.*

**roman de concierge** *(P)*. Dime-novel, cheap novel.

**romanichel** *sm.* *(P)*. Vagrant gipsy.

**rombière** *sf.* *(Sl)*. Derogatory term for a woman. *Une vieille rombière,* an old woman, an old trout.

**rompre les oreilles à q.** *(P)*. Same as : *casser les oreilles à q.*

**ronchonner** *v.* *(P)*. To grumble, to gripe, to chew the rag, to chew the fat.

**ronchonneur** *sm.* *(P)*. Ill-humored complainer, grumbler, griper, "belcher", "hollerer".

**ronchonnot** *sm.* *(P)*. Old griper, old belcher.

**rond** *sm. (Sl).* Five-centime coin, nickel.

**rond (être)** *(Sl)*. To be drunk, to be " plastered ", to be " jagged up ".

**rond-de-cuir** *sm. (P).* Nickname for a government clerk, esp. for one who likes routine office work.

**rond-de-cuirisme** *sm. (P).* Red tape.

**rondins** *sm. pl. (Sl).* Breasts. *Une belle paire de rondins.*

**rondouillard** *sm. adj. (P).* Short and stockish fellow.

**ronfler** *v. (P).* Same as : *gazer. Ça ronfle,* it's going all right, everything is working smoothly.
*(Sl).* To sleep, to do a doss.

**ronflette** *sf. (Sl).* Nap, snooze, forty winks.

**ronger les sangs (se)** *(P).* To worry a lot, to eat one's heart out.

**ronger son frein** *(P).* To control, to repress one's feeling, one's impatience ; to fret oneself.

**roploplos** *sm. pl. (Sl).* Woman's breasts, " ninnies ".

**roquet** *sm. (P).* Dog, pooch.

**rossard** *sm. adj. (Sl).* Bad guy, skunk.

**rosse** *sf. (P).* Inferior horse, a palooka.

**rosse** *adj. (Sl).* Nasty, mean (person), mean, low-down (trick).

**rossée** *sf. (P).* Beating, licking, " shellacking ".

**rosser** *q. v. (P).* To beat, to thrash, to dust one's jacket, to tan one's hide.

**rosserie** *sf. (P).* Mean or nasty trick, action, or remark.

**rossignol** *sm. (Sl).* Unsaleable goods (usually old or shopsoiled). Skeleton key.

**rot** *sm. (Sl).* Burp.

**roter** *v. (Sl).* To burp.

**rotin** *sm. (Sl).* Five centimes, one *sou.* See : *pas un rotin*).

**rôtir le balai** *(Sl)*. To kick over the traces, to lead a dissipated, dissolute life.

**rôtir le cuir (se)** *(Sl).* To sunbathe.

**rotoplots** *sm. pl. (Sl).* Woman's breasts, " ninnies ", " titties ".

**roublard** *sm. adj. (P).* Foxy, tricky, shifty, an unusually shrewd person, slicker.

**roublardise** *sf. (P).* Trickery, craftiness.

**roue (faire la)** *(P).* To show off, to strut.

**rouflaquette** *sf. (Sl).* Comma-shaped lock of hair stuck on temple. Also : side-whiskers, burnsides.

**roulant** *adj. (P).* Very funny, comical.

**roulante (cuisine)** *sf. (P).* Rolling field kitchen, bean gun.

**rouleau** *sm. (P).* See : *au bout de son rouleau.*

**rouler** *v. (P).* To best s.o., to cheat, to gyp, to rook.
*(Sl).* To lead a loose life, to prostitute oneself.

**rouler (se les)** *(Sl)*. To laze, to shirk duty.

**rouler dans la farine (se les)** *(Sl)*. Same as : *rouler (se les).*

**rouler les r** *(P).* To roll one's r's.

**rouler sa bosse** *(P)*. To travel, to knock around.

**rouleuse** *sf. (Sl)*. A dirty, dissipated woman, a prostitute of the lowest class.

**roulure** *sf. (Sl)*. A dirty slut, a prostitute of the lowest class.

**roupie de sansonnet** *(P)*. Same as : *roupie de singe*.

**roupie de singe** *(P)*. Worthless thing, not worth a red cent.

**roupiller** *v. (Sl)*. To sleep, to "pound one's ear".

**roupillon** *sm. (Sl)*. Nap, forty winks.

**rouquin** *sm. (Sl)*. Red wine (usually of cheap quality).

**rouscailler** *v. (Sl)*. To grouch, to gripe, to bitch, to "kick".

**rouscailleur** *sm. (Sl)*. Grouch(er), griper, grouser.

**rouspétance** *sf. (P)*. Protestation, bitching, bellyaching, gripe, kick(-back).

**rouspéter** *v. (P)*. To object, to "kick", to holler, to protest, to raise hell.

**rouspéteur** *sm. (P)*. Complainer, groucher, griper, chronic grouser.

**Rousse (la)** *sf. (Sl)*. Police.

**roussin** *sm. (Sl)*. Cop.

**roustisseur** *sm. (Sl)*. Crook, chiseler, sharper.

**R.P.F.** Abbr. of *Rassemblement du Peuple Français*, French political party (right wing).

**ruban de queue** *sm. (P)*. Road meandering like a ribbon through the country-side.

**rubis sur l'ongle** *(P)*. Cash on the barrel(head), cash on the nail.

**rudement** *adv. (P)*. Jolly. *Rudement bien*, jolly well.

**ruer dans les brancards** *(P)*. To protest, to "kick".

**ruisseau** *sm. (P)*. Gutter.

**ruminer** *v. (P)*. To mull over.

**rupin** *sm. adj. (P)*. Wealthy man, swell, "swellegant".

# S

**sable dans les yeux (avoir du)** *(F)*. To be sleepy (said of sleepy children).

**sabler le champagne** *(P)*. To drink, to swig champagne.

**sabot** *sm. (P)*. Bungler.
*(Sl)*. Animal cage (carnival sl.).

**sabotage** *sm. (P)*. Bungling, scamped work.

**saboter** *v. (P)*. To ruin, to spoil, to "ball up", to "louse up".

**saboteur** *sm. (P)*. Botcher, bungler.

**sabrer** *v. (Sl)*. Same as : *saboter*, to botch, to bungle, to "louse up", to "gum up".

**sac (un)** *sm. (Sl)*. 1.000-franc bill.

**sac (avoir son)** *(Sl)*. Same as : *culotte (avoir sa)*.

**sac à malices** *(P)*. Artful individual. Magician's wonder-bag.

**sac d'os** *sm. (Sl)*. Skinny person, rackabones, rattlebones.

**sacquer** *v. (P)*. Same as : *saquer*, to dismiss, to fire, to hand one the can.

**sacrebleu!** *(P)*. Same as : *sacristi!*

**sacré bon sort de bon sort !** *(P)*. Mild oath.

**sacredié !** *(P)*. Same as : *sacristi !*

**sacrée tapette (avoir une)** *(P)*. To be an exaggerated talker, a chatter-box, a "chinner".

**sacripant** *sm. (P)*. Scoundrel, rascal, "skeesicks". Braggart.

**sacristi !** *(P)*. Gosh ! Darnation ! (More often : *sapristi !*).

**sacristie** *sf. (Sl)*. Sitting-room, anteroom of musicians in a theater.

**saint-frusquin** *sm. (P)*. The whole kit, the whole (ca)boodle, the whole toot and scramble.

**sainte-nitouche** *sf. (P)*. *Elle fait*

— 174 —

*la sainte-nitouche,* she looks as if butter would not melt in her mouth.

**Sainte-Touche** *sf. (P).* Pay-day.

**Saint-Glinglin** *sf. (P). A la Saint-Glinglin,* never. *Jusqu'à la Saint-Glinglin,* till hell freezes over and the cows come skating home over the ice, till there is skating in hell.

**Saint-Honoré** *(P).* Syrup coated, crown-shaped cake with cream buns, the French national cake.

**saisir la balle au bond** *(F).* To seize opportunity.

**saisir le taureau par les cornes** *(F).* Same as : *prendre le taureau par les cornes.*

**saisir l'occasion par les cheveux** *(F).* To take the occasion by the forelock.

**salade** *sf. (P).* Hell of a mess, holy mess, foul-up, confusion. Ex. : *Quelle salade !* What a mess !

**salade russe** *sf. (P).* A variant of *salade.*

**saladier** *sm. (Sl).* Messy individual, "mussy" guy.

**salamalecs** *sm. pl. (F).* Kow-tow. *Faire des salamalecs :* to kow-tow.

**salaud** *sm. (Sl).* Dirty skunk, dirty stinker, son of a b..., s.o.b., a "louse".

**sale** *adj. (P).* Bad, rotten, lousy, foul, unpleasant, etc. Ex. : *Sale temps,* rotten, lousy weather.

**salé** *adj. (P).* Too expensive.

**sale coup** *sm. (P).* Dirty trick, nasty trick.

**sale coup pour la fanfare** *(P).* Very unpleasant surprise that upsets one's apple cart.

**salement** *adv. (Sl). C'est salement bon marché,* it's dirt-cheap, very cheap.

**salement bon marché** *(Sl).* See : *salement.*

**sale moineau (un)** *sm. (P).* Bad egg, heel.

**sale temps** *sm. (P).* Foul weather, lousy weather.

**saligaud** *sm. (Sl).* Dirty dog, dirty skunk.

**salir le nez (se)** *(Sl).* To get drunk. (See : *nez sale (avoir le).*

**salmigondis** *sm. (P).* Medley, omnium gatherum.

**salopard** *sm. (Sl).* Dirty skunk, dirty stinker, dirty dog.

**salope** *sf. (Sl).* Insult for a woman.

**saloper** *v. (Sl).* To bungle (a piece of work).

**saloperie** *sf. (Sl).* Nasty trick, nastiness, dirty trick.

**sang dans les veines (avoir du)** *(F).* To be alert, peppy, a live wire.

**sang de navet** *(P). Avoir du sang de navet,* to lack blood, to be anaemic, gutless, yellow-streaked.

**sans autre forme de procès** *(F).* Without any ceremony, quite simply and without further ado. Ex. : *Ils nous ont chassés sans autre forme de procès,* we were turned out neck and crop.

**sans blague !** *(P).* Excl. expressing surprise : No kidding ! Really ? Is that so ? "Izzatso ?"

**sans crier gare** *(F).* Without the slightest warning.

**sans doute** *(F).* Most probably.

**sans faire ni une ni deux** *(P).* Without much ado.

**sans rime ni raison** *(F).* Without rhyme or reason.

**sans sourciller** *(P)*. Without batting an eyelash.

**sans tambour ni trompette** *(F)*. On the q. t., without the slightest fuss.

**sans un (être)** *(Sl)*. To be stony-broke, busted, cleaned up, to have not a penny to bless oneself with.

**saoul** *adj. (Sl)*. See : *soûl*.

**saperlipopette !** *(P)*. Gee ! bless me ! (mild expletive).

SAPIN ATTENDANT LE CLIENT.

UNE BONNE SAUCÉE.

**sapin** *sm. (P)*. Four-wheeler, cab. *(Sl)*. Coffin. *Ça sent le sapin :* said of a tuberculous cough, " graveyard " cough.

**sapristi !** *(P)*. Same as : *sacristi !*

**saquer q.** *v. (P)*. To dismiss, to fire one.

**sardine** *sf. (P)*. Stripe worn on the sleeve of a military uniform.

**saucée** *sf. (P)*. Shower, heavy rain.

**saucer (se faire)** *(P)*. To get wet to the skin.

**saucisse** *sf. (P)*. Captive balloon, " sausage ". Stupid person, blockhead, dumbbell.

**saucisse de Frankfort** *(P)*. Hot dog.

**saucisson** *sm. (Sl)*. Woman, " blimp ", " broad ".

**sauf le respect que je vous dois** *(P)*. With your permission, with all respect to you.

**sauter** *v. (P)*. To become suddenly mad, angry, to flare up.

**sauter aux yeux** *(P)*. To be clear, plain, obvious.

**sauterie** *sf. (P)*. Dance, hop, hoe-down.

SAUTERIE.

**saute-ruisseau** *sm. (P).* Notary's errand-boy.

**sauteur** *sm. (P).* Unreliable fellow, weathercock ".

**sauteuse** *sf. (P).* Flighty girl, " dizzy ".

**sauver (se)** *v. (P).* To go away, to flee, to "beat it ", to scram.

**sauvette (à la)** *(P).* Said of certain street-vendors who are selling cheap articles without license. *Vendre à la sauvette*, to sell goods in the street without having a license.

**savate** *sf. (P).* Bungler.

**savater** *v. (P).* To bungle, to " louse up ". (See : *cochonner*).

**savetier** *sm. (P).* Bungler, unqualified worker.

**savoir nager** *v. (P).* To know what's what, to be in the know.

**savoir se retourner** *(P).* To be resourceful, up to snuff.

**savoir sur le bout du doigt** *(P).* To know thoroughly, to have at one's fingers' end.

**savoir y faire** *(P).* To have a way with.

**savon** *sm. (P).* Scolding, bawling-out, " going-over ".

**savonnage** *sm. (P).* Same as : *savon*.

**savonner la tête à** *(P).* Same as : *passer un savon*.

**scène de ménage** *(P).* Spat between husband and wife.

**schlague** *sf. (P).* Beating, " shellacking ", (as a punishment).

**schlass** *adj. (Sl).* Drunk, tight, " plastered ", " blotto ".

**schlingoter** *v. (Sl).* A variant of *schlinguer*.

**schlinguer** *v. (Sl).* To stink, to " hum ", to smell strongly.

**schlipoter** *v. (Sl).* Another slang variant of *schlinguer*.

**schloff** *sm. (P).* Bed. Ex. : *Aller au schloff*, to go to bed, to hit the hay.

**schnaps** *sm. (Sl).* Liquor, booze.

**schnick** *sm. (Sl).* Same as : *schnaps.*

**schnock** *sm. (Sl).* Same as : *duch(e)nock*.

**schtimmis** *sm. pl. (Sl).* Derisive nickname for the inhabitants of Northern France.

**scie** *sf. (P).* Anything plaguing, annoying. *Quelle scie !* Botheration ! Hit song, pop song known and sung by everybody.

**scier le dos** *v. (Sl).* To bore one to death, to weary, to plague one.

**scribouillard** *sm. (P).* Office employee, " quill-driver ". " pen-pusher ", " ink splasher ".

**Sébasto (le)** *(Sl).* Vulgarism for *Boulevard Sébastopol* in Paris (near the Central Market).

**sec (être à)** *(P).* Same as : *sans un (être), fauché (être)*.

**sec comme un coup de trique** *(P).* Thin, skinny individual, rackabones.

**sèche** *sf. (Sl).* Cigarette, " pill ", ciggie.

**sécher** *v. (Sl).* To wait in vain. To be stumped, unable to give a correct answer to the professor's question (school sl.).

**secouer (se)** *v. (P).* To hurry. *Secoue-toi un peu !* Hurry up ! make haste !

**secouer les puces à q.** *(P).* To reprimand, to bawl out, to tell a thing or two, to make it hot for one.

**secouer ses puces** (Sl). To stretch oneself.

**secret de Polichinelle** (F). Open secret, no secret at all.

**sellette** sf. (P). See : sur la sellette (être).

**semaine des quatre jeudis (la)** (F). Never ! When hell freezes over and the cows come skating home over the ice.

**semer** v. (Sl). To drop s.o., to blow s.o., to shake one off, to toss (throw) over, to get rid of s.o. Ex. : Sème-le ! Drop him ! Shake him off !

**semer la zizanie** (P). To sow discord.

**s'en aller de la caisse** (Sl). Said of a tubercular person, a "lunger". (See also : tubard).

**s'en aller en eau de boudin** (Sl). To fail utterly.

**s'en aller la queue basse** (P). To go off feeling small and humiliated.

**s'en aller les pieds devant** (P). To die, to "go home feet first".

**s'en balancer** (Sl). A variation of s'en battre l'œil.

IL S'EN COLLE PLEIN LA LAMPE.

**s'en battre le coquillard** (Sl). Not to care a damn, not to care a hoot.

**s'en battre l'œil** (Sl). Not to care a fig, couldn't care less.

**s'en coller plein la lampe** (Sl). To have a lavish meal, a "tuck-in". (Same as : s'en mettre plein la lampe).

**s'en contre-ficher** (Sl). Je m'en fiche et m'en contre-fiche, I don't give a damn ! I couldn't care less !

**s'en croire** (P). To be self-conceited, to be chesty, to get a swelled head.

**s'en donner** (P). To have a good time, fine time.

**s'en faire** (P). To worry (one-self grey).

**s'en ficher** (P). Not to give a damn.

**s'en ficher comme de sa première chemise** (P). Not to care a fig, couldn't care less.

**s'en flanquer une bosse** (Sl). A variant of s'en payer une bosse.

**s'en fourrer jusque là** (Sl). To eat a lavish meal, to eat everything from soup to nuts.

**s'en jeter un coup derrière le bouton de col** (Sl). To have a drink, to toss (off) a drink.

**s'en jeter une derrière la cravate** (Sl). A variant of preceding entry.

**s'en laver les mains** (P). To decline responsibility, to wash one's hands of the affair.

**s'en lécher les bab(ou)ines** (P). See : babouines.

**s'en mettre plein la lampe** (Sl). To fill one's stomach, to eat everything from soup to nuts, to eat a copious meal.

**s'en moquer** *(F)*. A coll. variant of *s'en ficher*.

**s'en moquer comme de l'an quarante** *(P)*. Same as : *s'en ficher comme de sa première chemise*.

**s'en mordre les doigts** *(F)*. To rue it. Ex. : *Vous vous en mordrez les doigts !* You shall rue it !

**s'en payer une bosse** *(Sl)*. To have an awfully good time, to have a lot of fun.

**s'en payer une tranche** *(Sl)*. A variant of *s'en payer une bosse*.

**sensas** *adj. (Sl)*. Jim-dandy, la-de-la.

**sens commun** *(F)*. Horse sense.

**sens dessus dessous** *(P)*. In disorder, in confusion, helter-skelter.

**s'en tamponner le coquillard** *(Sl)*. Not to give a damn, not to care a hoot.

**s'en taper** *(Sl)*. Not to care a darn.

**sentir le sapin** *(P)*. To be seriously ill, to be at death's door.

**sentir les coudes (se)** *(P)*. To be united ; to help one another.

**septième ciel** *(P)*. The pinnacle of happiness, seventh heaven.

**sergot** *sm. (Sl)*. Policeman.

**série noire** *(P)*. Losing streak, series of accidents or losses.

**serin** *sm. (P)*. Dum cluck, chump.

**seriner (q. ch. à q.)** *(P)*. To teach one something by dint of repeating.

**seringue** *sf. (Sl)*. Submachine gun.

**serrer la boule (se)** *(P)*. Same as : *serrer la ceinture (se)*.

**serrer la ceinture (se)** *(P)*. To go without food, to tighten the belt.

**serrer la ceinture d'un cran (se)** *(P)*. Same as : *serrer la ceinture (se)*.

**serrer la cuiller à q.** *(Sl)*. To shake hands with.

**serrer la pince à q.** *(Sl)*. Same as : *serrer la cuiller à q.*

**serrer la vis à q.** *(P)*. To subject s.o. to a (more) severe treatment, to put the screws on.

**serrer les coudes (se)** *(P)*. To help, back up, one another.

**serrer le sifflet à q.** *(Sl)*. To strangle one, to throttle one.

ET J'TE SERRE LE SIFFLET.

**serrer les fesses** *(Sl)*. To resist, not to yield (although terribly frightened), to endure bravely, without showing emotion.

**serrés comme des harengs dans une boîte à sardines** *(P)*. Packed like herrings in a barrel, packed absolutely full.

**service, service !** *(F)*. Duty is duty !

**sexe faible** *sm. (F)*. Fair sex.

**sexy** *adj. (P)*. Hot stuff, sexually provocative.

**S.F.I.O.** Abbr. of *Section Française de l'Internationale Ouvrière,* the French branch of the International Workers Association.

**shake-hand** *sm. (F).* Oddly enough "hand-shake" has bean distorted in French into "shake-hand". Used chiefly by certain snobs affecting some knowledge of English.

**sibiche** *sf. (Sl).* Cigarette, "pill", ciggie.

**sidi** *sm. (Sl).* Arab, Algerian.

SIDI.

**sieur** *sm. (P).* See : *drôle de sieur.*

**siffler un coup** *(Sl).* Same as : *siffler un verre.*

**siffler un verre** *(Sl).* To drink a glass in one stroke, bottoms-up, to "throw" a glass.

**sifflet** *sm. (Sl).* Throat.

**sifflet (se rincer le)** *(Sl).* To wet (moisten) the whistle, to drink a glass.

**sigue** *sf. (Sl).* 20-franc gold coin.

**simple comme bonjour** *(P).* Very simple, couldn't be simpler.

**singe** *sm. (Sl).* Corned beef, canned beef. Boss.

**singeries** *sf. pl. (P).* Monkey shine.

**sinoque** *adj. (Sl).* Crazy, daffy, cracked, goofy.

**sire** *sm. (P).* Ex. : *Un triste sire,* a sad case, a sad specimen of a guy.

**sirop de grenouille** *sm. (Sl).* Water (joc. term.).

**sirop de parapluie** *sm. (Sl).* A variant of *sirop de grenouille.*

**siroter** *v. (P).* To drink, to tipple, to swizzle.

**siroter un godet** *(Sl).* To sip a glass, to swizzle. (Also : *siroter un pot).*

**situation intéressante (être dans une)** *(P).* Applied to a woman when *enceinte,* expecting.

**Six jours (les)** *sm. pl. (P).* Six-day racing, six-day grind, bicycle race lasting six days and six nights.

**six-quatre-deux (à la)** *(P).* Same as : *va-comme-je-te-pousse (à la).*

**smala(h)** *sf. (P).* Tribe, large family, caboodle. *Toute la smala(h),* the whole tribe, the whole caboodle.

**SMIG** Abbr. of *Salaire Minimum Interprofessionnel Garanti,* guaranteed minimum salary.

**S.N.C.F.** Abbr. of *Société Nationale des Chemins de Fer Français,* French Railroads.

**soiffard** *sm. (P).* Drunkard, "stew", "rumpot".

**soigné** *adj. (P).* Thorough, suitable, proper, neat, well finished. (Often used sarcastically, f. i. : *Il a reçu une raclée, q. ch. de soigné,* he had a thorough thrashing, a " shellacking ".

**sonné** *adj.* *(Sl).* Crazy, cracked.

**sonner** *v.* *(Sl).* To beat up, to thrash, to give hell to, to " put (one) through the hoop ".

**sonner les cloches à q.** *(Sl).* To reprimand severely, to bawl out.

**sornettes** *sf. pl.* *(P).* Bunk, baloney, foolish windy talk.

**sorti de la cuisse de Jupiter (se croire)** *(F).* To think too highly of oneself, to imagine oneself to be of exalted birth, to think no small beer of oneself.

**sortie** *sf.* *(P).* Violent scene. Ex. : *Il a fait une sortie,* he raised hell, kicked up a shindy, he made hell pop loose.

**sortir** *v.* *(P). Il nous a sorti une histoire incroyable,* he pitched us an incredible story.
*(Sl).* To boot out, to give the Grand Bounce.

**sortir de ses gonds** *(P).* To lose one's temper, to lose patience, to fly off the handle.

**sot à vingt-quatre carats** *(P).* Prize sap, dumbbell.

**sot en trois lettres (c'est un)** *(P).* In plain language, he is a sap.

**sot-l'y-laisse** *sm.* *(P).* Pope's nose, parson's nose (the hind part of a roast fowl, a savory mouthful).

**sottises** *sf. pl.* *(P).* Abuse. Ex. : *Dire des sottises à q.,* to shower abuse on one.

**souche** *sf.* *(P).* Silly person, chump, dumbbell, dumb cluck.

**soudard** *sm.* *(P).* Trooper. *Vieux soudard,* old trooper (mostly pej.).

**sou du franc (le)** *(P).* Market-penny. Secret commission given by tradesmen to servants for purchases (one *sou* for each franc spent).

**soufflant** *sm.* *(Sl).* Revolver, oscar, roscoe, " rod ".

**soufflé** *adj.* *(Sl).* Very much surprised, amazed, taken aback, struck all of a heap, flabbergasted. Impudent, bold, crusty, cheeky. Ex. : *T'es soufflé, toi !* You have some cheek !

**souffler q. ch. à q.** *(Sl).* To take, to pinch s. th. from under one's nose.

**souffler sa chandelle** *(P).* To die, to kick the bucket, to " turn the lights off ".

**souffler sa veilleuse** *(P).* Same as : *souffler sa chandelle.*

**soufflet** *sm.* *(F).* Slap in the face.

**souffre-douleur de q. (être le)** *(F).* " Goat ", scapegoat, victim ; butt of one's jokes.

**souillon** *sm.* *(F).* Slut, kitchen wench.

SOUL COMME UN POLONAIS.

**soûlard** *sm. (Sl).* Same as : *soûlot.*

**soûl comme trente-six mille hommes** *(Sl).* Dead drunk, drunk as a boiled owl.

**soûl comme une bourrique** *(P).* Same as : *soûl comme un Polonais.*

**soûl comme un Polonais** *(P).* Dead drunk, merry as a Greek.

**soûlographe** *sm. (Sl).* Same as : *soûlot.*

**soûlographie** *sf. (Sl).* Dead-drunkenness. (See also : *cuite).*

**soûlot** *sm. (Sl).* Drunkard, " soak ", " stew ", " lush ", " souse ", " boozehound ". (Syn. : *pochard, soûlard, soûlographe).*

**soupçon** *sm. (P).* Teeny-weeny bit of. Ex. : *Donnez-moi un soupçon (ou une larme) de kirsch.*

**soupe au lait (être)** *(P).* Said of a person who gets angry, flares up, easily or suddenly, quick tempered.

**souper** *v. (Sl).* Ex. : *J'en ai soupé de ta fiole !* I am fed up with you !

**souple comme un gant (être)** *(P).* Said of a very accommodating person.

**sourd comme un pot (être)** *(P).* Deaf as a door-knob.

**sourde oreille (faire la)** *(F).* To turn a deaf ear.

**souris** *sf. (Sl).* Derisive for : woman, girl.

**sous** *sm. pl. (Sl).* See : *galette.*

**sous clé** *(P).* Under lock and key.

**sous la table** *(P).* Under the table, secretely.
*(Sl).* Dead drunk.

**sous-maîtresse** *sf. (P).* Brothel hostess, Madame.

**sous-off** *sm. (P).* Non-commissioned officer, non-com, N.C.O.

**sous pression (être)** *(P).* To be under heavy pressure, heavy strain.

**sous-verge** *sm. (P).* Second in command, straw boss.

**souteneur** *sm. (P).* Pimp, " cadet ".

**soutenir mordicus** *(P).* To affirm doggedly, stoutly, with all one's might and strength.

**soutirer** *v. (P).* To worm out of, to squeeze out of, to screw out of, to wheedle out of.

**squelette ambulant** *sm. (P).* Skinny person, human (walking) skeleton.

**stratège du Café du Commerce** *(P).* Parlor (cracker-barrel) strategist, an " Arthur Donovan ".

**stratège en chambre** *(P).* Parlor strategist, an " Arthur Donovan ".

**subito presto** *(P).* Very quickly, lickety-split, " pronto ".

**suçon** *sm. (P).* Trace left on the skin by a long kiss, " strawberry kiss ".

**sucre (du)** *sm. (Sl).* Something easy, easy job, " sugar ", " pushover ", " duck soup ".

**sucrer** *v. (Sl).* To arrest, to capture, to " pinch ". Ex. : *Ils se sont fait sucrer,* they got " nabbed ".

**sucrer (se)** *v. (P).* To get the largest part of the " gravy ", to get rich, to amass a fortune by profiteering.

**suer l'orgueil** *(P).* To stink of pride.

**suer sang et eau** *(P).* To strain every nerve, to labor under very great strain, to toil and moil.

**\* suer une (en)** *(Sl).* To dance.

**surboum** *sf. (P).* Joc. name for the so-called " surprise-party " (see this word).

**sur des roulettes** *(P).* Easily, " on wheels ".

**surin** *sm. (Sl).* Knife, " chive ".

**suriner** *v. (Sl).* To knife, to wound with a knife.

**surineur** *sm. (Sl).* Chiv(e)-man.

SURINEUR.

**sur la paille (être)** *(P).* To be in utter poverty, penniless, on the rocks.

**sur la sellette (être)** *(P).* To be under cross-examination.

**sur le flanc (être)** *(P).* To be bushed.
*(Sl).* To sleep, to be in bed.

**sur le pavé (être)** *(P).* To be destitute, out on the sidewalk, totally ruined, broke.

**sur le sable (être)** *(Sl).* To be broke, to be on the rocks, on the bum.

**sur les dents (être)** *(P).* To be pooped out, extremely tired. Also : hard pressed by work or business.

**sur les doigts** *(P).* See : *donner sur les doigts.*

**sur les genoux (être)** *(Sl).* Exhausted, dog-tired, run ragged.

**sur les rotules (être)** *(Sl).* Same as preceding entry.

**sur le tapis (être)** *(P).* To be under consideration, to be on the carpet.

**surpat** *sf. (P).* Joc. name for the so-called " surprise-party " (see this word). Same as : *surboum.*

**surprise-party** *sf. (P).* Informal social gathering of young people, party to which usually every member contributes some drink or food.

**surrincette** *sf. (Sl).* Second drink of liquor after coffee (at the end of a meal).

**swing** *adj. (Sl).* Hep, hip, " far-out ", (as in " far-out cats ").

**sympa** *adj. (P).* Congenial, popular, good sport.

**s'y prendre mal** *(F).* To go the wrong way about one's work.

**système** *sm. (P).* Ironic and disparaging term for the constitutional régime of the fourth French Republic.

**système D** *sm. (P).* Unscrupulous wangling. (See : *employer le système D*).

# T

**tabassée** *sf. (Sl).* Thrashing, licking, beating, a " dose of strap oil ", " shellacking ", a good going-over.

**tabasser** *v. (Sl).* To beat up, to give a thorough beating, thrashing, " shellacking ".

**table rase** *(F).* Clean sweep.

**tabou (être)** *(F).* To be taboo.

**ta bouche !** *(Sl).* Shut up ! Knock it off !

**ta bouche bébé, t'auras une frite** *(Sl).* Pop. catch-phrase meaning : Shut up ! Cut it off !

**tâche (mourir à la)** *(F).* To die in harness.

**tache d'huile (faire)** *(P).* To spread gradually (like a grease spot on a sheet of paper).

**tacot** *sm. (P).* Old car, jalopy, old crate, flivver.

**tailler (se)** *(Sl).* To scram, to make oneself scarce, to flee.

VIEUX TACOT.

**tailler une bavette** *(P).* To chat, to have a little chat with, to shoot the breeze.

**taire sa gueule** *(Sl).* To keep one's big mouth shut. *Tais ta g...* Button up your lip ! shut up ! lay off !

**taire son bec** *(Sl).* To shut up, to " button up one's lip ". (See : *ferme ton bec !*).

**tais-toi donc ! (taisez-vous donc !)** *(P).* Oh, come off !

— 184 —

**taloche** *sf. (P).* Slap in the face, box on the ear.

**tambouille** *sf. (Sl).* Food, " grub ", " chow ", " eats ".

**tambour battant** *(P). Mener une affaire tambour battant,* to handle an affair smartly without loss of time.

**tam-tam** *sm. (P).* Ballyhoo, hullabaloo. *Faire du tam-tam,* to raise a hullabaloo about s. th., beating the tom-toms.

**tannant** *adj. (Sl).* Tiresome, annoying, boring (thing or individual), nuisance.

**tanner** *v. (Sl).* To pester, to bother, to make one tired, to vex, to plague s.o.

**tanner le cuir** *(Sl).* To give a thorough beating, to wallop, to thrash, to tan one's hide.

**tante** *sf. (Sl).* Pederast, catamite, third-sexer.

**tapé** *sm. adj. (Sl).* Mentally unbalanced, nutty, crackpot, screwy, loco, cockeyed, cuckoo, loony.

**tape à l'œil** *sm. (P).* Well presented but intrinsically worthless article, as in *c'est du tape à l'œil.*

**tape-cul** *sm. (P).* Trot. *Faire du tape-cul,* to trot. Gig (light two-wheeled carriage).

**tapée** *sf. (P).* Great quantity of, large amount of, " oodles of ".

**taper** *v. (P).* To borrow, to " mooch ", to touch s.o. for money, to make a touch. To put the " bite " on, to put the " buzz " on.
*(Sl).* To stink, to " hum ", to smell strongly.

**taper (se)** *(P).* To stand oneself, to treat oneself to, to " blow " oneself to. Ex. : *Il se tape un bon dîner,* he treats himself to a good dinner.

*(Sl).* Ex. : *Vous pouvez vous taper, mon vieux,* you may whistle for it, boy (=you may try hard to get it, nothing doing !).

**taper (s'en)** *(Sl).* Not to care a fig (a damn).

**taper dans le tas** *(P).* To pick at random (out of a bunch, out of a group, etc.).

**taper dans l'œil** *(P).* To take one's fancy, to please highly.

**\* taper du saladier** *(Sl).* To have bad-smelling breath, halitosis.

**taper la cloche (se)** *(Sl).* To eat a lavish meal, to have a regular blow-out, eatfest.

**\* taper le cul par terre (se)** *(Sl).* To be happy and content. Usually in negative : *Il n'y a pas de quoi se taper le cul par terre,* there is no cause for contentment, joy, satisfaction.

**taper le derrière par terre (se)** *(Sl).* A less vulgar variant of preceding entry.

**taper sur les nerfs** *(P).* To get on one's nerves, to get in one's hair.

**taper sur le système** *(Sl).* To irritate, to weary s.o., to be a nuisance to s.o.

**taper sur le ventre** *(P).* To be too familiar with.

**tapette** *sf. (P). Avoir une tapette,* to be a chatter-box. Ex. : *Elle a une tapette, une de ces tapettes !* Isn't she a real chatter-box !

*(Sl).* Catamite, male homosexual.

**tapeur** *sm. (P).* Constant borrower. "moocher", free-loader, bummer, sponger. Pianist (in dancing establishments).

**tapin** *sm. (Sl).* Prostitute, "hooker". (See also : *faire le tapin*).

**tapineuse** *sf. (Sl)*. Same as : *tapin* : streetwalker, prostitute.

TAPINEUSE.

**tapis** *sm. (Sl)*. Drinking joint, dive, "flash house", usually frequented by members of the so-called " *milieu* ", prostitutes, etc. (back-room often used for card or dice gambling).

**tapis vert (autour du)** *(F)*. In a conference (round-table conference).

**tapisserie (faire)** *(P)*. To be a wall-flower (at a dance).

**taquet** *sm. (Sl)*. Blow in the face.

**taquiner le goujon (ou l'ablette)** *(P)*. To angle, to fish (to " tease " the fishes with the bait).

**tarabiscoté** *adj. (P)*. Too elaborate, doctored up. Ex. : *Je n'aime pas les plats tarabiscotés, épicés*, I don't like food doctored up with much spice.

**tarabuster** *v. (P)*. To pester, to plague.

**taratata !** *(P)*. Joc. exclamation denoting incredulity. *Taratata !* Baloney ! Oh, yeah ! I don't believe it ! Hoity-toity !

**tarte** *sf. (Sl)*. Slap in the face.

**tarte** *adj. (Sl)*. Lousy, " crummy ", " cheesy ". The reverse of good-looking.

**Tartempion** *(P)*. Joe Doakes, John Doe, John Q. Public, anybody.

**tartignolle** *adj. (Sl)*. " Cheesy ", lousy, " crummy ".

**tartine** *sf. (P)*. Long rigmarole, long and tedious story, letter, article, etc. See also : *en faire une tartine*.

**tartiner** *v. (P)*. To make a story, a speech, a letter, etc. longwinded or uselessly long and tedious.

**tartouillard** *adj. (Sl)*. Same as : *tartignolle*.

**tartouse** *adj. (Sl)*. Lousy, inferior.

**tassé** *adj. (P)*. *Deux heures bien tassées*, two solid hours. *Un repas bien tassé*, a generous, plentiful meal.

**tasser** *v. (Sl)*. To give, to dish (out), to let one have (it), to give one a bad time. Ex. : *Qu'est-ce que je lui ai tassé !* I gave him hell ! I gave him what-for !

**tasser (se)** *v. (P)*. To settle down. Ex. : *Ça se tassera*, things will settle down.

**tata** *sf. (P)*. Aunt(ie).
*(Sl)*. Pederast.

**tatanes** *sf. pl. (Sl)*. Shoes, " kickers ".

**tâter le terrain** *(P)*. To feel one's way, to feel how the land lies.

**tatouille** *sf. (Sl)*. Thrashing, hiding, licking.

**taule** *sf. (Sl).* Jail, jug. Cheap room or dwelling place.

EN TAULE.

**taulier** *sm. (Sl).* Owner of a bordello, of cheap and poorly furnished flats.

**taulière** *sf. (Sl).* Feminine form of *taulier*.

**taupin** *sm. (P).* Student-candidate for *Ecole Polytechnique*, student fitting for the E.P.

**teigne** *sf. (P).* Insult for a bad person. Ex. : *Quelle teigne !* What a pest !

**teinté (être)** *(Sl).* To be drunk, to be tight, to be boozy-woozy.

**Tel qui rit Vendredi, Dimanche pleurera** *(F).* He that laughs on Friday will weep on Sunday.

**tempêter** *v. (P).* To get angry, to fret and fume, to raise hell.

**temps de chien** *(P).* Heavy rain, awfully bad weather.

**temps de dire ouf (le)** *(P).* Very quickly, in a jiffy.

**tendre la perche à q.** *(P).* To attempt to help s.o. who is in a fix or in difficulties.

**tenir à carreau (se)** *(P).* Same as : *garder à carreau (se).*

**tenir à q. ch. comme à la prunelle de ses yeux** *(P).* To cherish s. th. like the apple of one's eye.

**tenir la chandelle** *(F).* To act as a panderer, to pander to a person's vices.

**tenir la dragée haute à q.** *(F).* To make s.o. pay a high price for.

**tenir la jambe** *(Sl).* To pester, to bore, to tire one, te be a nuisance.

**tenir la queue de la poêle** *(P).* To be in charge of running the house.

**tenir le bon bout** *(P).* To hold the better end of the stick.

**tenir le coup** *(P).* To stick it (out).

**tenir le crachoir** *(P).* To hold forth, to speechify, to patter, to talk a blue streak. Ex. : *Notre hôte a tenu le crachoir pendant toute la soirée.*

**tenir le haut du pavé** *(F).* To rule the roost, to boss the show.

**tenir les cordons de la bourse** *(P).* To finance.

**tenir sa langue** *(P).* To hold one's tongue.

**tenir sur ses gardes (se)** *(P).* To watch out, to look out, to be on one's guard.

**terminer en queue de poisson (se)** *(P).* See : *finir en queue de poisson.*

**têtard (être)** *(Sl).* To be a victim, "bagholder", dupe. To be arrested, to be "nabbed". (Syn. : *être chocolat*).

**tétasses** *sf. pl. (Sl).* Flabby breasts.

**tête à claques** *(P).* Face with an insolent expression, face one would like to slap.

**tête à coucher dehors avec un billet de logement dans sa poche (avoir une)** *(P).* Said of a very ugly face, face that'll stop a clock.

**tête à gifles** *(P).* Same as : *tête à claques.*

**tête-à-tête** *(P).* Strictly private conversation.

**tête à X** *(P).* Individual particularly gifted for mathematics, mathematical whiz.

**tête de cochon** *(Sl).* Stubborn person, pig-head, mule.

**tête de lard** *(Sl).* Same as : *tête de cochon.*

**tête de linotte** *(P).* Harebrain, birdbrain, rattlehead, scatterbrain.

**tête de mule** *(P).* Same as : *tête de pioche.*

**tête de pioche** *(P).* Stubborn individual, pig-headed person.

**tête de pipe** *(P).* Chump, blockhead, funny face. Guy, person, individual. *Compter des têtes de pipes,* to count noses.

**tête de Turc** *(P).* One who is the target of continuous attacks or mistreatment.

**tête de veau** *(Sl).* Bald head, " billiard ball ".

**tête dure (avoir la)** *(P).* To be dull-witted. See also : *comprenette dure.*

**tête près du bonnet (avoir la)** *(P).* To be irritable, easily angered.

**tettes** *sf. pl. (Sl).* Nipples.

**teuf-teuf** *sm. (P).* Very old automobile, flivver, tin Lizzie, model T.

**Thomas** *sm. (P).* Chamber pot.

**Thomas l'incrédule** See : *Je suis comme Thomas, je suis incrédule.*

**thunard** *sm. (Sl).* Same as : *thune.*

**thune** *sf. (Sl).* Old 5-franc coin (silver). (Similar in U.S. : cart wheel).

THUNE.

QUELLE TIGNASSE !

**thurne** *sf.* *(Sl)*. Same as : *turne*.

**ticket** *sm.* *(Sl)*. 1.000-franc banknote. Ex. : *Deux cents tickets*, two hundred thousand francs.

**tiffes** *sm. pl.* *(Sl)*. Hair, "fur".

**tifs** *sm. pl.* *(Sl)*. Same as : *tiffes*.

**tignasse** *sf.* *(P)*. Dirty long hair, "thatch", "fur".

**timbré** *adj.* *(P)*. Crazy, cracked, mentally unbalanced.

**timbre fêlé (le)** *(Sl)*. Crackpot.

**tinette** *sf.* *(Sl)*. Sanitary soil-tub.

**tintouin** *sm.* *(P)*. Worry, worriment, headache.

**tiquer** *v.* *(P)*. To show a sign of astonishment (or disapproval).

**tirage** *sm.* *(P)*. *Il y a du tirage*, there is some hitch in the business. *Il y a du tirage entre père et fils*, there is friction between father and son.

**tiré à quatre épingles** *(F)*. Spick and span.

**tire-au-cul** *sm.* *(Sl)*. Same as : *tire-au-flanc* (but much stronger).

**tire-au-flanc** *sm.* *(P)*. Lazy person, bum, shirker, goldbrick(er), "feather merchant" (in the army).

**tirebouchonnant** *adj.* *(Sl)*. Very amusing, very funny, funny as a barrel of monkeys.

**tirebouchonner (se)** *(Sl)*. Same as : *gondoler (se)*.

**tire-jus** *sm.* *(Sl)*. Handkerchief, "wipe".

**tirelire** *sf.* *(P)*. Piggy bank. *(Sl)*. Head, "knob", "noggin".

**tiré par les cheveux** *(P)*. Far-fetched.

**tirer** *v.* *(Sl)*. To pick pockets.

**tirer (se)** *(Sl)*. To go away, to leave, to "beat it", to scram.

**tirer au cul** *(Sl)*. Same as : *tirer au flanc* (but much stronger).

**tirer au flanc** *(P)*. To shirk one's duty, to "goldbrick", to take the lazy way of doing a job.

**tirer des flûtes (se)** *(Sl)*. To leave hurriedly, to take an airing, to "take it on the lam", to scram.

**tirer des pattes (se)** *(Sl)*. Same as : *tirer des flûtes (se)*.

**tirer des plans sur la comète** *(P)*. To make all sorts of plans for the future (particularly hypothetical or impossible ones).

**tirer la couverture à soi** *(P)*. To take all the bed-cover, hence : to look after one's own interest at the expense of others.

**tirer la langue** *(P)*. To be near exhaustion.

**tirer l'échelle** *(P)*. *Après ça, il faut tirer l'échelle*, that's the limit, nothing can be compared with that.

**tirer le diable par la queue** *(P)*. To be in a tight corner, hard-up, behind the eight-ball.

**tirer les marrons du feu** *(F)*. To accomplish something at great risk to the benefit of others, to be one's cat's-paw.

**tirer les pincettes (se)** To leave hurriedly, to scram.

**tirer les vers du nez** *(P)*. To pump, to squeeze secrets out of a person, to extract information by roundabout questioning.

MONSIEUR TIRE SA FLEMME.

**tirer sa flemme** *(P)*. To laze, to idle, to idle away one's time.

**tirer son épingle du jeu** *(P)*. To get unharmed out of a fix, out of a bad job, to back out.

**tirer une bordée** *(P)*. Same as : *bordée (être en)*.

**tirer une épine du pied à q.** *(P)*. To render a great service, to get one out of a fix.

**tireur** *sm. (Sl)*. Pickpocket, "dipper", "picker", "stripper".

**tisane** *sf. (Sl)*. Beating, severe thrashing, "shellacking", licking.

**titi** *sm. (P)*. Paris street child.

**Titine** *sf. (Sl)*. Tommy gun, submachine gun.

**toc** *sm. adj. (P)*. False jewelry, ape-ware, jitney, junk, "tripe". Ugly, mean, punk.

**tocante** *sf. (Sl)*. Slang term for an old fashioned watch, "turnip" (also : *toquante*).

TITI PARISIEN.

**tocard** *sm. (P)*. Rank outsider, poor horse (races).

**tocard** *adj. (Sl)*. Worthless, dud, punk, jitney, junk.

**tocasson** *adj. (Sl)*. "Cheesy", jitney.

**t'occupe pas du chapeau de la gamine !** *(P)*. Mind your own business ! Mind what you are about !

**tôle** *sf. (Sl)*. Jail, jug. Cheap dwelling-place. (Also spelt : *taule*).

**tôlier** *sm. (Sl)*. Same as : *taulier*.

**tôlière** *sf. (Sl)*. Same as : *taulière*.

**tomate** *sf. (Sl)*. Face, red nose.

**tomber à pic** *(P)*. To arrive (to come) in the very nick of time.

**tomber bien** *(P)*. *Tu tombes bien !* you are coming in the very nick of time ! (sometimes pej.).

**tomber dans le bouillon** *(Sl)*. To fall into water.

**tomber dans le panneau** *(P)*. To fall into the trap, to drop in for it.

**tomber dans les pommes** *(P)*. To faint (away), to keel over.

**tomber de Charybde en Scylla** *(F)*. Out of the frying-pan into the fire, out of the smoke into the smother, out of the thunder into the lightning.

**tomber des hallebardes** *(P)*. See : *il pleut des hallebardes*.

**tomber des nues** *(P)*. To be flabbergasted, greatly surprised, astonished.

**tomber de son haut** *(P)*. To be flabbergasted.

**tomber en digue-digue** *(Sl)*. To faint, to swoon.

**tomber la veste** *(P)*. To take off, to remove, one's coat. *Tombons la veste !* Off with the coat !

**tomber pile** *(P)*. To come in the very nick of time.

**tomber sur le casaquin** *(Sl)*. To jump at, to attack, to "light into", to give a sound thrashing.

**tomber sur le paletot** *(Sl)*. To jump at one's neck, to "sail into", to "pitch into".

**tomber sur le poil** *(Sl)*. To attack one unexpectedly, by surprise. To give a thrashing.

**tomber sur un bec (de gaz)** *(Sl)*. To fail, to come a cropper, to fall flat.

**tondre (sur) un œuf** *(P)*. To be a miser, a skinflint. Ex. : *Il tondrait (sur) un œuf*, he's tighter than a drum.

**tonneau des Danaïdes** *(F)*. Endless, profitless task, a Danaidean task, to pour water over a duck's back.

**tonnerre (du)** *(P)*. "Knock-out", something admirable, surprising, sensational, remarkable.

**ton nez remue !** *(P)*. You are telling a lie ! (Joc.).

**ton père n'était pas vitrier** *(P)*. Joc. fling meaning : "You make a better door than a window".

**tonton** *sm. (P)*. Uncle.

**topo** *sm. (P)*. Sketch, summary description of a geographical position.

**toquade** *sf. (P)*. Fancy. Infatuation. Passing fad, craze.

**toquante** *sf. (Sl)*. An old-fashioned watch, "ticker", "turnip".

**toquard** *sm. (Sl)*. Another spelling for *tocard*.

**toqué** *sm. adj. (P)*. Mentally unbalanced person, crackpot, cracked.

**torchée** *sf. (Sl)*. Fight, scrap, fracas.

**torcher** *v. (P)*. To botch, to "louse up", to scamp.

**torchon** *sm. (P)*. Slattern, untidy wench.

**torchon brûle (le)** *(P)*. Tiff between husband and wife.

**torchonner** *v. (P)*. Same as : *torcher*.

**tordant** *adj. (P)*. Exceedingly comical, amusing, very funny, funny as a barrel of monkeys.

**tord-boyaux** *sm. (Sl)*. Inferior liquor, booze, "pizen", "poison", "tanglefoot", "A-bomb juice".

**tordre (se)** *(P)*. To laugh heartily, to laugh oneself sick.

**tordre comme un bossu (se)** *(P)*. To laugh heartily.

**tordre comme une baleine (se)** *(P)*. A variant of *tordre comme un bossu (se)*.

**tordu** *sm. (Sl).* Goof. Péj. for any disliked person.

**tordu** *adj. (Sl).* Cracked, crazy, goofy.

**torgn(i)ole** *sf. (Sl).* Slap in the face. Thrashing, beating, "shellacking".

**torpilleur** *sm. (Sl).* One who borrows often money.

**tortillard** *sm. (P).* Local (train), generally slow, stopping many times, at many places.

**toto(s)** *sm. (pl.) (Sl).* Louse, grayback, lice, bugs, "coots".

**toubib** *sm. (P).* Doc(tor), "croaker".

**touche** *sf. (P).* See : *drôle de touche.*

**touche (faire une)** *(Sl).* To attract special attention from one of opposite sex.

**touchons du bois !** *(P).* Let's touch (knock) wood ! (Popular excl. on striking a wooden object in order to avert bad luck).

**touiller** *v. (P).* To stir.

**toupet** *sm. (P).* Impudence, effrontery, insolence, "sass", audacity, "crust", cheek, "gall".

**toupet (avoir du)** *(P).* To have some cheek.

LE TOUR.

**toupie** *sf. (Sl).* Frump, woman (term of abuse for a woman or a girl). *Vieille toupie,* old frump.

**Tour (le)** *(P). Le Tour de France,* national bicycle race.

**tour de bâton** *sm. (P).* Secret commission, "kick-back".

**tour de bête** *sm. (P).* Promotion for long service (and not for particular merit). Ex. : *Attendre son tour de bête.*

**tour de passe-passe (un)** *sm. (P).* A clever (smart) trick, gimmick, legerdemain, hanky-panky.

**tourlourou** *sm. (P).* Young soldier, young doughfoot, rookie.

**tourlouzine** *sf. (Sl).* See : *filer une tourlouzine.*

**tournant** *sm. (Sl). Il est dans un sale tournant,* he is seriously compromised, in a pretty mess.

**tournée** *sf. (P).* Beating, licking, thrashing.

**tournée des grands ducs (la)** *(P).* Table topping, visiting nightclubs during the course of an evening.

**tourner autour du pot** *(P).* To beat around the bush, to shilly-shally.

**tourner au vinaigre** *(P).* To get sour, to turn sour, to get spoiled.

**tourner casaque** *(P).* To turn one's coat, to bolt, to flop. (Syn. : *retourner sa veste*).

**tourner de l'œil** *(P).* To faint (away), to keel over.

**tourner la tête** *(P).* To turn one's head, to overexcite one.

**tourner les pouces (se)** *(P).* To be idle.

**Tour Pointue (la)** *(P).* Police jail, "cooler".

**tourte** *sf. (P).* Stupid person, dumbbell, muff.

**tout battant neuf** *(P).* Bran(d) new, spanking new.

**tout bêtement** *(P).* Simply.

**tout chose** *(P).* Out of sorts. Ex. : *Se sentir tout chose,* to feel out of sorts.

**tout craché** *(P).* Spit and image, spitting image of.

**tout cuit (c'est du)** *(Sl).* It's an easy job, a " pushover ". A sure bet (in a race), a cinch, a sure victory.

**tout de go** *(P).* At once, off hand.

**tout doux** *(P).* Same as : *piano-piano.*

**toute la boutique** *(P).* The whole kit and caboodle, the whole shebang, the whole boodle, the whole smear.

**toute la sainte journée** *(P).* All the blessed day, from morn till night.

**toute pompe (à)** *(P).* P.D.Q. pretty damn quick.

**tout feu tout flamme pour q. ch. (être)** *(P).* To carry a torch for.

**tout flambant neuf** *(P).* Bran(d) new.

**tout le bataclan** *(P).* Same as : *tout le bazar.*

**tout le bazar** *(P).* The whole kit and (ca)boodle, the whole shebang, the whole mess, the whole toot and scramble ; lock, stock and barrel.

**tout le bout du monde (c'est)** *(P).* Extreme limit, utmost.

**tout le tremblement** *(P).* Same as : *tout le bazar.*

**tout le tremblement et son train** *(P).* All that jazz. (See also : *tout le bazar*).

**toutou** *sm. (P).* Dog, little dog, pooch.

**Tout-Paris** *(P).* The " whipped-cream " of Paris Society.

**tout un plat** *(P).* See : *en faire tout un plat.*

**tout venant (du)** *(P).* Pell-mell, from all sources and origines.

**trac** *sm. (P).* Fright, fear, jim-jams.

**trac (avoir le)** *(P).* To be frightened, to be in a funk.

**train** *sm. (Sl).* Posterior, fanny.

**train (être dans le)** *(P).* To be hep (on, to), to be " in ". (Syn. : *être dans la note, à la hauteur*).

**traînasser** *v. (P).* To idle away one's time, to loaf, to louse around.

**train des maris (le)** *(P).* Same as : *train jaune (le).*

**traînée** *sf. (Sl).* Low-class prostitute.

**traîne-patins** *sm. (Sl).* Hobo, bo, bum. Mediocre bike racer (Syn. : *traîne-pattes*).

**traîner la savate** *(P).* To idle, to loaf around.

**traîner q. dans la boue** *(P).* To vilify one.

**traîner ses guêtres** *(P).* A variant of *traîner ses patins.*

**traîner ses patins** *(Sl).* To loaf around, to monkey around, to louse around.

**train jaune (le)** *(P).* " Yellow train ", husbands' train : sarcastic term for a train taken by husbands over the week-end, in summer time, to go and see their wife at the sea-side or at any other summer resort.

**train onze (le)** *(Sl)*. Legs. *Prendre le train onze*, to walk, to go (on foot).

**traintrain** *sm. (P)*. Daily routine (of work, life, etc.), daily grind.

**traiter q. de haut en bas** *(P)* To high-hat one.

**traits (faire des)** *(Sl)*. See : *faire des traits*.

**tralala** *sm. (P)*. Whoop-de-do.

**tranche** *sf. (Sl)*. Silly person, chump.

**tranche (en avoir une)** *(Sl)*. To be a dumbbell, to be hopelessly dumb.

**tranquille comme Baptiste** *(P)*. Very quiet.

**traquette** *sf. (Sl)*. Fright, funk.

**traquette (avoir la)** *(Sl)*. To be frightened, to "get the wind up".

**traquouse** *sf. (Sl)*. Same as : *traquette*.

**travail** *sm. (Sl)*. Burglary, "crack", "bust".

**travail de Romain** *(P)*. Tremendous undertaking.

**travailler comme un cheval** *(P)*. Same as : *travailler comme un nègre*.

**travailler comme un nègre** *(P)*. To drudge, to slave.

**travailler comme un sabot** *(P)*. To scamp, to bungle, to botch.

**travailler d'arrache-pied** *(P)*. To work hard, to plug.

**travailler de la chéchia** *(Sl)*. Same as : *travailler du chapeau*.

**travailler du chapeau** *(P)*. To be eccentric, crazy, a screwball, a crackpot, to have a screw loose.

**travailler du chou** *(Sl)*. Same as : *travailler du chapeau*.

**travailler du pick-up** *(Sl)*. To talk nonsense, to talk baloney.

**travailler pour des prunes** *(P)*. To work for nothing, in vain, without profit.

**travailler pour la peau** *(Sl)*. Same as : *travailler pour des prunes*, but stronger.

**travailler pour la tringle** *(Sl)*. Same as : *travailler pour des prunes*, (but stronger).

**travailler pour le roi de Prusse** *(P)*. Same as : *travailler pour des prunes*.

**travailleurs du chapeau (les)** *(P)*. Crackpots.

**travail sur la planche (avoir du)** *(P)*. See : *il y a du travail sur la planche*.

**traviole (de)** *(P)*. Awry, askew, screwy, cockeyed.

**treize à la douzaine** *(P)*. Baker's dozen.

**trembler comme une feuille** *(P)*. To tremble like a leaf.

**tremblotte** *sf. (P)*. Jitters, fright, extreme nervousness.

**trémousser le popotin (se)** *(Sl)*. To dance, to (w)rassle, to toss a leg.

**trempe** *sf. (P)*. *Les hommes de sa trempe*, men of his stamp. *(Sl)*. Beating, thrashing.

**trempé comme un canard** *(P)*. Wet as a drowned rat.

**trempé comme une soupe** *(P)*. Same as : *trempé comme un canard*.

**trempée** *sf. (Sl)*. Beating, licking, hiding.

**trempé jusqu'aux os** *(P)*. Wet to the skin.

**trempette** *sf. (P)*. Little piece of bread, generally long and thin, sippet (to soak in a soft boiled egg).

**trente et un (se mettre sur son)** *(P)*. See : *mettre sur son trente et un (se)*.

**très peu pour moi !** *(P)*. Sarcastic remark for a refusal : No ! I'm not having any !

**trève de plaisanterie !** *(F)*. Stop joking !

**tricard** *sm. (Sl)*. Ex-convict for whom certain towns or zones are prohibited.

**tricoter des gambettes** *(Sl)*. To dance, to sling the feet, to toss a a leg, to run fast.

CE QUI S'APPELLE
TRICOTER DES GAMBETTES.

**tric-trac** *sm. (Sl)*. Shady deal, shady business.

**trié sur le volet** *(P)*. Hand-picked, very carefully selected.

**trifouillée** *sf. (Sl)*. Thorough beating, licking, thrashing, " shellacking ", " strap oil ".

**trifouiller** *v. (P)*. To rummage.

**trimard** *sm. (Sl)*. Highway.

**trimarder** *v. (Sl)*. To walk aimlessly from place to place, to bum, to tramp, to be on the tramp.

**trimardeur** *sm. (Sl)*. Hobo, bum.

**trimballer** *v. (P)*. To drag, to tote.

**trimer** *v. (P)*. To work hard, to drudge, to sweat like a nigger, to toil, to slave.

**trimer comme un mercenaire** *(P)*. To drudge, to slave.

**tringle (la)** *sf. (Sl)*. Nothing (at all). (See : *travailler pour la tringle*).

**trinquer** *v. (Sl)*. To get a thrashing, a punishment, to get it in the neck, to get the rap, to get a jail sentence.

**tripaille** *sf. (Sl)*. Woman's flabby breasts.

**tripatouiller** *v. (Sl)*. To tamper with, to monkey with. Ex. : *Tripatouiller les comptes*, to doctor the accounts ; *tripatouiller des boissons*, to dope up, to fake, to adulterate drinks.

**Tripatouillis-les-Oies** *(P)*. Podunk, nickname for a hicktown.

**tripes** *sf. pl. (Sl)*. Flabby breasts.

**triple buse** *(P)*. Very stupid person, " saperoo ".

**triple galop (au)** *(P)*. Same as : *toute pompe (à)*.

**tripot** *sm. (F)*. Illicit gambling joint, gambling hell, clip joint, gaff-joint.

**tripotage** *sm. (P).* Unscrupulous manipulation, " hoopie-scoopie ".

**tripotée** *sf. (P).* Great quantity of, heaps of, scads of, oodles of. Beating, thrashing, licking, hiding.

TRIPOTÉE.

**tripoter** *v. (P).* To deal dishonestly with money, to embezzle. To monkey with, to mess around with.

**tripoteur** *sm. (P).* Grafter, boodler, grifter, finagler.

**triquée** *sf. (Sl).* Thrashing, shellacking. See also : *filer une triquée.*

**triquer** *v. (Sl).* To beat up, to thrash, to shellac, to lambast.

**trisser (se)** *v. (Sl).* To flee, to duck out, to clear out, to scram, to " do a Houdini ", to " fly the coop ".

**trogne** *sf. (Sl).* Face, " mug ", " clock ", " conk ".

**trombine** *sf. (Sl).* Face, " mask ", " dish ". Head, " bun ", " noggin ", " noodle ".

**trompette** *sf. (Sl).* Face, " mug ", " pan ".

**tronche** *sf. (Sl).* Face, " dish ", " pan ", " mug ". Head, " bun ", " nob ", " nut ". Fool, jug-head, dumbbell.

**trône** *sm. (P).* Chamber pot, " throne ".

**trop jeune !** *(P).* Young and inexperienced, not dry behind the ears, wet behind the ears, having no experience. Sometimes : not enough, below the mark.

**troquet** *sm. (Sl).* Barkeeper, wineseller, " boozer ". (Truncated form of *mastroquet*).

**trotter (se)** *v. (P).* To go away, to leave, to clear out, to " beat it ", to scram.

**trotter dans la cervelle** *(P).* *Ça me trotte dans la cervelle depuis des années,* it has been bugging me for years.

**trottin** *sm. (P).* Errand-girl in the fashion business.

**trottoir (faire le)** *(P).* Same as : *faire le tapin.*

**trou** *sm. (F).* Small provincial town, one-horse town, jerkwater town, a " filling station ".

**trou à la lune (faire un)** *(P).* To abscond, to duck out, to decamp in order to evade payment of bills, to " shoot the moon ".

**trouble-ménage** *sm. (Sl).* Ordinary red wine.

**trou de balle** *sm. (Sl).* Anus.

**troufignard** *sm. (Sl).* A variant of preceding entry.

**troufignon** *sm. (Sl).* Same as : *troufignard.* Hind end, fanny.

**troufion** *sm. (Sl).* Soldier, buck private.

**trouillard** *sm. (P).* Yellow-streaked individual, fraidy-cat.

**trouille** *sf. (Sl).* Intense fear and dread, funk, blue fear, "cold feet ".

**trouille (avoir la)** *(Sl)*. To be scared, funky, to have "the shakes", the jitters, to get chicken.

**trouilloter** *v. (Sl)*. To stink, to smell strongly.

**trou normand** *sm. (P)*. Glass of liquor between two courses.

**trousselin** *sm. (Sl)*. Posterior, fanny, pratt, seat of the pants.

**trousser bagage** *(P)*. To depart hurriedly, to decamp, to "do a Houdini", to take a powder, to "fly the coop".

**trouver à qui parler** *(P)*. To find one's master, to pick a tartar.

**trouver un bon filon** *(P)*. To strike a bonanza, to strike oil.

**trouver visage de bois** *(P)*. To call and find no one at home, to find the door locked.

**truand** *sm. (Sl)*. Ruffian, rough, tough.

**truc** *sm. (P)*. Gadget, thinguma-bobs, what-you-may-call-it, watchama-callit. Something the name of which cannot be recalled.

**truc à la gomme** *sm. (Sl)*. Monkey business. Indefinite worthless thing.

**truffe** *sf. (Sl)*. Big nose, "schnozz-le", "schnozzo(la)".

**trumeau** *sm. (Sl)*. Woman, "broad" (generally : *un vieux trumeau*).

**truqueur** *sm. (Sl)*. Bunco man, bunko artist, gypster, cheat, chiseler.

**truqueuse** *sf. (Sl)*. Harlot, low class prostitute, "hooker".

**tubar(d)** *sm. (Sl)*. Tubercular person, "lunger".

**tubards** *sm. pl. (Sl)*. Tip at the races, tip-off.

**tube** *sm. (Sl)*. Top hat, "chimney" (hat).

**tuer la poule aux œufs d'or** *(F)*. To kill the goose with the golden eggs.

**tuer les mouches à quinze pas** *(Sl)*. To have strong halitosis (bad breath strong enough to kill the flies).

**tuer le temps** *(P)*. To kill time.

**tuer le veau gras** *(P)*. To kill the fatted calf. (Biblical allusion : to celebrate the home-coming of an absentee).

**tuer le ver** *(Sl)*. To take an early morning bracer, an "eye-opener".

**tuile** *sf. (P)*. An unexpected mishap, unexpected unlucky event, nasty blow, "nick". Ex. : *Quelle tuile !* What a nasty blow !

**tu l'as dit, bouffi !** *(Sl)*. You said it ! you bet ! you said a mouthful ! you are darn tootin' !

**tu ne m'as pas regardé !** *(P)*. Exclamation denoting indignation, refusal, negation, contempt or anger. (Retort to a displeasing remark).

**tu ne voudrais pas ! (vous ne voudriez pas !)** *(P)*. Polite but categorical denial : certainly not, I certainly won't !

**tu parles !** *(P)*. And how ! you bet ! (Sometimes jocularly : *Tu parles, Charles !*).

**tu parles, Charles !** *(P)*. See : *Tu parles !*

**tu parles de... !** *(P)*. *Tu parles d'un jeu !* Strange play, I should say ! (Sarcastic remark).

**tu peux te fouiller ! (vous pouvez vous fouiller !)** *(P)*. You can whistle for it !

**tu peux te taper ! (vous pouvez vous taper !)** *(P).* A variation of *tu peux te fouiller !*

**tu peux toujours courir ! (vous pouvez toujours courir !)** *(P).* Another pop. variation of *tu peux te fouiller !*

**turbin** *sm. (Sl).* Work, hard work.

**turbiner** *v. (Sl).* To work hard.

**turlupiner** *v. (P).* To make uneasy, to worry. Ex. : *Cette idée me turlupine,* this idea makes me sort of uneasy.

**turlututu, chapeau pointu !** *(P).* Ironical fling meaning : Oh, come off, I don't believe it ! Hoity-toity ! (Similar interj. : *taratata !*).

**turne** *sf. (Sl).* Old ramshackle house, any place where living conditions are bad. Student's room, particularly in the *Ecole Normale Supérieure.*

**tu t'en ferais crever !** *(Sl).* You can try hard, my boy, you will never get it !

**tuyau** *sm. (P).* Tip-off, tip, pointer, dope, wire, low-down. *Où as-tu eu ce tuyau ?* Where did you get that dope ?

**tu t'entêtes et t'as tort (Totor) !** *(P).* Joc. fling and alliteration meaning : Don't be so pigheaded ! (so obstinate, so stubborn !).

**tuyau de poêle** *sm. (P).* Top hat, top(per), "chimney-pot".

**tuyauter** *v. (P).* To tip off, to give a pointer, to give the dope.

**tuyauter (se)** *v. (P).* To obtain information, to dope out.

**type** *sm. (P).* Guy, "ghee", bloke, any man. *Un brave type,* a reg'lar guy.

**type épatant (un)** *(P).* A remarkable fellow, a lollapaloosa.

**type fichu (un)** *(P).* A gone coon, goner.

**type louche** *(P).* Shady character.

**typesse** *sf. (Sl).* A derogatory slang term for a woman or a girl : "broad", "tart", "tomato".

# U

**Ugène** *(P)*. Nickname for Eugène (pop. or low-class pronunciation).

**un de ces quatre matins** *(P)*. One of the coming days, in the near future.

**une autre paire de manches (c'est)** *(P)*. It's a different proposition.

**une Telle** *(P)*. Substitute name applied to any woman : *Madame une Telle*, Mrs So-and-so.

**unité** *sf. (P)*. One million francs.

**un peu jeune (c'est)** *(P)*. Not (quite) up to the mark, below the mark.

**un peu là** *(P)*. Strong, "corn-fed", a chunk of a ; to have guts, to be courageous.

**un Tel** *(P)*. Substitute name applied to anyone : *Monsieur un Tel*, Mr. So-and-so, Joe Doakes.

**urf** *adj. (Sl)*. Swell, dandy.

**urger** *v. (P)*. *Ça urge*, it's urgent.

**user sa salive** *(P)*. To waste one's breath.

# V

vacciné avec une aiguille de phono (être) *(Sl)*. To be a chatter-box, (said jocularly of one who chatters without interruption).

* **vachard** *sm. adj. (Sl)*. Lazy person, lazy dog. Nasty, scurvy.

* **vache** *sf. (Sl)*. In sing. rude slang word for a fat woman. Insult for a wicked individual, swine. In plural : insult for policemen.

* **vache (être)** *adj. (Sl)*. To be a swine to s.o.

**vache à lait** *(P)*. Milk-cow, "sucker".

* **vache à roulettes** *sf. (Sl)*. Po-liceman on wheels, cycling cop. (Syn. : *hirondelle*).

* **vacherie** *sf. (P)*. Scurvy trick, dirty trick. *Faire une vacherie à q.*, to play a dirty trick on one, to play s.o. dirt.

* **vaches ! (les)** *interj. (Sl)*. Swine !

**va-comme-je-te-pousse** *sm. (P)*. Lazy, unenergetic person, poke.

**va-comme-je-te-pousse (à la)** *(P)*. In a happy-go-lucky way.

**vadrouille** *sf. (Sl)*. Drinking spree, binge.

**vadrouiller** *v. (Sl)*. To loaf aim-lessly or in quest of fun.

**vadrouilleur** *sm. (Sl)*. Bum, bo, boomer.

**vadrouilleuse** *sf. (Sl)*. Prostitute, "hooker".

**valise (faire la)** *(Sl)*. To go away, to leave, to clear (check) out, to jilt.

**valoir dix** *(P)*. See : *Ça vaut dix.*

**valoir le coup** *(P)*. To be worth-while, to be worth one's while.

**valoir son pesant d'or** *(F)*. To be worth one's weight in gold.

**vanné** *adj. (P)*. Dog-tired, exhaust-ed, all in, dead-beat, frazzled, bushed.

**vanner** *v. (P)*. To tire, to poop out, to fag out, to drag out.

**vaseux** *adj. (P)*. Out of sorts. *Se sentir vaseux*, to feel out of sorts. "Woolly". Ex. : *Une réponse vaseuse*, a vague, unclear answer ; *des idées vaseuses*, "woolly" ideas. Anything vague and inaccurate.

**vasouiller** *v. (P)*. To be unable to give a correct answer, to be stumped. (School sl.).

**\* va te faire foutre !** *(Sl)*. Go to hell ! Scram out of here !

**va t'en voir s'ils viennent !** *(P)*. Nothing doing, you can wait till hell freezes over !

**va t'faire cuire un œuf !** *(Sl)*. Go to the dickens, go you know where !

**vautour** *sm. (P)*. Usurer, a Shylock, loan shark.

**veau** *sm. (Sl)*. Inferior horse (racing).

**vécé** *sm. (P)*. W.C., wash-room.

**veiller au grain** *(P)*. To watch out and be ready for any emergency, to keep one's weather eye open, to keep a sharp look-out.

**veinard** *sm. adj. (P)*. Lucky (individual).

**veine** *sf. (P)*. Luck, lucky chance, fluke.

**veine (avoir de la)** *(P)*. To be lucky.

**veine de cocu** *(Sl)*. Remarkable, extraordinary luck.

**veine de cocu (avoir une)** *(Sl)*. To be exceptionally lucky.

**veine de pendu (avoir une)** *(P)*. To be particularly lucky, to be "hit with a horseshoe".

**Vel d'Hiv** *(P)*. *Vélodrome d'Hiver*, arena for mass meetings and citadel of indoor athletics in Paris.

**vélo** *sm. (P)*. Bicycle, bike.

**velours** *sm. (P)*. *Faire des velours*, to make the wrong *liaison* (in speaking French), f.i. : *trop-z-aimable*, instead of *trop aimable*. Fluff.

**velours (du)** *(P)*. Something easy, "velvet", "duck soup", a "snap", "pushover", "tipover". Delight.

**vendre** *v. (P)*. To betray, to sell out.

**vendre la mèche** *(P)*. To spill a secret, to spill the beans, to blow the gaff.

**vendre sa salade** *(P)*. To make one's living according to one's trade.

**vendu** *sm. (P)*. Traitor.

**venette** *sf. (P)*. Fear, funk. Ex. : *Avoir la venette*, to jitter (through fear).

**venir à bout de q. ch.** *(P)*. To lick. Ex. : *Venir à bout d'un problème*, to lick a problem.

**venir à la rescousse** *(P)*. To come to the rescue.

**venir aux coups** *(F)*. See : *en venir aux coups*.

**venir aux mains** *(F)*. See : *en venir aux mains*.

**venir comme des cheveux sur la soupe** *(P)*. To be far-fetched, very inappropriate.

**vent dans les voiles (avoir du)** *(P)*. To be slightly drunk, to be rather "on", "lit up a bit", "half-cocked".

**vent de q. ch. (avoir)** *(P)*. To get wind of.

**vente à tempérament** *(F)*. Installment plan, installment selling.

**ventre à terre (aller ou courir)** *(F)*. To ride like mad.

**ventrée** *sf. (Sl)*. Lavish meal, "blow-out". Ex. : *S'en mettre une ventrée*, to eat a lavish meal.

**venu au monde un Dimanche** *(P)*. Said of a lazy person. Ex. : *Il est venu au monde un Dimanche*, he was born tired.

**verbe haut (avoir le)** *(F)*. To speak firmly and loudly, to be bossy, dictatorial.

**vérité de la Palice (la Palisse)** *(F)*. Self-evident truth, platitude, truism. (See also : *lapalissade*).

**verni** *adj. (P)*. Lucky. *Etre verni*, to be lucky, in the fat.

**verre dans le nez (avoir un)** *(P)*. To be drunk, slightly tight, boozy.

**verser des larmes de crocodile** *(F)*. To shed crocodile tears.

**vert (être)** *(Sl)*. To be a victim.

**vert-de-gris** *(Sl)*. Old nickname for a German soldier (on account of the color his uniform).

LA VEUVE.

**vertes et des pas mûres (des)** *(P)*. *Risqué* or smutty stories, raw stuff, blue gag.

**veuve (la)** *sf. (Sl)*. Guillotine.

**vidage** *sm. (Sl)*. Dismissal, firing (of a person).

**vidé** *adj. (Sl)*. To be penniless, broke. To be fired from an employment.

**vider** *v. (Sl)*. To dismiss, to fire, to boot out, to blackball.

**vider le calice jusqu'à la lie** *(F)*. Same as : *boire le calice jusqu'à la lie*.

**vider le zinc** *(Sl)*. To bale out (airman slang).

**vider son sac** *(P)*. To confess.

**vider un glass** *(Sl)*. To drink a glass (of liquor).

**vie de bâtons de chaise** *(P)*. Dissolute, fast and loose life, high-stepping. *Mener une vie de bâtons de chaise*, to lead a disorderly life.

**vie de chien** *(F)*. Dog's life.

**vie de galère** *(F)*. A variant of *vie de chien*.

**vie de patachon** *(P)*. Same as : *vie de bâtons de chaise*.

**vieille (la)** *sf. (Sl)*. Mother, the old lady.

**vieille baderne** *(P)*. Old fogey. (See : *baderne*).

**vieille barbe** *(P)*. Fuddy-duddy.

**vieille branche** *(P)*. Old friend, old cock, buddy, pal.

**vieille cloche** *(P)*. Same as : *vieille branche*.

**vieille culotte de peau** *(P)*. An overscrupulous and griping army officer.

VIEILLE CULOTTE DE PEAU.

**vieille noix** *(P)*. Old dodo, old goof(y).

**vieille perruque** *(P)*. Old-fashioned individual, old frump, old mossback.

**vieille toupie** *(P)*. Same as : *vieux tableau*.

**vieux (le)** *sm. (Sl)*. Father, the old man, pop.

**vieux (mes)** *(Sl)*. My parents, my folks.

**vieux bahut** *(Sl)*. Old, worn-out car, jeloppy, jitney car.

**vieux birbe** *(P)*. Old dodo.

**vieux clou** *(P)*. Old typewriter, old and bad machine, old car.

**vieux comme Hérode** *(F)*. As old as the hills.

**vieux de la vieille (un)** *(P)*. Old-timer.

**vieux jeu** *adj. (P)*. Old-fashioned, behind the times, " old hat ", " razz-matazz ". *Un individu vieux jeu*, a square, back number.

**vieux marcheur** *(P)*. Old dissolute man, old rooster, old *roué*, **old** buck.

VIEUX MARCHEUR.

DANS LES VIGNES DU SEIGNEUR.

**vieux ronchon** *(P).* Old buzzard, old grouch.

**vieux tableau (un)** *(P).* Old frump.

**vif-argent dans les veines (avoir du)** *(F).* Restless, bustling. (Said of a person who can't stand still for a minute).

**vignes du Seigneur (être dans les)** *(F).* To be boozy-woozy, drunk.

**vinasse** *sf. (P).* Inferior, low-grade wine.

**vingt-deux !** *interj. (Sl).* Look out ! " Beat it " ! Scram ! Zex ! (Interj. in case of danger). Ex. : *Vingt-deux, les flics !* Beat it ! The cops are coming !

**vin triste (avoir le)** *(F).* To be dull in one's cups.

**violon** *sm. (P).* Jail, pokey, " coop ", " cooler ".

**violon d'Ingres** *sm. (F).* Secondary talent or hobby in which a person takes more pride than in his (her) chief profession. (According to a French legend, Ingres, a famous French painter, is said to have taken more pride in his secondary talent as a violin player than in his matchless art of painting).

**vioque** *adj. (Sl).* Old, stale, out of date.

**virée** *sf. (P).* Joy ride, trip, automobile tour.

**virer** *v. (Sl).* To dismiss, to fire, to boot out, to kick out. *Tu vas te faire virer, mon gars !* You will be kicked out neck and crop, my boy !

**viser** *v. (Sl).* To look.

**vissé (mal)** *adj. (Sl).* In an ugly mood.

**visser q.** *(P).* To put the screws on.

**vitriol** *sm. (P).* Low grade liquor, booze, " rat poison ", " vitriol ".

**vivoter** *v. (F).* To live from hand to mouth, to scrape along, to live on a very limited income, to vegetate.

**vivre au jour le jour** *(F).* To live from hand to mouth.

**vivre aux crochets de q.** *(P).* To live at another's expense, to sponge on s.o., to chisel.

**vivre de l'air du temps** *(F).* To live on (almost) nothing.

**vivre sur un grand pied** *(F).* To live in luxury, to lead an elegant life.

**voir de dures** *(P).* See : *en voir de dures.*

**voir de raides** *(P).* See : *en voir de raides.*

**voir les étoiles en plein jour** *(P).* Same as : *en voir trente-six chandelles.*

**voir les feuilles à l'envers** *(P).* Petting party under a tree.

**voir rouge** *(P).* To see red, to be mad.

**voir trente-six chandelles** *(P).* See : *en voir trente-six chandelles.*

**voir venir q. avec ses gros sabots** *(P). Je te vois venir avec tes gros sabots !* I see your little game, bud !

**voiture des quatre saisons** *(F).* Push cart of a street vendor (chiefly for vegetables, food or flowers).

**voiture pie** *(F).* Light police patrol car equipped with radio set including transmitter, squad car.

**voix au chapitre (avoir)** *(F)*. To have one's say.

**voix de mêlé-cass** *(Sl)*. Sore throat voice, raucous voice. (Syn. : *voix de marchande de poissons*).

**vol à la tire** *(P)*. Business of a pickpocket, pocket picking, " touch ".

**vouloir prendre la lune avec les dents** *(P)*. Attempting impossibilities, " pipe dream ".

**vous êtes orfèvre, Monsieur Josse** *(P)*. Fling at one who gives you advice not to serve you but rather his own interest. (Semi-proverbial col-

VOL A LA TIRE.

UN VRAI DE VRAI.

**volant** *sm. (Sl)*. Trapeze performer.

**voler de ses propres ailes** *(F)*. To go it on one's own, to stand on one's own.

**voleur comme une pie** *(F)*. Thievish as a magpie.

**vouloir décrocher la lune** *(P)*. To reach for the moon.

**vouloir être à cent pieds sous terre** *(F)*. To be terribly ashamed (or embarrassed), to feel like thirty cents.

loquialism taken from *l'Amour Médecin*, by Molière).

**vous me faites rire !** *(P)*. You make me laugh ! Pop. excl. meaning : You are talking nonsense ! or : I don't believe what you say ! Don't fool me !

**vous m'en direz des nouvelles !** *(P)*. Popular phrase meaning : Make your own experiment and you will tell me what you think of it. Ex. : *Goûtez ce fromage, vous m'en direz des nouvelles,* just taste this cheese, you will be surprised (you will tell me) how delicious it is !

**vous voulez rire !** *(P)*. Pop. excl. denoting disbelief, negation, denial.

**vous y êtes !** *(F)*. Right you are ! You said a mouthful !

**voyageur** *sm. (P)*. Commercial traveler, drummer, field man.

**vrai de vrai** *(Sl)*. Fancy man, souteneur, pimp. Man of the so-called " *milieu* ".

**vraiment ?** *(P)*. Izzatso ? Really ?

**vue de nez (à)** *(P)*. See : *à vue de nez*.

# X

**X (l')** *(P). Ecole Polytechnique.*
*Un X,* student at the *Ecole Polytech-*
*nique.* (See also : *pipo*).

# Y

**y a pas plan** *(Sl)*. No go ! No sale ! No soap !

**y être** *(P)*. To understand. Ex. : *J'y suis,* I understand, I got you.

**yeux de merlan frit** *(Sl)*. See : *faire des yeux de merlan frit.*

**yeux plus gros que le ventre (avoir les)** *(P)*. To bite off more than one can chew.

**y laisser des plumes** *(P)*. To lose money in a venture, in a business deal, at gambling, etc.

**y mettre son grain de sel** *(P)*. To put in one's two cents worth, to chip in.

**youpin** *sm. (Sl)*. Derogatory slang term for a Jew, Yid.

**yoyoter de la mansarde** *(Sl)*. To be crazy, to talk nonsense, to goof off, to be dingdong daffy.

**y passer** *(Sl)*. Said of a woman who succombs to a male petter.

**y perdre son latin** *(F)*. To be at one's wits' end, to be at a loss, to be nonplus(s)ed. Ex. . *J'y perds mon latin,* I can't make head or tail of it.

**y regarder à deux fois** *(P)*. To think twice about.

**y tâter** *(Sl)*. To touch, to " feel " a thing. *Tâtez-y !* Just feel it !

**Yvans** *sm. pl. (P)*. An obvious nickname for Russians, " Russkies ". (More often : *Popofs*).

# Z

**zanzi** *sm. (Sl)*. A gambling game played with three dice, game of craps with three dice, " galloping dominoes ".

**zanzi-bar** *(Sl)*. A crap joint.

**zazou** *sm. (P)*. Zoot-suiter of the early Forties, sharpie. Also : rock'n-roller.

**zèbre** *sm. (P)*. Man, guy, " ghee ". *Un vieux zèbre,* an old guy. *Un drôle de zèbre,* a queer guy. (See also : *filer comme un zèbre*).

**zéro** *sm. (P)*. No-account, unimportant individual, nonentity.

**zéro en chiffre** *sm. (P)*. Nonentity, mere nobody, washout, bum.

**zéro fini** *(P)*. Same as : *zéro en chiffre.*

**zéro pointé** *(P)*. In education : 4 - F, " goose egg ".

**zieuter** *v. (P)*. To have a looksee, to peel an eye at, to " get a load of ".

**zigomar** *sm. (Sl)*. Same as : *zigoto.*

JEUNE ZAZOU.

**zigoto** *sm. (Sl)*. Individual, guy, geezer, " ghee ".

**zigoto (faire le)** *(Sl)*. To play the fool.

**zigouiller** *v.* *(Sl)*. To murder, to kill, to "erase", to "wipe out", to "blot out", to bump off.

IL LE ZIGOUILLE, MA FOI !

**zigue** *sm.* *(Sl)*. *Un bon zigue,* an honest guy, a reliable fellow.

**zinc** *sm.* *(P)*. Bar, bistro, public-house. Counter of a bistro. Ex. : *Prendre un verre sur le zinc,* to have a drink at the counter (of a bistro).
*(Sl)*. Airplane, "crate", "bus". (Syn. : *coucou*).

**zone** *sf.* *(P)*. Ground cleared after the city's fortifications (round Paris) were torn down ; here lived not long ago, in cheap huts, the petty junkmen of Paris.

**zouave (faire le)** *(P)*. To play the wag (fool).

**zozo** *sm.* *(P)*. Naive, gullible person, "cluck", Johnny Sap.

**zozores** *sm. pl.* *(Sl)*. Ears, "flappers".

**zut !** *interj.* *(P)*. Excl. of contempt or anger : Dammit ! Shucks ! Hell !

**zyeuter** *v.* *(P)*. Same as : *zieuter.*